SALFORD CROSS.

[*From a painting by Ralston.*

SALFORD THROUGH THE AGES.

The "Fons et Origo" of an Industrial City.

BY

CHARLES P. HAMPSON.

Introduction by the
Rev. Canon PETER GREEN, M.A.

SEPTCENTENARY FIRST EDITION, 1930.

E. J. MORTEN (Publishers)
Didsbury, Manchester, England

First Printed 1930 by
SALFORD CITY REPORTER

Republished 1972 by
E. J. MORTEN (Publishers)
10 Warburton Street, Didsbury,
Manchester, England
From the First Edition 1930

ISBN 0 901598 66 6

Printed in Great Britain by
Scolar Press Limited, Menston, Yorkshire

*To my Father and Mother,
who first taught me to love
my native town.*

Preface

BY

The Rev. Canon Peter Green, M.A.,

Chaplain to H.M. The King, Canon of Manchester, Rector of St. Philip's, Salford, and Rural Dean of Salford.

WHEN Mr. Hampson honoured me with an invitation to write a short Preface to his history of " Salford Through the Ages," I wondered what qualifications for the task I could be supposed to possess. There can be few men with less knowledge of archeology and topography than I, few men less skilled in deciphering ancient manuscripts or reconstructing the half-forgotten legends of the past. A little reflection however convinced me that even I, a Southerner born and bred, yet possessed one genuine qualification for the task to which I had been called. I have lived for nearly thirty years right in the middle of central Salford, and have come to love the city and its inhabitants, and to be proud to call myself, even if only by adoption, a Salford citizen.

Many people, rushing through one or other of the big industrial and merchantile cities of the North, on their way perhaps to the moors and lochs of Scotland, see little to attract them in our crowded, smoke-grimmed streets, and wonder at the passion of local patriotism which burns in our hearts. It will be one of the things which this book will effect to make people understand that patriotism and perhaps to envy it. There are plenty of places in England which would be called pleasant residential centres which thirty years ago were open fields. What historic associations, what romance can there be in these collections of trim villas ? Leaving London, of course, and a few other of the great towns of the South perhaps, out of account, what have most of England's cities to set against the rich fulness of past history and of present life which Salford can boast ? Some of them have the like background of historical interest and association, but to-day they are quiet backwaters, lacking our full strenuous life of thought and of action. Some are busy centres of industry, but they are creations of to-day or at best of yesterday. In Salford we have the fulness of life of a great centre of industry ; a manufacturing city ; a mercantile city ; a port ; and we have a past which stretches back to the dim beginnings of our race and nation.

Mr. Hampson leads us from the earliest days of pre-historic man, past Briton and Saxon and Dane, through the chequered history of the city he loves, down to the present day. And how much there is to tell. Here we have Guy Fawkes and Ordsall Hall ; here we have the gallant gentlemen who were " out in the Forty-five," and went bravely to the block or to exile for the fated house of Stuart. Then we have the record, nowhere perhaps to be read and interpreted more clearly than in Salford, of that grim Industrial Revolution which was the cause of so much that is good in our own day, as well as of so many of our most intractable problems and social diseases. To many, even among those who know something of English social and economic history between 1760 and 1840, the details of the " Cripple Mill " and of the " White Slave Factory " will be something new. And through the long record of Salford life and Salford doings readers will not be slow to remark, and perhaps to wonder at, the way in which the life of the spirit, the activity of the scientific discoverer, or the poet and hymn-writer, of the social reformer and the champion of civil and religious liberty, has burned strongly and glowed brightly among our hard-headed, warm-hearted merchants and mechanics.

Nor would I wish strangers who may read this book— Salford citizens will not need my warning—to suppose that we are altogether lacking even in Salford in external beauty obvious to the bodily eye as well as to the eye of imagination. The first thing that the visitor from the South has to learn is how beautiful even Blake's

" DARK SATANIC MILLS "

can look on a winter's morning early, or late on a winter's afternoon—when, lit up, the long rows of windows make an adjective " dark " the least appropriate one possible. And fine judges of beauty have spoken to me of the grace of tall factory chimneys, slender columns of darkness against the pale lemon sky of early dawn or the richer tints of the sunset. And even by the prosaic light of day there are many nooks and corners in old Salford where the man with an eye for beauty, coming suddenly round a corner, is struck with some old building, some relict of the past, such as Mr. Hampson has described in more than one passage of his book.

And always, blending with memories of the past and touched with gleams of beauty of the present, there is the full, rich, strenuous, eager life of a great community spinning the threads of the life of to-morrow, as the men of the past span the threads which make the warp and woof of our life to-day. Mr. Hampson's love for Salford, his conviction that he is indeed a citizen of no mean city, is infectious. It should reveal to many Salford citizens the only half-realized thoughts of their own hearts. No lover of our city should be without his volume, and it may well win for Salford lovers who as yet have never known her.

CONTENTS

PROLOGUE.—IN THE BEGINNING.

BOOK ONE.—PREHISTORIC TO 1230 A.D.

CHAPTER I.........................Men of the Long Ago.

CHAPTER II................. When the Romans Came.

CHAPTER III ....A Town of Saxon Kings.

CHAPTER IV...................Early Christian Influences.

CHAPTER V........................Salford in Domesday.

CHAPTER VI.........................After the Conquest.

CHAPTER VII. ....The Monks of Kersal Vale.

CHAPTER VIII. ....A Free Borough.

CHAPTER IX...............................The Charter.

List of Illustrations.

"Salford Cross," from a drawing by Ralston....*Frontispiece.*

Woden's Cave at Ordsall 33

Plan of Salford in Anglo-Saxon Times.............. 51

Ordsall Hall 69

Bull's Head Inn, Greengate 87

Hatton's Shop, Chapel Street, with Watchman's Box.. 99

Agecroft Hall 107

Crabtree's House at Broughton Spout 125

Trinity Church, 1635 143

View of Salford about 1690 143

Kersal Cell 163

Kersal Hall 183

Old Houses, Riverside, Greengate 197

Oak Hall, Cross Lane 217

Plan of Salford in 1740........................... 235

Old Blackfriars Bridge 253

The New Bayley 271

Salford Through The Ages.

INTRODUCTION.

TO its own people every place is a Zion, a vineyard for
the labours of its well beloved, and both love and labour
wax the greater when they are fortified by knowledge.
For an ancient town Salford is singularly unknown even to its
own people. Looked upon usually as a rather grim product
of the Industrial Age there is little enough to suggest that
beneath the grimy shroud and smoky grey-webbed veil lie
hidden the rich hues of Old Romance, and few of the countless
thousands who day by day take their busy way about her
streets, ever pause to think they are treading historic mould
where life was cradled in the dawn of time, and the drama
of human existence has been played unceasingly through
the centuries' changing forms.

Looking on Salford for the first time the fastidious may
not be attracted by her present-day appearance, although
that is neither better nor worse than any other city where
industry reigns supreme, but lingering awhile in our midst
even the stranger catches something of a far off whispering
charm and ceases to wonder at, even though he may not
understand, the passionate devotion of even the lowliest of
our people of this well-beloved town.

Ever since, as a tiny child, I first learned tales of Old
Salford at a Granny's knee, this home of my fathers has been
to me in very truth, an enchanted place, and whether with a
schoolboy's questing mind, or later with thoughts more
mature, but interest sharpened rather than dimmed, it has
been a never ceasing joy to wander about her odd nooks
and corners, and draw from out her half forgotten past magic
fragments, that, pieced together like some wondrous jig-saw
puzzle, reveal the faint but clear presentment of our ancient
city, this ageless mother whose echoing voice through the
mist of ages her children hear so clearly in these later days
summoning their service in love to enrich her heritage in the
great days that lie before.

For a city is compounded not of bricks and mortar and trade and the complex of many activities. It is the breathing life of countless human souls, of lives lived well and laid down without fear, blindly perhaps, but none the less truly striving to interpret within their local orbit a world "apparelled in celestial light." Their material forms pass with their day, but a fragment of their spirit remains behind to inspire and reinforce the progress of the generations who succeed.

It is in no mere archæological or antiquarian interest that this book is now sent forth, but rather to meet that hungry longing expressed by so many of our people in these days when new opportunities seem about to dawn for this, our city, to know something more than has hitherto been available of the time-old community, in which they have been born and brought up, or whence they have been led to serve. To be a citizen of no mean city was a boast that even an Apostle did not scorn. I hope my fellow citizens may find in the pages which follow their ample justification for a legitimate pride, and gazing through this casement on the illustrious past of one of England's oldest towns, each one will find anew the glowing vision in what our sires wrought, and a deeper strength of purpose to walk worthily where the trail has been blazed so well.

My thanks are due and are here gratefully rendered to all who have helped in so many ways to facilitate the compilation of this, the first published record of an authentic Salford history, and particularly would I thank Mr. Alfred Hobson, the City Librarian and his Staff at the Royal Free Library, Peel Park, to whom no trouble has been too great to facilitate my pleasurable task.

In the Beginning.

ON a rugged sandstone bluff which strikes aside the
wide, rough, roaring torrent pouring headlong down
from the melting snows of the uplands on its way to
find the sea, a man is standing, gazing out over the desolate
chill drenched land. Trackless morass, wild inhospitable vista
of spreading virgin forest, marshy fen, low-lying scrub,
bleak moors rising to low hills and merging at length into
grey horizon. Above the moan of the wind come the howls
and shrieks of bear and boar, wolf and reindeer, as in the
forest the brute things seek and find their prey.

Short of stature, dark of skin, the lonely nameless
adventurer, pioneer of an advancing tide he wots not of,
stares out with eyes that see beyond the immediate outlook,
and with deep thoughts stirring within that long-shaped
head with its mass of curly raven hair.

Here would be a perfect dwelling-place, easily accessible
yet defended from attack by the swiftly-flowing river and the
impassable morass, sheltered by the surrounding hills, and
sloping to catch the fullness of the sun's warming rays by
day, giving the ground a warmth against the chill of the
night. Caves to house many families, plain-land to be tilled
and sown, flocks of sheep on the moors, fish from the river,
and the forest to provide meat and fuel and clothes.

The screen of oncoming night draws down upon the view,
the man gathers his meagre outfit into one of the caves,
and the building of the city has begun. For this lone figure
is the true father of our Salford, and to-day we stand upon
that self-same spot, dreaming and planning too, for the
building still goes on, and, indeed, will never end until in some
far age, immeasurably beyond our ken, the " civitas dei "
raises its proud fanes and the divine purpose is revealed in
our common life. So do we well to pause and search back
to the very beginning of our life here, learning by the sign-
posts of the past a greater wisdom for the journey still before.

BOOK   ONE
Prehistoric   to
1230 A.D.

CHAPTER I.

Men of the Long Ago.

PALEOLITHIC life never extended beyond the fringe of the South Midlands, but when the glacial area moved northward and climatic conditions made human habitation possible in the parts of these islands in which we now dwell, the Iberian Colonists of the New Stone Age left their homes on the Mediterranean coast following the northward call to the unknown lands released from the grip of the ice gods by mighty stirrings of the restless bosom of the earth. Crossing the narrow seas in light canoes fashioned out of tree trunks came these Neolithic adventurers, distinguished from the men of the old Stone Age by a higher degree of culture which, savage and primitive though it be, heralds the dawn of later civilisation. No longer merely a hunter, a human savage contending with the brute creation, Neolithic man had subjected and tamed the ox, the sheep, the goat and the pig. He knew how to till the ground to make it yield him food. He had acquired the art of moulding the clay of the earth and firing it to make utensils for his domestic use. Rough and rudimentary though this may have been, it marks the beginning of progress of northern mankind, of man's struggle with Nature and with himself, sometimes winning, sometimes thwarted, but rising unbowed from every setback to something greater still, proudly if with slow and bitter travail marking a nearer accomplishment.

That the site of what we now call Salford was occupied by these early people we have tangible proof that must thrill even the least imaginative in the beautifully-executed stone weapons of these men that have been found. It is easy to realise why this site would attract them if we study its natural features and the appeal it would inevitably make to a people whose prime requirements were accessibility, shelter, provision and defence. It forms truly an ideal position, and it is reasonable to surmise that for a period of at least ten thousand years human life has existed on this very site.

Their dwellings would be the caves which in those days honeycombed the soft rock, but which the process of erosion by wind and weather have in the course of the centuries utterly destroyed. Each cave would be the home of one family, the larger ones serving the communal purposes for council, worship and amusement. The instinct for mutual defence caused groups of families to unite into a clan under a chief, but it was not until a much later age that any idea of civic organisation developed. The idea of God was unknown, but burial customs suggest that there was a firm belief in some form of hereafter, and the spirits of earth and air and sky were worshipped and propitiated.

Something like two thousand years before the Christian era, the Neolithic Age gave place to a form of living in which the knowledge of metals played a dominant part. Whether the Bronze Age was merely the out-growth of the increasing knowledge of the earlier age or the introduction of a new race of people will never be known, but certain it is that the new knowledge of the working of metals played a big part in elevating primitive life, providing the means for greater food production, a more tolerable system of living and consequently increased population. Spirit worship was still the religious expression, and the sun which conferred light and warmth was the deity which claimed the chief allegiance. It helps a realisation of the antiquity of our life in this place to recall that when in Israel of old the prophets of Baal were gathered on Mount Carmel crying aloud to the God of Fire " and cutting themselves after their manner . . . till blood gushed out upon them " ; our early forbears were assembled for the same heathen rites twice a year on Buile Hill, where a great fire was lighted and human sacrifices made to appease that great and mighty spirit whose warming rays brought forth the harvest fruits, and whom they besought that in the dark winter days he would not depart utterly from them. Here was no Elijah, however, to point them to some better thing. At these festivals a large cake was baked and distributed, a custom we still perpetuate, for our Lancashire " parkin " is merely the ancient Celtic word for " cake."

" Going West " is a familiar enough term of our modern speech. So is preserved an ancient significance. In all ages adventurers have gone forward into the unknown in obedience to the impulse to seek the land that lies beyond the setting sun. So there came from the East about 400 B.C. a continuous wave of Celtic invaders bringing with them besides a higher mental superiority and a wider culture, that which through the ages has been the dominant factor in progress and prosperity, the art of forging and working in iron. This immigration marks the first stirrings of historic life. An Aryan people, they had a definite system of civic organisation. The social tie became closer knit with the family as the political unit, and groups of families, many of them large enough to be petty tribes, welded together under a ruler, partly elective, partly hereditary, known as the " Rix," who had his seat at a central place or " city," whence the people of the various tribes were called at certain times of the year for council, worship and the administration of justice, the main system of government alike as of religion being in the hands of that mysterious priesthood, the Druids. Dismiss from your minds the history book fable of the ancient Britons as naked woad-painted savages, and remember rather what travellers like Pytheas have recorded of the high standard of British agriculture and civilisation generally.

The most powerful of the Brythonic nations was the Brigantes, who dominated the Voluntii and the Sistuntii of the north-west. On the banks of the " Irguile," " the winding torrent," in which name they have left an indelible impress of their possession, the Brigantes had one of their strongholds. A powerful settlement of warriors and husbandmen, with social castes of freemen, bondmen and dependents or slaves, no longer cave-dwellers, but living in rough circular houses of timber thatched with heather and turf. One hundred and twenty-five years after the hurried arrival in Britain of Julius Cæsar and his equally hurried departure, this British " city " felt the first attacks of a foreign invader when Petilius Cerealis, in 71 A.D., was sent north to subdue the troublesome Brigantes. To what extent he succeeded in reducing the Irwell stronghold is not known, but retiring to Isurium, the chief capital of the Brigantes, he left the natives to carry on a guerilla warfare for seven years until the arrival of the great Agricola himself.

Such was the first rude beginnings of our town as an actual civic unit, in the days when Boadicea, in the east of Britain, was harrying the Roman invaders, and when further still in the East, beyond the seas, was being enacted the greatest tragedy the world has ever known.

CHAPTER II.

When the Romans Came

IN the time of the Emperor Antoninus Augustus there was compiled a great road book of the Roman Empire known as the Iter of Antoninus. Therein appear certain references to a place quite obviously in what we to-day call Lancashire. These references have several variations. In the 2nd Iter occurs the word "Mamucium," and in the 10th Iter "Mancunium." It is generally conceded that the latter is intended to apply to the fort of Agricola at the point where the Medlock falls into the Irwell, but in their anxiety to find a way out of the difficulty created by the first-mentioned name local antiquarians have been troubled by much searching of mind, even to the extent of creating an imaginary pre-Roman British town at the junction of the Irk and the Irwell. It has apparently never occurred to them to consider that the name "Mamucium," a Latinised form of a Celtic term meaning "the mother town," may more reasonably be taken as referring to the place across the river which for centuries had been the main settlement of the ancient inhabitants of these parts. I therefore venture to assert that the earliest name under which our Salford is revealed to historic notice is that which appears in the Iter II. of the old Roman road book, and, further, that it was the presence of this powerful native settlement threatening communication between Deva and Eboracium that caused Agricola to erect a fort at Castlefield, to which was given the name of "Mancunium," the camp or station by the mother town, whose troublesome inhabitants were thereby held in check.

Far more potent than any military station, however, was the genius of Agricola in winning the conquered Britons to accept the rule of Rome and the heightened civilisation that was brought in its train, and for a period of three centuries we can imagine the Celtic city transformed more and more by Roman influences carefully mating with the ancient British stock, the ruder dwellings giving place to Roman villas, trackways made into roads, and the ancient governing rules welded into a strict legal code which is the basis of all British administration to-day. Little, unfortunately, survives in our midst (although much may still lie beneath the surface awaiting the spade of the investigator bringing it to light) except the Centurion's Ring found in Murray-street and the ancient Roman roads.

From the Castlefield Camp the Romans drove a road, crossing the river by a probably existing ford and along the site of our present Regent-road, dividing into two forks at about Cross Lane, passing on either side of Buile Hill, which provided a useful outlook station, and going thence one in the direction of Coccium (Wigan) and the other towards the mouth of the Mersey. Another road left the castrum by the north gate, and, skirting the bank of the river (present-day Deansgate), followed the high land to the north-west in the direction of Ribchester, passing on the way the low hill, Rainsough, on which another outpost station was set corresponding to the similar eminence on the opposite side of the valley at Buile.

The religion of the Roman soldiery was the Persian cult of Mithras worship, which at one time was the great rival of Christianity. The temples of Mithras were usually made within caves or chambers below the ground. On the opposite bank of the river from the Castrum was a great natural cave, and here, on the fringe of the woodlands in whose dark depths the Druids had practised their awesome rites, the troops of the First Frisian Cohort who formed the garrison, set up their altar to Fortuna Maxima.

The Romans may have taught our Celtic forbears much of imperishable value, but in the greater luxury of living they introduced was sapped that "rude greatness of soul." When, therefore, the Goths were clanging at the gates of the Eternal City, and the Brito-Romans, in common with all troops of the Empire, were recalled to the defence of the capital, little of the old-time fighting spirit remained in those left behind, and the province of Maxima Cæsariensis, the Roman territorial designation of this district, fell under the onslaughts of the wild barbarians from further north.

The Arthurian legends are the only faint pin-pricks of illumination which light the period of British history after the Roman withdrawal. King Arthur may be but a shadowy historical figure, but there is not the slightest doubt that there was at this time a great leader who drew the ancient elements together and re-established a Celtic kingdom in the West. At the same time there came from across the North Sea a bold race of sea-faring adventurers, to whom the defenceless Brito-Romanos turned for defence against the Scottish savages, only to find that these new defenders were conquerors, too, and, having routed the northern hordes, themselves possessed the land, coming over in ever-increasing waves until they outnumbered the Britons.

CHAPTER III

A Town of Saxon Kings.

THE civilisation of Rome was a settled order of things, spreading itself wherever its arms advanced, and although the Roman occupation laid the foundations, if we are to seek the real formative influences of our national life they will be found in that period of perpetual war and tumult which marks the settlement of the Saxon in the land. No longer dominated by a paramount authority, the country was divided into contending kingdoms whose development varied according to local racial tendencies and the power of the strong right arm.

One hundred years after Hengist settled his marauding Saxons in Kent, the north-east was invaded by a new race, who came over in a body from their Jutland homes with thoughts of colonisation rather than to ravage and to slay. In 547, these Angles, under Ida, established the Kingdom of Bernicia, to be followed by a further tribe under Aella, who created a new Kingdom in what we to-day know as Yorkshire, but was then British Deira. Gradually spreading themselves over the Midlands, the Kingdom of Mercia was founded. Aethelfrith, grandson of Ida, married the daughter of Aella, and forcibly united the crowns of Bernicia and Deira into one Kingdom of Northumbria. Then began the incessant sanguinary conflict that was to maintain for centuries, the duel for supremacy between Northumbria and Mercia.

Aella had a young son, Eadwine, who, to escape the tyrant Aethelfrith, was placed under the protection of Cadvan, King of North Wales. Aethelfrith overcame Cadvan at the Battle of Chester in 613, and so gained a footing on the western sea, driving a wedge between the Britons of Wales and the Britons of Cumbria.

With these facts in mind we shall better appreciate the strategic importance of the lands lying between the Ribble and the Mersey, a sort of buffer state, the key to which was the town that kept the gateway and bordered the contesting kingdoms. Such a town would assuredly be possessed always by whomsoever was the dominant king ; and perhaps we can trace here the origin of the indisputable fact that whilst there were bondmen and slaves elsewhere, the men of Salford have always been free, with no other overlord than the King himself.

It also reveals the explanation of the notion of defence stressed in almost the whole of our local place names, and, not the least, it explains the name the town then received and which has endured unchanged for over fourteen hundred years.

"Names," says Locke, "are not a mere description of things themselves, but of our concepts of them." To attempt to explain local place names, therefore, by some matter-of-fact interpretation is to miss the very important point that these names were more often than not conferred originally by a people of romantic mind, who gave thereto something of their own outlook and personality, and, often enough, meant to convey in the naming some significant attribute. If British influence is traceable in the names of natural features such as hills and rivers, the permanent naming of towns was almost entirely the work of the Saxons, and a careful examination of such names will often reveal a special characteristic in the seeming commonplace.

Dr. Murray, of Oxford, perhaps the greatest authority on such matters, has pointed out that the name of Salford has practically remained unaltered in form, and is so written in Domesday. After pursuing many interesting conjectures, only to reject them, it seems most reasonable to believe that the name is derived from two Anglo-Saxon words, " *soel* " (the hall), and " *ord* " (the prince). The significance of this interpretation is emphasised when we come to examine other adjacent place names. Immediately contiguous on the south side is Ordsall, originally "Woerdsal," the warding or guarding place of the hall, commanding the South Ford and the approach from Cheshire. To the north, occupying a similar strategical position guarding the approach along the Irwell Valley is " Caersael "—the fort of the hall. Joining these two outposts, and surviving still in part, is a way bearing the significant name of " Waellnaess "—the wall or rampart along the high land. The river formed a protective barrier on three sides of the town, and the open western side, where met the ancient roads along the high ridges on each side of the valley, would be defended by this fortified rampart.

What is to-day known as Mode Wheel was, anciently, the Manor of Shoresworth, a name derived from " Sceaweard "— the advanced look-out post. Here was, until quite recent times, a " Campfield," whence the garrison outpost, concealed in their forest eyrie, would be able to observe all that passed along the great military highway from Chester.

" Penulton " was " the village beyond the ramparts," between which and the Shoresworth woods stretched a fertile meadow, " Saedleah," our present Seedley. Clustering around the ford which carried the road from Waellnaess across the river to connect with the Roman road, formerly the old British track that is now Bury Old Road, was " Buhrton," " the village by the camp or fort." At the junction of these two roads was a " Camp," from which the present Camp Street derives its name, and the site of which was occupied for centuries by farm buildings. Hard by was a natural eminence known as Barrow Hill, and further along the Tetlow Brook the city boundary still embraces a singular, rectangular excrescence once known as " Camel Field." Six hundred feet north of Broughton Camp was " Foghcastle," " the fort on the hill," and the same distance to the west of the latter was " Rainshow," " the shielding hill," overlooking the Agecroft Ford. On the hog's back ridge extending from Foghcastle to Caersael was Castle Hill, whereon was, within recent times, a conspicuous artificial escarpment resembling the Mode Wheel Camp. It has been suggested that these various landmarks are survivals of the Roman agrimensorial or surveying system, but it seems far more probable that they indicate the main points of the Saxon defences command- ing the Northern and Eastern approaches, as Woerdsael and Sceaweard did on the south.

Still another trace of this idea of defence survives in one of our existing street names. At what dim period of time the trackway that is now Oldfield Road was first trampled out by the feet of men cannot be known, but its antiquity may be gauged from its name, indicating " the pathway across the Houldfield "—" the place of great strength " forming the encampment of the regular army or militia— " the fyrd," maintained perpetually in and about the town. The western side of this fortified enclosure abutted on the Waellnaess, and its outline may be roughly traced in the remarkably regular rectangular area bounded by Oldfield

Road, Regent Road, Cross Lane and The Crescent, which latter originally bore the illuminating name of Broken Bank. Military valour in those days was the only test of citizenship, the thegn of every five hides of land had to supply one combatant, and all males capable of bearing arms were enrolled in the "fyrd." Girded with the support of this great force, the King-Lord in his capital could count himself secure.

Where, then, was the site of the Anglo-Saxon Royal Hall that conveyed so great an import to the early town, but which has been swept away into the limbo of the forgotten past without one single trace remaining. Careful study of the various possibilities suggests one site in particular, the free and somewhat rugged upland now covered by the Adelphi.

Almost entirely embraced by the bend of the river, its situation at the junction of the two ridges of high land flanking the course of the Irwell gave an uninterrupted prospect along the river valley to the distant Winter Hill, and southwards, a wide view over the Cheshire Plain. Significant also is the fact that from this position ran the ancient paths to the fords at Ordsall, Stanyhurst and Broughton, and to the Roman road through South Lancashire.

It was eminently a site that would commend itself for such an important building as the High Hall ; and here we can picture the Anglo-Saxon ruler in his high-gabled, timbered Mead Hall, like Hrothgar in the Beowulf saga, the epic strains of which, sung by the minstrels, thrilled and inspired King and warriors alike in the Court and the camp, wielding dominion over the surrounding lands twelve centuries ago.

Who was the first Saxon King to establish himself here ? It is well within the bounds of credence to suggest that the building of the original hall was the work of Aethelfrith, shortly after the Battle of Chester, and concurrent with the beginnings of the Kingdom of Northumbria, of which the town of Salford would form the western outpost between the hills and the seaboard.

Around the Hall would be grouped the domestic apartments, the dwellings of the Radmanii or Royal Guard, and the hutments of the lowly serfs, the menials of the Court, the whole contained within a pallisaded fence. Beyond this fence, clustered in groups, dwelt those who were entitled to live within the protection of the overlord, the villeins, or small farmers, the Bordars, who were cottagers possessing some small portion of soil under the obligation to serve the Hall with eggs and poultry, and all whose business attached them to the Court, and the life of a market town.

In 872 the whole of the district fell into the hands of the Danes, who divided the lands amongst their followers. This was confirmed by the Peace of Wedmore, by which the sovereignty of Alfred was limited to the southern and western parts of England. It is incorrect to speak of Alfred as the originator of the system of Hundreds. The Anglo-Saxon administrative system was not created by any one person or during any one age, but grew by degrees, and it is probable that for long enough before the time of Alfred the Great, the Salford Hundred had been in existence, taking its name from its capital town. In 923 Edward the Elder, son of Alfred, having reconquered Mercia, set himself to subjugate Northumbria and Cumbria, and having apparently taken Salford, sought to strengthen his hold upon the town by sending soldiers to rebuild the old Roman Fort across the river which had long lain in ruins. Could we but lift the veil we should most probably see this Royal Burgh a cockpit of that incessant sanguinary struggle for Northumbrian supremacy in which move the figures of Eadgar, Sweyn and Canute. Certain it is that in common with similar Saxon Burghs, it was thriving and free, a stronghold of trade, where self-government was matured in a turbulent age, its men, the Burhwara, having privileges of a higher order than the ceorls, electing their local officers headed by the Gerefa (the early mayor or reeve), keeping their own watch and ward, constituting the " fyrd " or defence force, and from the fact of living in a state of society developing a social influence. So in Salford a thousand years ago was the free spirit of local government being developed with the king exercising seignorial rights over all.

CHAPTER IV.

Early Christian Influences.

A N ancient tradition asserts that in the Fifth Century, Germanus, Bishop of Auxerre, visited Britain to repel the Pelagian heresy, and was accompanied through the West of Britain by St. Patrick. The record of their journeyings asserts that, refused admittance to a walled city, they encamped at a distance beyond, on the banks of a stream wherein they baptised their converts, calling this water " Gidea Broc," " the brook where homage was rendered to God." The Gilda Brook forms the present boundary between Salford and Eccles, the latter place doubtless deriving its name from the " cell " or hermitage then established, the first ecclesiastical building of the district, and the reference to the " walled city " seems likely to be to the fortified town of Salford with its great ramparts at Waellnaess. The Ladywell, on the Salford-Eccles boundary, whence the villagers of Eccles up to quite recent times derived their water supply, but now unhappily converted into a railway pumping station, is believed to be the actual spot where the saints laboured in their holy mission.

It was the custom of the early missionaries to establish a feldekirk, by setting up a cross near to a camp or town, where they used to preach Christianity. Within the bounds of the Anglo-Saxon town of Salford sites of three such crosses are recorded, at Cross Lane, White Cross Bank and Greengate (where later the Town Cross stood), a fact that is not surprising when it is considered what a populous centre of civil and military interests the town of those days was.

These early crosses were doubtless first set up in the seventh century, when Eadwine, son of Aella, and successor of Aethelfrith on the Northumbrian throne, married Aethelburga of Kent, and was persuaded to embrace the Christian faith, extending his patronage and protection to Paulinus, who was created Archbishop of York. Then commenced an intensive missionary campaign on the part of Paulinus, as a consequence of which the whole of this northern realm forsook Woden for a higher worship.

Mention has previously been made of the Great Cave of

WODEN'S CAVE AT ORDSALL.

FROM A DRAWING MADE ON
THE SPOT IN 1780 BY BARRITT.

Ordsall wherein the Roman soldiery worshipped. When the pagan Saxons first settled here they transformed this cave into a place of devotion to Woden, their supreme deity, to whom sacrifices were made by the travellers using the near-by ford. Hence the name of Woden's Den, by which it has been known for centuries since. When Christian influences began to prevail, this rocky cell became a hermitage of Christian monks, and Dr. Hibbert Ware believes that it was used as a chapel by the monks of the Cluniac order prior to their establishment at Kersal by Hugh de Burun in the reign of Stephen. A description of the cave in 1780 has been left by Barritt, who says : " . . . on part of the rock much labour has been bestowed in ornamenting it with Runic characters, and in one part the sacred initials, I.H.S., in rude text three feet long . . . a few shields ornamented with crosses, and near the south end the faint remains of a shield with a sword handle across it." It may be recalled that it was in this cave that Bess Orton, in Ainsworth's novel, died in the arms of Guy Fawkes. Like many another precious relic of Old Salford, the Cave, whose site was approximately the land bordered now by Ordsall Lane, Everard Street, Oldfield Road and Woden Street, was destroyed by iconoclastic hands, James Hall, the Quaker dyer, who built his house "Sunnyside," on Ordsall Hill, in 1808, destroying the cave to save his land from antiquarian trespass.

The conflict between Northumbria and Mercia had developed into one between Christianity and paganism, and Penda, the heathen King of Mercia, uniting with Cadwallon, King of North Wales, defeated Eadwine at Heathfelth in Yorkshire in 633. Two years later Oswald succeeded in re-establishing the supremacy of Northumbria, and seven years later this Champion of Christendom met Penda at Masafelth. If, as is generally believed, this place was our Lancashire Makerfield, is it too much to surmise that it would be from the Royal Burgh of Salford that the sainted King went forth to battle and whence his body would be born back from the stricken field ? Penda met his fate in 654 at Winwaedfelth, near Leeds, at the hands of Oswin, Oswald's successor, who thus established the triumph of Faith in Britain.

Thus within a comparatively short radius of Salford were fought the three decisive Christian battles of this realm.

CHAPTER V.

Salford in Domesday.

The clearest knowledge we have of Saxon England is
that which is contained in the survey of the kingdom made
by William I. in 1080—1086 and called the " Domesday
Boc." Norman Commissioners were sent into each county,
juries summoned in every hundred, and a faithful and
impartial record made of everything appertaining to the land
and its ownership. What we know to-day as South
Lancashire was surveyed under Cheshire as " Intei Ripam et
Mersha," that is, " The Lands between Ribble and Mersey,"
and of the six hundreds into which this territory was divided
at the time of the Domesday Survey, Salford is the only one
which retains its ancient area unchanged.

The following is the translation of the actual record in the
Survey concerning Salford :—

" King Edward (the Confessor) held Salford. There
" are three hides. And twelve carves of land waste.
" And forest three miles long and the same broad. And
" there are many hays and an aery of hawks. King
" Edward held Radcliffe for a manor. There is one hide
" and another hide belonging to Salford. The Church of
" Saint Mary and the Church of Saint Michael held in
" Mamecestre one carve of land free from all customs
" save Danegeld.

" To this manor there belong twenty-one berewicks
" held by as many thanes as manors. In which there
" were eleven hides and a half and ten and a half carves
" of land. The woods there are nine miles and a half
" long and five miles and one quartern broad.

" One of these thanes Gamel, holding two hides in
" Racedham (Rochdale) had them free from all customs
" save these six : Theft, Heinfare, Forestal, Breach of
" the King's Peace, Destroying Boundary firmly placed,
" Remaining behind after oath taken to fight. For these
" the amends were forty shillings. Others of these lands
" were free from all customs save Danegeld and are now
" partly free from Danegeld.

" The whole manor of Salford, with the hundred,
" paid thirty-seven pounds four shillings. There are
" now in the manor, in the demesne two ploughs and
" eight serfs, and two villeins with one plough. This
" demesne is worth one hundred shillings.

" The land of this manor is held by the knights, of
" the gift of Roger of Poictou. Nigel has three hides
" and half a carve of land. Warin two carves of land.
" And another Warin one carve and a half. Goisfrid
" one carve of land. Gamel two carves of land. In
" these are three thanes and thirty villeins and nine
" bordars and a priest and ten serfs. Among them all
" they have twenty-two ploughs. It is worth seven
" pounds. The men of this manor of Salford did not
" work by custom at the hall of the king ; nor did they
" reap in August. They only made one hay (enclosure
" for deer) in the wood. And they were subject to the
" forfeitures for bloodshed and for the violation of
" women. They shared in the other customs of other
" superior manors."

The land between Ribble and Mersey, as has been
previously noted, had by force of conflict passed from
Northumbria to Mercia about 923, and although the
connection thus wrought with the more settled Midlands
had borne fruit to some little extent, the district had little
attraction for the Norman settlers. In consequence, it
passed through the Conquest almost unscathed and with
practically no displacement of the Saxon and Danish Thanes
from their ancestral estates. The Hundreds into which the
district was divided were actually the great manors anciently
established, and loosely termed " shires " in the absence of
any over-riding shire organisation, whereby the whole district
would have been incorporated in the general administrative
system of the kingdom.

The Manor of Salford at the Domesday Survey embraced
an area of 350 square miles with an estimated population of
35,280. Only a small portion of this vast area was cultivated,
the remainder being covered by great stretches of forest,
of pasture lands, and of dreary uncultivated wastes such as
the moors and the hill country. Salford itself was Royal
Demesne as was the sub-manor of Radcliffe, and there were
twenty-one sub-manors in thanage.

Domesday was merely a rate book, hence the tantalising paucity of descriptive detail.   As the centre of administration, the only place that could be termed populous in the light of those days was the town that lay around about the Manor House, the place of meeting as well as the market for the scattered peoples of the Hundred. The Norman Commissioners were concerned only with recording the ownership of the land as the basis of taxation, and it is not strange, therefore, that whatever urbanities existed should have been omitted from the Survey.   The absence of these particulars has led local historians into conjectures which seem hardly feasible, even to the extent of supposing an important Saxon town of Mamecestre and ignoring entirely the actual existence of the town from which the whole district drew its name.   It is surely time that many of these fallacies were re-examined in a less prejudiced light and just meed rendered to Salford, the indisputable capital of these parts throughout Saxon times.

As the administrative centre, it is inconceivable that the Salford of those days would be without its Church or Churches, and I suggest that the Domesday reference to the Churches of Saint Mary and Saint Michael should be read as applying to the Saxon Churches within the Royal Burgh of Salford which had presumably been endowed with a carve of glebe land on the opposite side of the river in a district whose designation was derived from its contiguity to the old fort. This seems a far more reasonable conclusion that the many ingenious but rather strained attempts that have been made to fix elsewhere the situation of these much-debated edifices.

Domesday is the great source of English historical knowledge, a document that has no parallel elsewhere, and it is with no uncertain thrill of pride that we glean from this survey, bare and scanty though the details concerning this district be, the importance of Salford even in those days half-way twixt the Romans and ourselves, and conjure up a picture of king and nobles riding to the chase in Salford Forest where our hard-pressed teeming population now seeks with difficulty for room to live.

CHAPTER VI

After the Conquest.

A T one fell stroke William achieved perhaps the most dramatic act of the Conquest. By declaring forfeit the estates of all who had resisted his assumption of the Crown he secured possession of the whole soil of England, except that held by the ecclesiastics, as terra regis. Since all land now belonged to the king, a Royal Manor no longer had the significance of Saxon times, and we find Salford passing, along with other extensive grants, into the hands of Roger de Poictou, who was at the same time invested with privileges of an earl exercising under the king all the attributes of regal state in the domains assigned to him. Roger divided the Hundred of Salford amongst a select number of " Barones comitatus," but retained Salford itself in demesne, and demesne it has always remained, as Professor Tait points out, whether Roger's fief was in the hands of the crown or of some great subject. Salford never owed obedience to a superior beneath the rank of an earl, and since Henry of Lancaster became King Henry IV., the King of England has continuously been the Lord of Salford.

Towards the end of William's reign, for some unestablished reason, the King resumed Roger's fief, but it was regranted by William Rufus only to be forfeited again when in 1102 Roger joined the rebellion of his brother, Robert de Belleme, and was in consequence banished the kingdom, his estates reverting to the Crown.

The town and wapentake of Salford then passed to William Peverel, Lord of Nottingham, the illegitimate son of the Conqueror. Joining Stephen against the claims of the Empress Maud, William Peverell, at the battle of Lincoln, fell into the hands of Ranulph Gernons, Fourth Earl of Chester, who then assumed the Lordship of Salford. A state of anarchy at this time held the land and the claims of the Earl of Chester were hotly disputed by William Peverel the younger, but Ranulph was as subtle as he was brave and secured confirmation of his possession from Stephen, Maud and Henry of Normandy (afterwards Henry the Second).

Ranulph died on December 16, 1153, as the result, it is said, of poisoning at the hands of William Peverel in revenge for having seized his estates.

The troublesome reign of Stephen had now come to an end, and at the time that Thomas à Becket became Chancellor of England under Henry II., Salford was receiving a new lord in the person of Hugh Kelvilioc, the fifth Earl of Chester, who, in 1181, was succeeded by his son, the famous Ranulph de Blundeville.

The Lancashire Pipe Rolls and other old records, such as the Lancs. Inquests and Extents, throw an interesting light on Salford and its inhabitants about this time. In 1168 the men of Salford paid £14 10s. to the aid for marrying the King's daughter. In 1201 there was an increase of 4s. in the rent of the manor for the half-year. The assized rent of Salford in 1226 was 23s., and the vill, with its dependancies— Broughton, Ordsall and a moiety of Flixton—paid 112s. tallage.

King Henry III., on June 4th, 1228, granted a weekly market on Wednesdays, and an annual fair on the eve, day and morrow of the Nativity of Saint Mary, at his manor of Salford. This stimulated the growth of the town as a trading place, a development greatly assisted by the Charter of two years later, and significantly reflected in the increased rent, which in 1257 amounted to £12 a year. The receipts for a half-year are recorded as : Assized rent of the Borough, 65s. 3d. and 40d. ; perquisites of courts, 5s. 3d. ; toll of the Borough at farm, 40s.—113s. 10d.—to which was added 6s. 8d. paid by Agnes the Reeve's widow for the wardship of her daughter's land.

The extent made in 1346 shows that there were then 129 1/3 burgages, each rendering the 12d. yearly rent, and there were also a number of free tenants paying over £8 10s. for lands in Salford and adjoining it. The profits of the Portmote were valued at 12s. a year, making a total of nearly £16 a year. The free tenants were :—

Henry de Pilkington . . . . Three islands of land by the bank of the Irwell, by charter of Wm. de Ferrars to Robert, son of Thomas de Salford, at 6s. 8d. rent.

John Bibby ....The common oven, with four acres at 4s.

John de Radcliffe ....63 acres approved from the waste in Salford, Pendleton and Pendlebury at 31s. 6d.

Thos. de Strangeways..........15 acres from the waste.

John de Leyland ....5 acres at 2s. 6d.

Robt. Walker, John de Stanlow, and Adam Wright ....2 acres in common at 1s. 6d.

Henry de Bolton ....34 acres at 17s. 3d.

Roger de Mancestre ....6½ acres at 3s. 3d.

Henry Marche.................1 acre at 6d.

Robt. de Hur' ....2 acres at 12d.

Wm. Margotson ....1 acre at 6d.

Thos. de Pilkington ....2 acres at 12d.

Thos. Geoffreyson ....5 acres at 7s. 6d.

Henry, son of William de Salford 5½ acres at 2s. 9d.

All the above were obliged to grind the corn growing on these lands to the twenty-fourth measure, but had rights of pasturage and turbary.

Other tenants were Roger Dickeson, Maud Linals, and Ellen Shokes. John de Radcliffe and Henry de Pilkington held some other lands, the latter claiming the right to keep the pinfold, but he had also to provide lodgings at the lord's will in two of his burgages. Many of the free tenants held burgages also. The most considerable holders were John de Prestwich, with fourteen and a fraction, and Henry de Worsley, with about the same. Other holdings ranged from half a burgage up to five, and were held amongst others by Adam de Pendleton, Alexander de Pilkington, John de Oldfield, James de Byron, John, his brother, and the heir of Geoffrey de Trafford.

The Sherriff's compotus of 1348 shows a similar total to that of 1246, and, in addition, it states that John de Radcliffe had the water-mill at a rent of 66s. 8d.

When we turn to the Duchy Records, another interesting crop of place names and people is revealed. In 1337, Alexander de Pilkington released to Henry, Earl of Lancaster, his right in the waste for his two burgages, reserving turbary (the right to go upon the soil of another to dig and carry off turf) and free entry and exit. In return for a similar release by John, son of Ellen Chokes, the Earl in 1339 granted him

15 acres of the waste at a rent of 7s. 6d. In 1402, Ralph de Prestwich and Alured de Radcliffe had a license to build two mills on the Irwell, and this seems to have been renewed to the former in 1425 in the form of a lease for ninety years at 13s. 4d. a year. Henry de Buckley in 1414 had a lease of the toll of Salford at a rent of five and a half marks, and eleven years later, James de Prestwich succeeded him at the lower rent of 60s.

The Holtfield, Windlehey and Shawfoot are place names that occur repeatedly, and other surnames mentioned are Oldfield, Highfield, Bird and Grant.

Amongst the Hunt deeds are the following relating to lands in Salford :—

> 1397.—Regrant of a half burgage to Ellen, daughter of Alexander de Pilkington, lying between the burgage of Henry, son of John de Strangeways and that of Henry del Helde, with remainder to John Lancashire.
>
> 1399.—Emmota de Glazebrook gave to Henry del Helde and Emmota his wife a burgage between the burgage of John de Radcliffe called the Cornel Orchard, and that of John Bibby, called the Neldurs Acre.
>
> 1423.—Edmund de Trafford granted to Ralph, son of Ralph de Prestwich, his claim in land called the Gledeyard.
>
> 1447.—Grant by feoffees to Roger Bird of Salford of three acres of arable land and a meadow called Merevall.
>
> 1513.—Roger, son and heir of James Bird granted to Richard Hunt a burgage called the Cornel Orchard.

Records of various disputes amongst the inhabitants are shown in the Plea Rolls. John de Broughton and Agnes his wife, in 1274, recovered certain messuages and lands in Salford in the latter's right. In 1292, Geoffrey de Worsley and Agnes his wife were non-suited in a claim against Richard the Leycestre and others respecting a tenement in Salford. In 1346, John, son of Geoffrey Walker, claimed two messuages and lands against Ellen, daughter of Richard de Salford, Roger the Barker, and Margaret, widow of Richard de Worsley.

Joan, daughter of Thomas de Pilkington, in 1352, unsuccessfully claimed a messuage and land against Henry del Wood and Joan his wife. She alleged that her uncle,

Richard de Pilkington, chaplain, had demised the same to Joan with the stipulation that they might be redeemed on payment of £6. Henry del Wood and Joan his wife were plaintiffs against William de Highfield in 1354, and in 1357 recovered a tenement in Salford against Joan, daughter of Thomas de Pilkington, Cecily, his widow, and William de Highfield. Mather Newton, in 1432, acquired a toft in Salford from Henry Chadwick and Cecily his wife.

The Worsley family long held lands in Salford. In 1343, Henry de Worsley leased to Robert the Miller 1½ roods upon Sandywell, a rood in the Whitacre, 1½ acres on Ollerschagh and on Kolleschot, and 3 roods in the Middlefield between lands of John de Prestwich and Richard de Pilkington, chaplain, deceased, at a rent of 6s.

William, son of Walter de Salford, gave a messuage in Salford, held of the King by a rent of 12d. to his sister Agnes. She married one Roger Dikeson and had a daughter Emma, wife of Robert Bibby, whose son John Bibby claimed in 1394. Roger Dikeson, however, gave the messuage to Stephen the Cook and Joan his wife and Emma their daughter. Joan, as widow, transferred it to Wm. de Radcliffe, the occupier under him being Ellis del Helde in, or before, 1359. Ellis was outlawed for trespass, but his natural son Henry obtained possession and held it in 1394.

In 1338, Cecily, daughter of Roger the Barker granted two burgages in Salford to Geoffrey, son of Sir Henry de Trafford, and immediately afterwards Roger the Barker gave his lands to the same Geoffrey.

Thus in these yellowing parchments gleams a magic glow wherein the rude forefathers of our city, gathered to the dust more than half a thousand years ago, live again in their loves and quarrels and friendships, in alliances prompted often as not by increase of estate as much as of hand and heart.

CHAPTER VII

The Monks of Kersal Vale.

IT is interesting at this juncture to turn and observe certain developments in the ecclesiastical life of Salford. Woden's Den in Ordsall, it has been previously pointed out, had reverted, perhaps during the missionary efforts of Paulinus in these parts, from pagan to Christian use, and for long enough was an oratory attached to a hermitage of monks who kept the adjoining ford. Odin was still regarded with superstitious awe as shielding the wayfarer against the perilous accidents of flood and field, and the pious monks sought to turn this pagan belief to a more holy faith by themselves acting as guides and escorts across the ford and the perilous surrounding marshes of "trembling mud," through which Sir Lancelot is said to have pursued his quest of the giant Tarquin. Early in the reign of Henry the First, William Peverel, Lord of Nottingham and Salford, founded the Priory of Lenton in Nottinghamshire as a house of Cluniac Monks, and attached thereto the ancient oratory by the Ordsall ford, and further lands in the sequestered vale of Kersal. The fords of Ordsall and Kersal lay at either end of the Wallneys, the guard-way on the western fringe of the town which, intersecting the Roman road to Soccium and Verantium, connected by these fords with the roads to Condate and Ribchester respectively. It is probable, therefore that the Monks from Woden's Den kept also the passage of the Kersal Ford, and had, too, a small cell at the latter place, and perhaps a cave in the rock beneath the shadow of Rainshow fort.

In 1154 Hugo de Burun, Lord of Horestan in Derbyshire, gave a portion of his lands to the Prior of Lenton, and, undertaking the vows of the Order, retired as a solitary recluse to Kersal. Ranulph Gernons, on taking possession of the town of Salford, confirmed the monks in their possession. In 1780 a piece of parchment which had been used as the cover to an old book was found to be an original deed of Ranulph Gernons giving foundation to a religious house at Kersal, thus following the example of his predecessor, William

Peverel, the great benefactor of the Cluniac Order. With so influential a patron as Hugo de Burun as its first monk, the Kersal house was brought into repute and the Chapel of Ordsall fell into comparative disuse. Henry the Second, in 1182, duly confirmed the hermitage of Kersal to the monastery of Lenton, and a further charter of King John in the first year of his reign gave and granted to the Church of the Sacred Trinity of Lenton " to have and to hold it in ' puram et perpetuam elemosinam ' as freely, peaceably, quietly and honourably as Hugo de Burun had held the same."

In the same year that John gave his grant, Robert, the grandson of Hugo, married the heiress of Sir Richard Clayton and became the founder of the Lancashire Byrons.

The Cluniac Order at this time had become highly honoured and famous throughout Europe for its integrity and devotion, and the monks of Kersal, who not only fulfilled their duties at the fords, but were assiduous in the work of public education, must have had a marked influence on the social life of Salford of that day. Do we find in this fact the explanation of the strange lack of parochial facilities that is so marked a feature of Salford church life up to the seventeenth century. We have record that in the early days of the church which Robert Greslet built in Manchester the rector complained to the Prior of Lenton that his parishioners in that town, just then coming into being, preferred the offices of the monks of Kersal to his own, and it is very probable that the well-attested indifference of the whole of the secular clergy of that time may have caused whatever church had existed from Saxon days in Salford to have fallen into disuse and the townspeople to have sought their spiritual ministrations entirely from the revered religious community at Kersal.

In 1222, owing to the drain which foreign houses were making on religious houses in England, the Kersal Monastery was prohibited in common with all similar establishments from sending any tax or the goods of their houses out of the country. Nearly a century later it was seized by Edward the Third as an alien monastery but subsequently given back and made denizen, and in the reign of Henry V. released entirely from its obedience to the Abbot of Clugni. Kersal Cell is the only monastic house which is known to have existed in the Hundred of Salford.

CHAPTER VIII.

A Free Borough.

W E now draw nigh to the most momentous event in the early history of Salford, when Ranulph de Blundeville, sixth Earl of Chester and Lord of Salford, granted the Charter which made the town a Free Borough.

To understand the significance of this grant, it will be necessary to observe for a moment the administrative system then in operation. For the two centuries following the Conquest there had been little interference with the rules instituted by Edward the Elder, by which all men having a fixed residence were obliged to do suit and service at the King's Court and pledge themselves with their households and dependants to keep the peace. These courts were held locally in each shire at Easter and Michaelmas and presided over by the earl in the capacity of Shire-Reeve (*Prae Positus*).

The excessive powers with which the Sheriff was armed as the representative of the king often led to grave abuse. After the Conquest, the Hundred or Wapentake of Salford was split up into baronies, whose lords were permitted to hold their own courts, but the lords themselves were still required to render personal suit and service at the superior court of the Wapentake.

Salford at this time was not only the chief seat of jurisdiction, but also the chief market town of the district. In its vicinity were many landed proprietors, such as the Traffords, representing the upper classes of society, and large numbers of other individuals of gentle lineage in severely straitened circumstances. There were also the ceorles, who were freemen, but not of noble birth, and in the lowest class of all, the villeins, who were little more than slaves. In more or less degree, all these were suffering great impoverishment.

The Town and Wapentake of Salford were the hereditary possession of the Earldom of Chester, and Ranulph himself acted as the sheriff, except during the times he was absent at the wars when Salford was held in sergeantry, first by Elias Fitz Robert and later by William de Ferrars, who married Agnes, sister of the Earl. Ranulph is said to have had a deep attachment to the town of Salford and, feeling himself growing old, desired to confer upon it the jurisdiction and privileges of a Free Borough removed entirely from the interference of any who might succeed him in the shrievalty.

Ranulph de Blundeville has been described by Bishop Stubbs as almost the last of the great feudal aristocracy of the Conquest, his vast possessions and palatine jurisdiction making his position in the kingdom unique.

> " Ich can rhyme of Robyn Hode
> And of Randolf, Erle of Chestre "

sings Langland in the " Vision of Piers Plowman," and he was a popular hero immortalised in song and story. Married to the Constance of Shakespeare's " King John," he was thus stepfather to the murdered Prince Arthur. A great favourite of Cœur de Lion, he bore one of the three swords at that monarch's coronation. Foremost in rebuking John, he was chiefly instrumental in advancing the claims of young Henry the Third to the throne, and in 1219 he was confirmed Earl of Lincoln as well as Chester.

Such was the great noble who, fifteen years after the gathering on Runnymede, granted to his town of Salford for himself and his heirs " to the end of the world," that document which is one of the most important borough charters that England has to show.

By it Salford became a borough or mutually pledged town in which every inhabitant was to be sworn and enrolled as in pledge or bail, for his neighbour. And not a borough only but a Free Borough which indicates the importance of the privileges conferred. Of these the chief was the escape from the jurisdiction of the hated sheriff's tourn. The townspeople were to have a " Portmanmote " or Court of the Portmen, giving them independent jurisdiction over all civil and criminal matters concerning the town and its people. They were to have the power of choosing their own Reeve ; they would possess burgages of their own with power of sale or gift (with one exception, to which fuller reference will be made later) ; they were allowed to develop, unhindered, industrial arts and commercial pursuits ; they were to have the opportunity of serving the needs of the State in a wider form.

It was not altogether mere affection that caused Ranulph to elevate Salford to a leading position amongst the towns of the day. So great and leading a personality in the affairs both of Church and State was often pressed for money and men.

During his campaigns in France he had seen the communes or burghs there with chartered liberties developing in population and prosperity, and often enough rendering invaluable aid therefrom to the king or lord from whom they had derived their liberties and privileges. By creating the Free Borough of Salford he was desirous of attracting thereto the oppressed and impoverished peoples of the countryside, who, by taking up residence in the newly-privileged town and profiting by its municipal advantages, would vastly improve their social condition. What a prospect did the far-sighted Earl offer even to the villein, the wretched bondsman of lordly caprice. Here in Salford, should he succeed in escaping from his domain, would be a place of refuge where, if he dwelt without claim for a year and a day, he would be completely emancipated from servitude.

No longer a hapless serf, in Salford town he could seek in honest industry a means of better subsistence, and as a free burgess enjoy without molestation the rights to which his labour entitled him. And as to the villein, so in varying measure to all others of high caste and low caste who, by taking up burgages in the new borough, would become as the burghers of the free communes of France and make their contribution by talliage or by scot and lot to the defence of their country and the freedom of its institutions.

Wise and puissant Ranulph, though seven centuries divide his day from ours, the wheatsheaves upon our coat of arms will ever serve to remind us of the debt of gratitude we owe to the noble earl, whose badge they were, and who first set the infant feet of our Salford and his towards some better and more prosperous goal.

CHAPTER IX.

The Charter.

THE original document of Earl Ranulph—one of the most precious historical documents of the country—is jealously preserved in a locked chest in the Town Hall. A copy, together with a translation, hangs in the Royal Museum at Peel Park.

Its clauses fall under four headings which Dr. Hibbert Ware has most excellently explained as follows :

First, the charter explained the terms upon which a settlement might be procured by the acquisition of burgage tenures. Each person wishing to be enrolled as a burgher of Salford was to have one acre of land as his burgage, for which he was to pay by the year twelve pence for all service which to that burgage belonged, namely at the Nativity of our Lord, threepence ; at Mid-Lent, threepence ; at the feast of the Blessed John the Baptist, threepence, and at the feast of the blessed Michael, threepence.

If a burgess had not an heir he might leave his burgage to whom he listed ; but if he had an heir he could not give or pledge or sell his burgage to whom he chose without an option being given to the next heir to buy same. The widow of a burgess was allowed to remain in the house with the heir, and have necessaries so long as she remained without husband ; but if she re-married she might depart freely without dower, and the heir remain in the house.

The tenements of the borough could not be included in any debts liable to be distrained ; whoever would sell his burgage should pay fourpence and go freely without hindrance with all his chattels, and a third restriction was " that no burgage be alienated to religion."

The burgesses were to have free pasture in the woods, the plain and in all the pastures of Salford ; be free of pannage (toll for pasturing hogs) in the wood itself of Salford ; have, in reason, all the timber they required from the wood for building and burning. Besides these manorial advantages the burgesses had to perform certain customs as " boon work." And in order that an heir might not suffer unduly from an excessive relief payable before he came into his property it was declared that the heir should give no other relief than his arms, to wit, a sword, a bow, or a lance.

Secondly, the charter of Salford sought to promote the extension of commercial dealings. Then, as now, industrial professions were thought to be best protected by monopoly, and no one was allowed to exercise his trade in the wapentake except within the borough. The burgesses were, however, allowed to traffic in buying and selling with whomsoever they might, to hold markets and fairs without any toll except the curious toll of salt. It is interesting to note that the Lord Mayor of London, too, levied the twentieth part of whatever salt entered the port of London.

Thirdly, the charter provided a new and liberal system of internal jurisdiction. Before the charter was granted Salford was termed a Port, each inhabitant a " portman," and the prefect, who was appointed by the lord of the town, a " portreeve." Now the burgesses might choose a reeve for themselves, removable at the end of each year. Under the reeve was to be held a court leet or " Portmanmote " for the review of the frank pledge required from the burgesses, and to try all such cases as appertained to the indwellers of Salford exclusively. The reeve was to be known as the " Borough-reeve," thus inaugurating the long unbroken line represented by the present Mayor. If a debt was proved and the debtor failed to make payment by the eighth day from the reeve's order, he was to pay a fine in addition to the debt, of twelve pence to the lord and fourpence to the reeve. In charges of robbery and assault, the aggravated cases were to be referred to a superior authority of twelve knights of the Hundred.

Lastly, the charter was to enable the borough of Salford to better administer to the exigencies of the State, and the final clause of the charter indicates very clearly that it was part of Ranulph's purpose in creating the borough to assist him to meet the talliages which Henry the Third so frequently made to aid the supply of men for his foreign wars and the defence of Lancashire from the Scots.

The burgesses were bound to contribute to the public charges by paying their " scot," and to bear the " lot " of the place that is serving a turn in the wars, keeping watch and ward, and filling in succession the local offices of the

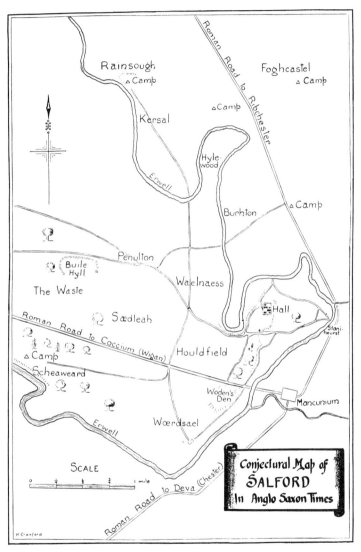

PLAN OF SALFORD IN ANGLO-SAXON TIMES.

borough. They were also required under a law of Henry the Second to provide themselves with armour and weapons.

That Earl Ranulph drew his inspiration largely from the French bourgs is seen in the burgage of uniform size and the rent and fines of twelve pence, all of which are derived from the customs of the Norman bourg of Breteuil.

Such were the privileges conferred upon the free burgesses of Salford, liberal in their day, and in some cases in advance of the age in which they were framed, and it may be worth while examining more closely, as affecting the later development of the town, the strange clauses in which burgages are forbidden to be sold or given to religion.

Perhaps the most important act of Ranulph's life was his resistance to the supremacy of the Pope. For years the Papal Domination had been increasing in England, the King himself had become a mere vassal of Rome, the country was suffering from the abuse by the ecclesiastics of that time of civil privileges. Led by the Earl of Chester a number of the principal noblemen determined to defend the free institutions of the country from the oppression of both King and Pope. So formidable was Ranulph regarded that when Pope Gregory demanded a tenth of the revenues of the clergy to enable him to wage war against the Emperor Frederic, the only part of the country that escaped the galling impost was the Palatinate of Chester. Included in the districts that were impatient of the yoke of Rome was therefore the town of Salford. Such a clause as appears in the charter is not known elsewhere, and in view of the prevalent feeling of the period, and especially the part taken in the matter by Ranulph himself, it is not unreasonable to surmise that the Earl deliberately precluded any burgage being utilised, even for the building of a new Parish Church in the town, and so deprived the Burgesses of an amenity for the provision of which they had to wait another four hundred years. At that time, on the opposite bank of the river, Robert Greslet had taken up his residence and was busily engaged in trying to establish a town on his estates. To get back into favour with the Pope, by whom he had been excommunicated, he built a church which was destined to become, in the absence of an edifice in Salford, the ecclesiastical centre of the district. How different might the later development of Salford have been but for those words in the Charter " religione excepta " !

Who were the friends whom Ranulph gathered round
him to witness his grant ? Their signatures alone make
the document beyond price. First of all was William de
Vernon, Justiciar of Chester from 1229 to 1232. The second
was no less a person than Simon de Montfort himself, the
man who, according to Freeman, gave to English freedom
its most lasting shape, the hero and martyr of England in
the greatest of her constitutional struggles. Pain de Chaworth,
the third witness, was a baron of Gloucestershire, and then
comes Fulk Fitz-Werine, the hero of the famous medieval
romance of " Foulques Fitz-Warin," wherein many remarkable
adventures are attributed to him. He was a great friend of
Earl Ranulph, with whom he went to Ireland and " there
did manie noble feates." Gilbert de Segrave was the son
and heir of Henry the Third's unpopular minister ; Walkelin
de Arderne was son and heir of Sir John Arderne, of Aldford,
in Cheshire, and later Marshal of the King's Household in
Gascony ; Roger Gernet was hereditary Chief Forester of
Lancashire. Then follow Richard de Vernon, Roger de
Derby, Galfride de Bury, Hugo de Biron (most probably the
great-grandson of the founder of the Kersal Monastery), and
Simon and John, clerks. We can see from these witnesses
that the granting of the Salford Charter was no mere item of
routine, but a noteworthy event of its day to whose
attestation were called the nobles of high rank, great possessions
and important judicial office, who attended the great Earl of
Chester in his semi-regal state.

Soon after signing the Charter, Ranulph was called away
to join the standard of the king in France, where he was one
of the five commanders entrusted with the command of the
Royal armies. Making a successful campaign in Anjou, he
recovered the possessions the folly of the king had lost, and,
returning to England, spent himself in moderating public
indignation against the action of the Pope in preventing
English natives being presented to benefices in favour of
Italian priests, and also endeavouring to bring the infamous
Hubert de Burgh to trial.

Ranulph de Blundeville's meritorious life came to an end
in 1233 and, being childless, his estates passed to his four
sisters, of whom Agnes, wife of William, Earl of Ferrars,
inherited Salford. William de Ferrars, sixth Earl of Derby,
now held Salford in chief of the king.

It should be pointed out that although eighty years after the granting of the Salford Charter, Thomas Greslet gave a charter to the town of Manchester, there is a wide difference in the status conferred by the respective documents. Manchester was not made a borough, but merely a market town with limited privileges, a fact that is very definitely declared by the inquisition taken in 1359 at the instance of the Duke of Lancaster when Roger la Warre claimed rights as the Lord of Manchester, to which the town was shown to have no title. It was then shown that the lord of Manchester had no judicial privilege except that of his court baron, that there could be no judicial officer appointed in Manchester whose authority was equal to that of the lord of the wapentake of Salford, that the jurisdiction of the wapentake of Salford and of the sheriff's tourn continued in force in all cases in the town of Manchester except as concerned the lord and his tenants, which relations were controlled by the court baron, of which the new Portmanmote of Manchester was but a subsidiary court. On the other hand, when Ranulph,—a Palatine Earl, be it remembered, and not a mere baronial lord,—granted a Portmanmote to the free borough of Salford he gave it a jurisdiction equal to that of the sheriff, and made it a completely independent entity within the Honour of Lancaster. In short, whilst Salford, in confirmation of its ancient status, received the name and title of a free borough, with all the rights, privileges and dignities attached thereto, Manchester occupied a much inferior position.

Translation of the Charter.

RANULF, EARL OF CHESTER AND OF LINCOLN, TO ALL NOW PRESENT AND TO THOSE WHO SHALL HEREAFTER HEAR OF THIS PRESENT CHARTER, GIVES SALUTATION.

I. Be it KNOWN that I have given, granted, and by this my present Charter have confirmed, that the Town of Salford may be a Free Borough, and that the Burgesses dwelling therein may have and hold all these Liberties underwritten :—

II. First, that every Burgess may hold One Acre of Land with his Burgage, and shall pay for each Burgage Twelve Pence per year for all rents pertaining to the said Burgage.

III. If the Reeve of the Town challenge any Burgess, concerning any plea, and the party challenged shall not appear at the day appointed, nor any other for him, in the Laghemoot, he shall forfeit to me Twelve Pence.

IV. If any Burgess shall sue another Burgess for any debt, and he has acknowledged the debt, the Reeve may appoint a day for him to appear (in Court), viz., the Eighth ; and if he comes not, he shall pay me Twelve Pence for forfeiture of the day, and pay the debt, and the Reeve Four Pence.

V. If any Burgess shall in anger strike or beat any other Burgess within the Borough without shedding blood, he may make peace for himself in view of the Burgesses, saving my right, viz., Twelve Pence.

VI. And if any one shall be sued within the Borough concerning any Plea, he shall not answer, if a Burgess to a bondman, or to any other, save in his own Portmannemoot, that is, concerning a Plea which appertains to the Borough.

VII. If any Burgess or other person accuse another Burgess of Theft, the Prefect shall summon him to answer and to stand Judgment in the Portemannemoot, saving my right.

VIII. If any one shall be sued by his Neighbour, or by any other person, concerning any matter which appertains to the Borough, and the complainant makes no appearance for three days, if the defendant shall have the testimony of the Reeve and of his Neighbours that his Adversary has failed to appear during those three days, he need give no answer to that plea, and the other shall be at the mercy (of the Lord of the Borough).

IX. Also no Burgess ought to bake Bread which is for sale, except at my Bakehouse, according to the reasonable Customs (of the Borough).

X. If I shall have a Mill there, the Burgesses may grind at such Mill to the Twentieth bushel ; and if I shall have no Mill there, they may grind wheresoever they wish.

XI. Likewise the said Burgesses can choose the Reeve from themselves whom they wish, and remove him at the end of the year.

XII. Also when any Burgesses shall wish to grant mortgage, or sell his Burgage, he may do so to any one, unless the Heirs wish to buy it, and then the nearest shall have the preference, saving my service, and so that it be not sold to Religion.

XIII. Moreover, the Burgesses may arrest their debtors for debts contracted in the Borough, if the debtor acknowledge the debt, unless they hold a Tenement in the Borough.

XIV. The Chattells of the Burgesses may not be detained for any other debts than their own.

XV. The aforesaid Burgesses also and all theirs, of whomsoever they may buy or sell, and wheresoever they may be within my lordships, whether at Fairs or Markets, shall be free from Toll, except the Salt Toll.

XVI. Whosoever shall break the Assize, whether of Bread or of Beer, shall suffer a forfeiture of Twelve Pence three times ; and the fourth time he shall perform the Assize of the town.

XVII. Also the said Burgesses shall have Common Free Pasture in the Wood, in the Plain, and in all the Pastures belonging to the Town of Salford ; and shall be free from pannage in the same Wood of the Town of Salford.

XVIII. The same Burgesses may take reasonably in the aforesaid Wood all necessaries for building and for burning.

XIX. Any one may also implead for his wife and for his family, and the wife of any person can pay his fine, to be made to the Reeve as he ought, and to follow the Plea for her husband, if he himself chance to be elsewhere.

XX. A Burgess, if he have no heir, can leave his Burgage and his Chattels, whensoever he dies, to whom he pleases, saving my right, viz., Four Pence and saving the service pertaining to the said Burgage be not alienated in Religion.

XXI. When a Burgess dies, his Widow shall remain in the House with the Heir and there have necessaries so long as she remains without a husband, and from the time she may wish to be married again, she may depart freely, without dower, and the Heir as lord shall remain in the House.

XXII. Also, when a Burgess dies, his Heir shall give no other Relief to me except Arms, viz., of this kind—a Sword, a Bow, or a Lance.

XXIII. No one within the Wapentake of Salford, as a Shoemaker, Currier, Fuller, or any such, may exercise his calling, except in the Borough, saving the liberties of the Barony.

XXIV. The aforesaid Burgesses, moreover, shall pay my Rent for the Burgages at four periods of the year, viz., the Nativity of Our Lord, Three Pence ; Midlent, Three Pence ; the Feast of the Blessed John the Baptist, Three Pence , and the Feast of the Blessed Michael, Three Pence.

XXV. All the above Pleas shall be decided before the Bailiffs of the lord of the Earl, upon view of the Burgesses.

XXVI. Whoever may wish to sell his Burgage, except to Religion, and to leave the Town shall pay me Four Pence, and go freely wheresoever he wishes, with all his chattels.

I, RANULPH, and my heirs, will guarantee all the aforesaid Liberties and Customs to the said Burgesses and their heirs against all men for ever, saving to me and to my heirs reasonable Tallage, except when the lord the King imposes a Tallage on his Boroughs throughout England.

In memory whereof to this present page I have affixed my seal Before these Witnesses : (1) SIR WILLIAM, Justiciar of Chester ; (2) SIMON DE MONTFORT ; (3) PAGAN DE CHAUWORTH ; (4) FULC, Son of Fitzwarrain ; (5) GILBERT DE SEGRAVE ; (6) WALKEL DE ARDERNE ; (7) RICHARD DE VERNON ; (8) ROGER GERNET ; (9) ROGER DE DERBY ; (10) GEOFFREY DE BURY ; (11) HUGH DE BIRON ; (12) SIMON and (13) JOHN, Scribes and many others.

BOOK TWO
A.D. 1230 to
A.D. 1700.

CONTENTS

BOOK TWO.—A.D. 1230–A.D. 1700.

CHAPTER I......................A Very Perfect Knight.

CHAPTER II............................The Golden Age.

CHAPTER III................The Possession of the Crown.

CHAPTER IV.... ....When the Night Watch Rode.

CHAPTER V...................Some Old Salford Manors.

CHAPTER VI......................Our Own Whittington.

CHAPTER VII......................The Maid of the Mill.

CHAPTER VIII....................................Ordsall.

CHAPTER IX........................Tragedy and Valour.

CHAPTER X.................................. Guy Fawkes.

CHAPTER XI.....................A Prince of Benefactors.

CHAPTER XII....................The Draper Astronomer.

CHAPTER XIII...............In the Seventeenth Century.

CHAPTER XIV. ....Kersal.

CHAPTER XV. ....The End of an Epoch.

CHAPTER XVI.....................The Portmote Records.

CHAPTER XVII.............The Records of the Wapentake.

CHAPTER I

A Very Perfect Knight.

IS it just mere chance or some deeper destiny that the ancient town of Salford should mark its beginnings as a Free Borough coincident with the emergence of the nation as a whole from obscurity into greatness ? For, indeed, they were momentous days which followed the granting of the Charter, when grave distractions lay upon the land, but days that pulsated with the vigour of a new-found national spirit, and an awakened intellectual life. Norman and Saxon, Briton and Roman, no longer separate streams finding each their lone course, but now joining their strains into one mighty torrent to be for ever England, a great race destined for victory and dominion beyond the ocean seas, but still groping, though not blindly, for a deeper unity and strength of purposes within the island realm.

Free labour was sweeping aside the ties of feudal tyranny, society in general was rousing itself to an effective resistance to oppression, the heritage of representative government was being hammered out in the fiery furnace, and, under pressure of the growing necessities of the community, in the Great Council a widening basis was developing in whose points of contact the growing aspirations of the conflicting orders of the nation were welded into one.

And the flooding tide of national vigour touched, too, the newly-elevated Lancashire town, stirring it to play its worthy part in the march of the times. As a borough, it was bidden by the sheriff to send two of its burgesses to take their part in the first English Parliament. We shall never know, perhaps at this distance of time, who then represented the voice of our town in the national deliberations, but it is sufficient to know with pride that our Salford was there summoned, even though we are told from one source that such poverty lay upon Lancashire in those times that no borough in the county could afford to send any of their burgesses to London.

Among those who accorded the greatest support to De Montfort was Robert de Ferrars, Earl of Derby, who, in 1254, had succeeded his father as Lord of Salford. Marching towards Chester at the head of 20,000 horse and foot de Ferrars was overcome and taken prisoner by the King's forces. Held in captivity for three years, he was offered his liberty on payment of a heavy fine, which, finding himself unable to meet, his lands became forfeit, and passing thence into the hands of Edmund Crouchback, Salford became an integral part of that surpassing power and splendour which was the House of Lancaster.

The war in Scotland and the rising of the Welsh were draining the resources of the country, and in 1282 John de Kierby, Bishop of Ely, visited Salford in course of his mission to explain the King's necessities to the people of Lancashire. Through the town, too, passed Edward the First himself when, menaced by the invasion of the Scots, the King came North to make his headquarters at Preston and enlist the men and money of Lancashire in his campaigns. Doubtless there were many Salfordians in the thousand men of Lancashire who were deputed to pursue Robert Bruce in his flight from the Rout of Perth into the fastnesses of Athol.

In 1296 the Borough of Salford was surveyed as held by the Earl of Lancaster and the profits estimated with rents of the town, including the " tollage, stallage, farm of the water mill, and the produce of a toft near the bridge," and in 1317, with other towns of Lancashire, the Reeve received a writ from the King to send as much money as the Borough could afford as " Loyalty Loan."

The fierce dispute between Piers Gaveston and certain of the great nobles raged more hotly in Lancashire than anywhere, ending finally with the execution of Thomas, Earl of Lancaster, and Lord of Salford, and the forfeiture of his estates. For a time Salford was held by the Crown, but one of the first acts of Edward the Third on ascending the throne was to reverse the attainder and reinstate Henry of Lancaster to the possession of all lands and lordships previously escheated, including the manor and lordship of Salford.

The distraction of the time was grievously intensified by three causes : Firstly, the discouragement of peaceful industry by the Scottish wars ; secondly, the difficulty of maintaining, by the decrease in villeinage, sufficient cultivation of estates to support the increasing population ; and thirdly, military habits had gained so complete an ascendancy that men were no longer able to settle down to the peaceful amenities of ordered existence. A new order of freeholders had been created to provide the requisite man-power for the wars. Base-born peasants had been endowed with small parcels of land in exchange for military service, and given the name of yeomen. In their distinctive garb of buff hide to differentiate them from warriors of more gentle birth, and armed with sword and dagger, bow and quiver, these men in intervals of campaigning flooded the land, offering their services to any disputant who would engage them. Some became outlaws, habiting the woods in bands and sallying forth to attack the civil officials and ecclesiastics whose avarice and tyranny were the terror of the impoverished husbandry and the suffering peasants. Hereabouts in the woodland districts of Lancashire and Yorkshire were the favourite fields of adventure for Robin Hood and his merry men, and oft enough the streets of Salford Town must have echoed with the frolics of these picturesque figures of medieval romance, and supplied the news for many an exploit in the adjoining greenwood.

With the ascent of Edward the Third to the throne, the anarchy of misrule gave place to more statesmanlike administration, and it was not long ere the young King fixed his attention on the internal state of his kingdom. In this seed time whence was born the first beginnings of industrial supremacy, it is impossible to overlook the part played therein by an eminent Salfordian of those early days.

Amongst the young knights, boon companions of Edward III., was one John Radcliffe, who enjoyed in marked degree the friendship of his lord and king. About the middle of the thirteenth century William de Ferrars II., nephew of Earl Ranulph, conveyed to David de Hulton the manor of Ordsall and a moiety of Flixton in exchange for Pendleton, for the homage and service of two marks of silver and the sixth part of a knight's fee. David's son, Richard, married Margery of Radcliffe Tower, who gave Ordsall to her favourite nephew, John, third son of her brother, Robert ; and John Radcliffe held Ordsall in capite, and by the service of a Rose. By his marriage to Joan, sister of the Earl of Kent, one of the founder members of the Order of the Garter, he achieved relation to the royal house, and during his sojourn in Hainault, attending on the king at his betrothal to Phillipa, he had formed many associations with the prosperous burghers of the Low Countries whose accumulated riches and power had been amassed from their expert knowledge of the arts of spinning, weaving and dyeing. Who could be a better intermediary therefore when the Flemings, under Jacob van Artevelde, were anxious for an alliance with the powerful King of England, who on his part, was equally desirous to facilitate commercial intercourse between Flanders and his own land ? Sir John, as he moved about the wealthy Flemish towns, oft, no doubt, thought of his own home town with the skilled labour of Flanders enriching its chartered liberties, and with a statesmanship equal to his gallantry on the field, he succeeded in gaining permission for certain Flemish craftsmen to leave their native land and settle here in Salford to teach their skill to the burgesses, widening immeasurably the scope of the trades to be practised solely within the borough. Thus to Salford belongs the honour of the birthplace in this land of the textile industry, and it is said that descendants of the first Flemish settlers are still employed at one of the local mills.

Sir John Radcliffe was a knight of the shire in 1340, and in 1347 we find him at the Siege of Calais with two knights, twelve esquires and fourteen archers. For his services in the French campaign he was granted the motto, " Caen, Creci, Calais," and on his return to England about 1350, he commenced the building of Ordsall Hall, on the site where centuries before had stood the ancient oratory by the ford, a religious connection that was re-established when in 1360, Sir John received from the Bishop of Lichfield a licence for the solemnization of divine worship in his chapel at Ordsall. So does that previous survival in timber and plaster link us in tangible form to the glorious days of Crecy and Geoffrey Chaucer, and to that very perfect knight, our own townsman, whom it should ever be our delight to honour and his memory to sustain.

The Descent of Ordsall Manor.

IN 1293, Richard, son of David de Hulton, was non-suited in claims against Edmund the King's brother, and against Adam de Prestwich for tenements in Ordsall (Assize R. 408, m. 3, 36).

Richard de Hulton for the sixth part of a fee in Ordsall and Flixton contributed 6s. 8d. to the aid of 1302 (Lancs. Inq. & Ext. i, 314).

The Hulton lands were partioned about 1330, Richard de Hulton releasing to John de Radclyffe all his claim in Ordsall and Flixton. During the absence of John at the wars, the manor of Ordsall was seized by Robert de Radclyffe, Thomas de Strangeways and Robert de Legh, the latter of whom had married Maud, widow of Richard de Hulton. Robert de Radclyffe was Sheriff of Salfordshire from 1337 to 1342, when he was succeeded by Sir John Blount of Hazlewood and Sodington. Robert de Radclyffe died suddenly 14th February, 1344, owing the King £149 14s. 8½d. for debts and licence to agree regarding the manor of Astley, and having at Ordsall on the day of his death ten oxen (worth 100s.) which Thos. de Strangeways took ; two oxen (worth 20s.) which William, son of Robt. de Radclyffe took ; and two horses (worth 13s. 4d.) which Richd., son of Wm. de Radclyffe took (L. T. R. Memo. R 117). John Blount took Robert de Radclyffe's claim to Ordsall under forfeit, by charter of Henry, Duke of Lancaster. In July, 1351, John de Radclyffe claimed the Manor of Ordsall, viz., a messuage, 120 acres of land, 12 acres of meadow, and 12 acres of wood. After prolonged litigation John de Radclyffe finally gained possession in 1354 (Duchy of Lancs. Assize Records i, m. 2). He had to defend his rights on several occasions against Robt. de Legh and Maud his wife, until in 1359 the latter released their claim in return for an annuity of 33s. 4d. during Maud's life. (Final Conc. Lancs. & Ches. Records ii, 162).

Sir John died in 1362 and was succeeded by his son Richard, who in addition to Ordsall, held in Salford by knight's service and 20s. rent, 40 acres of arable land. Richard was also Bailiff of Rochdale.

In an inquisition taken at Sir John's death, Ordsall is shown to be held by knight's service and a rent of 6s. 8d ; there were there a hall with five chambers, kitchen, chapel, two stables, three granges, two shippons, garner, dovecote, orchard, windmill, 80 acres of arable land and six acres of meadow.

Richard de Radclyffe married Maud (Matilda), daughter and heir of John de Legh, and thus the manor of Sandbach, a moiety of Mobberley, and other lands formerly belonging to the Ardernes came into the Radclyffe possession. For his second wife he married Sybil, daughter and heir of Robert de Clitheroe of Salesbury.

Richard met his death in 1380 by drowning in Rossendale Water, and was succeeded by his son John, who was then twenty-seven years of age. In 1385, John had the king's protection on his departure for Normandy in the retinue of his relative, Thomas de Holand, Earl of Kent and Captain of Cherbourg, when he was made a knight. He died in 1422, holding Ordsall and all the family estates with the exception of Shoresworth and Hope, which in 1396 he had granted as a marriage portion to his son John, who married Clemency, daughter of Hugh de Standish. He left a widow, Margaret— who quickly married Robert de Orrell—and three younger sons, Alured (died 1462), Edmund (died 1446), and Peter (died 1468).

Sir John Radclyffe who succeeded at the age of forty-four, died 26th July, 1442, leaving a widow, Joan, who had settled upon her lands, etc., in Flixton, Shoresworth and Tockholes, and was succeeded by his eldest son, Alexander, whose wife was Agnes, daughter of Sir William Harrington. Sir Alexander was Knight of the Shire in 1455 and died in 1475, leaving a son and heir, William, forty years of age, who died in 1498. The 40 acres of land in Salford valued a century before at 20s. a year at Sir William's death, were held for a rent of 50s. a year.

In 1444 there was an affray between the Radclyffes and the Booths of Barton, in which John and Hugh Radclyffe, brothers of Sir Alexander, were both killed.

CHAPTER II

The Golden Age.

L ET us step back a space of five and a half centuries and
picture ourselves in Salford Town on a bright June
morning—the Feast of Saint John the Baptist, in
the middle of the fourteenth century. There's a stir
and a bustle about the cobbled streets, though the hour
be early, and the good burgesses are hastening home to
breakfast after first Mass at the Chapel on the bridge.
Seven years have passed since the ravages of the second
visitation of the Black Death, and the state of the town
reflects the prosperity which the country as a whole was
now enjoying. A pleasant enough town, indeed, as we
survey it from the bridge, into the recesses of which we
have to press ourselves as a string of pack mules comes
across occupying all its narrow width. Ever since the
time of the pious St. Dunstan, the building of bridges has
been one of the duties of charity which the rich owe to their
poorer neighbours, and this Bridge of Salford had long before
replaced the ancient ford to give a better access to the growing
town.*

At one end of the bridge stands the Chantry Chapel, a two-
storeyed building ; the upper floor comprising the chapel
proper, approached from the bridge level and connecting by
an outer stairway to the lower storey at the level of the river.
This lower room was the Guildhall, the meeting-place of the
fraternity or guild in the town responsible for the maintenance
and preservation of the bridge. Adjoining was the small cell,
the single-roomed habitation of the Chantry Priest whom, in his
black cassock and square cloth cap, we see entering the Chapel
to say his office of Tierce, for between his daily tasks of
working for the living and praying for the dead, in a happy
mien of peace and prayer and poverty, keeping alight the
Christ ideal within the community, this devout scion of some
wealthy house has little leisure, e'en though beyond his
garden croft is all the excitement of the holiday fair, to which
most of the townsfolk are now wending their way.

---

* From old references it appears that the Bridge was a main
connecting link between the north of England and the South.

ORDSALL HALL.

Here are displayed the silken cloths of France and Flanders and the durable productions of the new and active Salford looms. From far and near have people come to buy and to sell and to coax the favours of the crowds. The juggler balancing his wheel and sword ; the acrobat, descendant of the Saxon Gleeman ; the musical girls tumbling for largesse, as was complained " Salome tumbled before Herod " ; the Bearward with his dancing bear, his monkey and his drum ; the tabourer ; the dancers ; the minstrel—all are represented at this gathering of merchandising and frolic, when the free spirit of the borough seeks a short respite from its labours at the great Salford fair.

We cross from Stanyhurst and the fair through Bell Gates and pass the house of Master Bothe, the chief burgess of the town, typical of the middle classes whose rise to wealth and power had finally destroyed the old feudal relations of society.

In the first year of the reign of Edward the Second a yeoman, John del Bothe, had married Loretta, a daughter and heiress of Sir Gilbert de Barton and his wife, the Lady Edith. Their son was Thomas del Bothe, who lived at Barlow in the parish of Eccles, and was rich in land and houses and cattle. He bought from Sarah de Waker-legh of Salford certain lands including a burgage at " Salforde Bridge Foote," where he erected a town house (the Booth Hall, which was demolished in 1821). The higher classes were more immersed in the diversions of the field, and, consequently, the cause of learning found its patrons chiefly in the wealthy yeomen. Thomas del Bothe was a striking example of this in the care he took in educating his children and assisting the higher arts of life. Of this pious and worthy Salfordian no less than four grandsons rose to high positions in Church and State. Ralph became Archdeacon of Durham and York ; John became one of the most saintly and munificent of the Bishops of Exeter ; William (who founded the Jesus Chantry in Eccles Church) rose to be Bishop of Lichfield and Cardinal Archbishop of York, whilst Lawrence was Dean of St. Paul's, Bishop of Durham, and the Lord High Chancellor of England, and so high in favour with Pope Nicholas V. that he was appointed to succeed his brother in the See of York, even though the King had specially recommended his chaplain for that dignity. Lawrence Booth adhered strongly to the Lancastrian side in the Wars of the Roses, being Chancellor of Queen Margaret and tutor to the Prince of Wales. Though suspect, as Bishop of Durham, to Edward IV., he was afterwards reconciled to him, becoming Lord Chancellor in 1473. Another grandson, Robert, married Douce Venables and succeeded to the Lordship of Dunham, and their effigies in brass with interlinked hands are to be seen yet over their burial place in the chancel of the Parish Church of Wilmslow. His grand-daughter, Margaret, married Sir John Biron, and thus became the ancestress of Lord Byron, the poet.

Thomas del Bothe by his will made in 1368, amongst numerous legacies, bequeathed £30 in instalments of £10 per year (£150 of present-day money) towards the repair of the Bridge of Salford, and further sums of £50 per year to endow chaplaincies at the Chapel on the Bridge at Salford and before the Altar of Saint Katherine in the Parish Church of Eccles " for the soul of Edward III., for the soul of Roger de Hulton, and for all benefactors of the said Thomas." We may presume he was the Warden of the Guild as well as the Borough Reeve, and that it was with a real sense of loss that after his death in 1369 his fellow townsmen would repair to the Chapel on the Bridge to pray fervently for the repose of his noble soul.†

We are now arrived at the Town Cross occupying the centre of the Green, whereon the rougher games of the people are in full play, and sturdy young townsmen are wrestling for a ram or a bull, a red gold ring, or a pipe of wine. Prentices and foresters engage in bouts of Quarter Staff play, and a merry tinkling of bells draws our attention to the Morris Dancers and a team of men going through the strenuous gyrations of the sword dance of their Saxon forbears. Truly the spirit of " Merrie England " is fully abroad this day. *" And what man beareth hym best, ywis, the prize shall bear away."*

Across the Green stands the court house where the Portmanmote sits to determine the affairs of the Borough and the Wapentake, and on the other side, Master Allen's

†NOTE .—Thos. del Bothe died apparently from violence as Ellen, his widow, appeared against John, son of Thos. de Hulme ; Robert, son of Richard de Worsley, and many others concerning her husband's death (Coram Rege R. 434, M110). There appears to have been a long-standing and continuous feud between the Booths and their neighbours in Barton. In 1345 Thos. del Bothe and Gilbert de Barton were involved in a case of assault and cattle seizure (De Banco R 344 M 21).

house has now been turned into the chief hostelry of the town with the sign of the Bull's Head, out of compliment to Sir John Radclyffe, whose crest it is, and who has recently built the houses adjoining as dwellings for the workmen he has brought from Ghent and Hainault, and who, by the industry and wealth they brought, are highly honoured in the town.

Green gate leads by Paradise Hill and Sandywells to Shaw Brows, where stands the Manor House whence a noble concourse is now making its way down to the town. For know ye not who is the Lord of Salford in these days but my lord Duke of Lancaster, even John of Gaunt himself, who, inheriting by the right of the Lady Blanche, his wife, has taken Salford under his special patronage. So is he come to visit his demesne and its new industries, and with him comes his lady mother, the good Queen Phillipa, and his wife, the Lady Blanche Plantagenet. Little do the burgesses realise, as they throng to acclaim the royal party that they are looking on both these gracious ladies for the last time and that within a year all England will be mourning their deaths.

The Duke has a special interest in the Flemish craftsmen, for not only have they come hither from his own birthplace, but he is hopeful, too, of using them in his plan towards concluding a treaty of peace with Flanders by which he may aid his eventual accession to the throne. In the gallant company that attends my Lord go many illustrious Salford names. There is Thomas del Bothe, of course, and Sir Richard Radclyffe, Richard de Langley of Agecroft, Sir Roger de Hulton, Sir John Biron, Galfride de Salford, Henry de Trafford, Henry de Workedslegh, Roger de Pilkyngton, and " clothed each in the livery of his solemn and great fraternity " the Weavers, the Fullers, the Dyers, the Tapisers. The craftsmen of the borough with their ladies, who out of their substance might wear, as decreed by the Statute of Apparel, " fur turned up with minever," rubbed shoulder by shoulder with those of humbler status in their blanket and russet.

Such importance did Salford achieve in those days that it is believed to have possessed its own Mint. In a document of Queen Elizabeth's time regarding the finding of certain treasure Trove in a plot of ground in Manchester, the find is described as consisting of " twenty-two ould Salford groats," (Manchester Court Leet Records, 7th April, 1575.)

The groat was a silver coin of the realm first issued in 1227, and the appellation of " Salford Groats " indicates quite obviously that at some time Salford had a licence from the King for the minting of a local silver coinage. These were sometimes called "croste (crossed) groats" from the cross on the reverse, which divided the coin into four quarters each of which could be broken off and used as legal tender. A groat was of the weight and value of four silver pennies or sterlings, and the name, a curious example of French-English, is derived from " le gros " sterling, the French " gros " retaining its vocal sound in the English " Groat " for great.

Every relic of the Salford of those days has been ruthlessly swept away, except the ancient inn of the Old Bull's Head, with its four-gabled frontage, its sandstone plinth, its oak beams now hard as rock, from which the workmen who built Manchester Church in 1422 slung their hammocks as they lodged within the old inn, the oldest building in the city to-day, carrying us back to days when in Salford Town there was a real fellowship amongst the burgesses, where arrogance and servility were unknown and individual dignity was maintained in a natural respect of man for his fellows, and a devotion to the common interest of the town. That spirit made Salford great in the golden age of its history. It is surely not without its significance to-day.

CHAPTER III

A Possession of the Crown.

WHEN in 1399 John of Gaunt died, his son Henry Bolinbroke at once returned from the banishment to which he had been committed by Richard the Second in the previous year. Landing at Ravenspur he was joined by the Duke of York and the Percys. Richard was taken prisoner and formally deposed by Parliament, and Henry of Lancaster succeeded to the throne as Henry IV. Thus begins that unbroken connection of Salford with the Royal House, which is sustained even to the present day, and on those several occasions in later years when the city has been privileged to receive royal visits, it was in no mere ordinary sense that the King was coming then amongst his own. Attempts have been often made, inspired as much by stupid jealousy as by ignorance, to challenge Salford's claim to the title of " Royal Borough." Whatever may be the official definition of so proud a title he would indeed be rash who would deny the appellation to a town which was not only a possession of Saxon kings, but has been, too, for five hundred years without a break, a demesne of the reigning house, and whose manorial court has been consistently " holden for our lord the king."

The status of the Duchy of Lancaster as a kingdom within a kingdom is well revealed in the Rolls of the Duchy which cover the period of the First Duke's administration, and in which occur several references to Salford. As for instance in 1351 it is recorded :

" John Blounte, of Hazlewood, Robt. Legh, and Thos. Strangeways came on their recognizance, at the suit of John Ratclif touching a tenement and lands in Salford. John Blounte answering that the premises were of the manor of Ordesale and that Henry, late Earl of Lancaster, father of Henry, the Duke, was seised of the lands, and granted the same by charter to the said John Blounte, as of the manor of Ordesale."

In 1354 is a grant by the Duke to William de Heghfeld and his heirs in perpetuity of 28 acres of land in Salford Waste, at 14s. rent, and tenants to do suit at the Lord's mill.

Two years later this was revised to a " rent of 11s. 6d. reserved and the remainder to Thomas Strangeways."

We note also the following :—

" Robt. de Legh and Matilda, his wife, paid 13s. 4d. for the Manor of Ordeshale."

" Grant of Land and Turbary in Salford."

" Grant of an Eschat in Salford."

" Grant of a Messuage and Lands in Salford which came into the Duke's hands by the death of Richard de Tetlowe, who was a bastard and died without heir.—— Remainder to Thomas de Strangewas."

Other grants made to persons specified were cancelled as the premises became leased by the Duke's Charter to John de Radeclif.

Another item runs : " Grant of Holtefeld in Salford," and probably refers to the Oldfield. In 1317 five roods in the Oldfield were released from Dower by Cicily, widow of William the Cooper of Salford to Randle the Miller, and in 1346 John de Oldfield was named amongst Salford tenants.

In the Close Rolls of John of Gaunt in 1380 is a mandate " to give seisin of the Manor of Urdesale, 3 parts of the Moiety of the town of Flixton, Tenements in Le Hope, Shoresworth, Le Holynhed, and Tokholes in Salford to John Radecliffe." It is difficult to identify the two latter places *, but Hope, of course, still retains its identity, whilst Shoresworth is the ancient name of the entity on the northern bank of the Irwell now known as Mode Wheel from a water corn mill which formerly stood there, and from the fact that it once contained a Campfield with a rampart and fosse is believed to have been a Roman outpost station and later a part of the Saxon defences of Salford.

At the close of the fourteenth century the public mind was chiefly exercised by the mission of Wycliffe, who has sometimes been termed " the morning star of the Reformation," and to whom John of Gaunt extended his patronage until the Duke could no longer support the extreme doctrines which were being advocated, and, further, because of the effect of

---

*This is because these manors have been presumed to be within Salford Borough when actually Salford Hundred should be understood. They obviously refer to Tockholes and Hollinshead in the valley of Roddlesworth, three miles south west of Blackburn. They are now comprised within the Hundred of Blackburn. The fourteenth century manor house is still standing and is used as a farm-house.

the preachings in engendering civil unrest. Under Henry IV. the Wycliffites, or Lollards, as they were coming to be called, were subjected to grievous persecution. The good burgesses of Salford would doubtless be well acquainted with the figures of Doctor Hereford and Master Ashton, who, in coarse attire and staff in hand, traversed the length of Lancashire preaching the new doctrines and proclaiming the virtues of poverty.

During this time the population of Salford was rapidly increasing, not only in size but in wealth. The yeoman, typified by Thomas del Bothe, by combining agricultural industry with commercial enterprise in the new industrial arts introduced from Flanders, were amassing great wealth and affluence, and their ranks were greatly added to by many of the reduced gentry, who preferred the opulence of commerce to the baneful distinction of poverty on their meagre holdings. Such was the Franklin of Chaucer's Tales, the progenitor of the eighteenth century squire, and to whom more than any other belongs the credit for the commercial enterprise of those days. He was famed alike for his hospitality as for his industry, and his house flowed all day long with good cheer. " There be no truer servant in the house than himself," says an old writer of the Franklin, and it was these numerous small landed merchant possessors in the vicinity of Salford that gave the place its character. Even many of the larger landed proprietors set their younger sons and brothers to the art of clothing, which, in the words of the old writer again, " was held in high reputation, both in respect of the great riches that thereby was gotten, as also of the benefit it brought to the whole common-wealth." The tiller of the soil, now finding a greater opportunity open to him as an artisan, crowded into the towns, and Salford in the Middle Ages was more populous than at any time in its history prior to the Industrial Revolution. When Henry the Fifth was winning undying lustre for the arms of Britain on the battle-fields of France, the wealthy clothiers of his Royal Borough of Salford were no whit behind Sir Richard Whittington and the citizens of London in pouring out their gold to sustain the King's campaign, and full many a gallant Salford yeoman proved the mettle of his pastures in the imperishable glory of Agincourt.

CHAPTER IV

When the Night Watch Rode.

THAT medieval Salford was to some extent a walled town, or, at any rate, had gates that could be closed at night or in times of trouble, is evident, inasmuch as the Port Mote Records show the maintenance of " Winchester Watch " as prescribed by the Statutum Wynton of Edward I. and Edward III. For instance, it is recorded that "the Constables . . . shall buy two bills on the Townes charges for to keep Winchester Watch with accordinge to former custome and that the watch shall go by the Bill from doore to doore as formerly it hath done." There are also mention at various times of the Broadgate, the Lower Gate, the Gate to Broughton, and the Gate to Ordsall. Once a year, on the evening of St. John's Day, was held the " Marching Watch," when the Constables of the Watch, attended by demilances, white-coated archers and pikemen would perambulate the bounds of the town. In the procession went also the Reeve with his attendants, and the whole was brought up with the town waits and morris dancers in picturesque array. The effect of the ceremony was heightened by the cresset train, the cresset being a flaming rope soaked in tar, in an iron frame held aloft on a shaft. Every house was decorated with garlands of greenery and flowers illuminated with oil lamps, bonfires were lighted in the streets, and before the houses of the wealthier burgesses were set tables laden with meat and drink, of which their neighbours and all passers by were invited to partake. The very name of " bonfire " tells us more eloquently than anything else of the spirit that pervaded this festival time, for, as Stow explains, " they were a sign of good amity amongst neighbours that being before at controversy, were there by the labour of others, reconciled and made friends." We may have outgrown many of the ideas in which our medieval ancestors implicitly believed, but out of the remote past they challenge us yet with what a good and pleasant thing it is to live together in unity.

The Hundred Years War with France was now no sooner brought to an end than an even more awful war broke out when, for thirty-five years upon their native soil, the people

of England engaged in mutual self-destruction under the
rival banners of the Red Rose and the White. Although
the War of the Roses is said to have made no difference in
the even flow of administration, it nevertheless had, as all
internecine strife must ever have, a devastating effect upon
the lives of all classes, high and low, and particularly must
its effects have been felt in the town that was so valued a
possession of the Lancastrian Royal House, where the
perilous fortunes of its Lord and his intrepid and gallant
Queen Margaret would be followed with more than the ordinary,
and something of a personal anxiety. Perhaps the most
striking feature, however, of this most remarkable epoch of
national history is that with the desolation of the great
families the gentry and the chief burgesses of the towns were
united into one class and the feudal system comes finally and
completely to an end. New and more distinguished houses
began to be built as family seats on the sites of the former
humble farmsteads, and among the local halls that were newly
built at this time were Agecroft, Beaucliffe, Hope and
Pendleton, none of which, alas ! are left to us, although
Agecroft Hall has now entered on a new and strange existence
thousands of miles across the world in far-away Virginia. It
is hard to forgive the City Corporation for letting this precious
relic pass from our midst when they had the original
opportunity of acquiring it as a public possession.

In Lower Chapel Street still stands, although no longer a
licensed house, the old King's Head. It was in the original
house here that Henry VII. stayed when, in 1495, he passed
through Salford on his way from visiting his mother, Margaret.
Countess of Richmond and Derby, at Lathom.

This was the year in which Sir William Stanley was
executed for taking part in a Yorkist plot against Henry,
whom he had largely helped to the throne at Bosworth Field.
Thomas Stanley, his brother, and Henry's step-father, had
been created Earl of Derby, but William was discontented
with the rewards given to him by the King, and eagerly
joined his support to those who were conspiring to put Perkin
Warbeck on the throne. It is said that Thomas Stanley
rode with the King from Lathom to Salford vainly pleading
for his brother's life. According to a curious rhyming
chronicle attributed to Humphrey Brereton, the Earl's Jester,
Thomas Stanley, unable to move the King to mercy, turned

back home again at Salford Bridge, leaving his son George,
Lord Strange, to whom Henry was much attached,* to
continue the suit.

> " Upon Salford Bridge I turned my horse again.
> My son George by the hand I hent
> I held so hard forsooth certain
> That his forefinger out of the joint went
> I hurt him sore ; he did complain."

Ordsall at the end of the fifteenth century was held by
Sir William Radclyffe, fifth in descent from the first Sir John.
Shortly before his death in 1498, Sir William, whose son John
had pre-deceased him, founded a Chantry at the Altar of
the Sacred Trinity in the Collegiate Church, and in the
following year Elizabeth, widow of John Radclyffe, bequeathed
to the Chaplain celebrating at the Trinity Altar a Mass Book
with cover and clasps, a cruet of silver with J.R. on the
cover, two towels, a vestment of green and white velvet with
bull's heads on the ophreys, and 3s. 4d. to buy a Sacring Bell.
This Chantry, which contained a rich window of the Trial
and Crucifixion, with symbols of the Trinity, became a place
of much devotion, especially to country people, for the
Radclyffes, well maintaining the traditions of the gallant
knight, their founder, were by their nobility of character
and generous benefactions very dear to the people of
Lancashire.

At the same time, Robert Chetham and Isabel his wife
founded a chantry at the altar of St. George in the Collegiate
Church, endowing it with Domville House, in Salford, and
other burgages and lands in Salford and Worsley. The
Chapel of St. George was later held with the Manor of Ordsall.

---

* Shakespeare makes Richmond to ask as his first thought after
the crown was placed on his head on Bosworth Field :—

> " Great God of Heaven, say amen to all !
> But, tell me, is young George Stanley living ? "

CHAPTER V

Some Old Salford Manors.

PENDLEBURY AND AGECROFT.

KING JOHN, in 1199, granted to Elias, son of Robert, the Manor of " Peneburi " together with Shoresworth and Hope. Elias was also Master Serjeant of Salford, and was a great benefactor to Cockersand Abbey in the Fylde. He was succeeded in his manors and serjeantry by his son Adam, and his grandson Roger. In 1274, Ellis, son of Roger, came to a violent death, and about 1291 by the marriage of Cecily, grand-daughter of Roger, to Adam de Prestwich, the manors passed to the latter family.

In 1350, the Prestwich estates, in default of male issue, passed, by his marriage to Joan de Tetlowe, to Richard de Langley, now settled at Agecroft. In 1374, during the minority of Roger, son of Richard and Joan de Langley, the estates were claimed by a notorious swashbuckler, Robert de Holland, but were seized by John of Gaunt, who held them in ward until Roger came of age. Roger died in 1394, when an inquisition post-mortem showed him to be possessed of Agecroft mansion and land, with land in Pendlebury, the manor of Shoresworth, and a tenement called Tetlowe in Burghton. He was succeeded by his son Robert, who at the age of fifteen had been married to Katherine de Atherton. Robert died in 1447, his mother being still alive and in possession of Tetlowe, which afterwards reverted to his widow, Katherine. His heir was his eldest son, Thomas, and his second son, Ralph Langley, was Rector of Prestwich and Warden of Manchester. At some time prior to this the Manors of Shoresworth and Hope had passed, presumably by marriage, to the Radclyffes of Ordsall, and in 1496, Robert Langley, grandson of Thomas, who had married Eleanor, daughter of William Radclyffe of Ordsall, succeeded to the Agecroft properties. Ten years before, Robert Langley had received a general pardon from Henry VII. when that monarch deposed Richard III., and an annuity of ten marks for services rendered and to be rendered.

This Robert Langley commenced to build Agecroft Hall on the site of an older house, a work that was completed by his grandson, for Robert died in 1527, the year that Wolsey fell. Robert, the grandson, who, in 1547, on the accession of Edward VI. was made a knight, was the last male of his line in possession. Three days before his death, in September, 1561, Sir Robert had given to trustees for his daughter Anne " the capital messuage or mansion house of Agecroft with its appurtenances in the vill of Pendlebury and also all the closes, lands, etc., in the vill aforesaid, commonly known by the several names of Old Agecroft, Lower Coppice, the Over Coppice, the Park, the Ryefields, the Sowerbutts, the Lumns, the Warths, the Crimbles, Aynesley, the Oxhey and the Little Oxhey ; also the water mill in Prestwich and the meadow called The Springs ; also common pasture and turbary on Swinton Moor." In 1571 Anne married William Dauntesy of West Lavington, Wilts., whose father had been Usher to Queen Katherine Howard.

The manor of Penelburi was also claimed by the Dauntesys, but eventually passed to the Coke family with Prestwich and Tetlow, and in 1780 was sold to Peter Drinkwater, of Irwell House, Prestwich.

A picturesque legend attaches to Agecroft Hall that the ghost of Thomas Langley, Cardinal Bishop of Durham, whose reputed bed was shown at Agecroft prior to being taken, on the removal of the hall, to the present home of the Dauntesy family in Dorset, laid a curse on the family for deserting the old faith, that the line should perish for want of an heir. Strangely enough, the estates passed through a very broken succession, and were eventually bequeathed by the last of the Dauntesys in 1811 to his cousins, the Hulls, each succeeding owner assuming the name of Dauntesy.

Agecroft is also credited with being the first place in England where tea was introduced. It is said that a member of the family, early in the seventeenth century, serving with the Navy in China, sent home a jar of " chaw," which he described as being highly esteemed by the Chinese. Unfortunately, he omitted to say how it should be used, and the Agecroft housekeeper, treating it as any other vegetable, drained off the liquor and served the boiled leaves. It is hardly surprising, under the circumstances, that the gift was not appreciated.

To a Langley is also attributed the introduction of clogs into Lancashire.

The Hall, which has now been transplanted, stick and stone, to America, formerly stood on the west side of the

Irwell Valley between the high ground of Kersal and Prestwich on one side and Pendlebury on the other. It was a very interesting example of timber construction standing on a low stone base, and built round a central courtyard. It had a wealth of carved ornament in the bay windows, excellent in design and typical of the early Tudor period. The windows of the Great Hall contained some ancient glass with the badges of John of Gaunt and of Edmund of Langley, Duke of York ; the Langley crest (a cockatrice), a red and white rose with stalks entwined, a crown, and initials H.E. signifying the union of the roses in the marriage of Henry VII. and Elizabeth of York.

HOPE.

Everyone in Salford is familiar with the handsome Georgian mansion of Hope Hall on the Eccles Old Road. In 1212, " le Hope " was held by Elias de Peneburi of Iorwerth de Hulton by a rent of 4s. Granted in 1319 by Thomas, Earl of Lancaster, to Sir Robert de Holland and Matilda, his wife, the manor of Hope was in 1324 amongst this knight's forfeited lands, and in 1380 Richard de Radcliffe of Ordsall held in The Hope a messuage and sixty acres of arable land by the service of £4 2s. per year. Along with Shoreworth, Hope continuously formed part of the Radcliffe possessions. In 1561, Katherine, widow of Sir William Radcliffe, is recorded as living at Hope. The manor gave its name to a family of whom Henry de Hope, in 1346, was charged with 6s. for " castle-ward " on account of a meadow in Pendleton held by him. Hope Hall is mentioned as an ancient house in 1595 when the estate was acquired by the Bradshaw family, in whose possession it remained until the eighteenth century, when Hope was purchased by Daniel Bayley, who built the existing mansion on the old site.

PENDLETON.

Jornechio de Hulton, in the first year of King John, exchanged the wood at Kereshall (the site of the hermitage of Hugh de Burun) for the village of Penelton, which latter was assessed as four oxgangs of land and held by the service of a sixth part of a Knight's fee. In 1251 the Hultons exchanged Penelton for Ordsall and part of Flixton, and ten years later

Robert de Ferrars granted to the Priory of St. Thomas the Martyr, Stafford, "the manor of Swineshurst and of the Walneys by Salford with the mill on the Irwell, the vill of Penilton with all the villeins holding the villeinage of the town, their chattels and sequel." The right of the Prior was called in question in 1292, when Master John de Craven was in possession, but the King, in 1295, confirmed the grant, and it was retained by the house until the Dissolution.

Maud de Worsley, in 1332, granted to the Prior her interest in lands, etc., in Penelton, Newhall, Woodhouses, Wallness and Swineshurst, and in 1339, Henry, Earl of Lancaster, gave the Prior 12 acres of heath in Salford and Penelton as recompense for the Priory's common of pasture on the heath. These estates were held in farm of the Prior by the Hollands, who took up residence at New Hall, and the bounds were described at the time as follows : From Wallness Pool to Broad Oak Snape following the lache to Wetsnape, by the Rowe Lache to Saltfield Clow as far as Wolfharp meanigate, thence by the high road (to Eccles) to Little Leyhead, and thence to Gildenaver Ford (Gilda Brook), and so by Tippesbrook (Folly Brook) to Bispeslowe (The Height), thence by the Black Lache to Alwine Mere to Redford and by the syke under Pendlebury Park to the Irwell and down this to the starting point.

At the Dissolution, Pendleton, as part of the Priory estates, was granted in 1539 to Rowland Lee, Bishop of Lichfield. On his death his property was divided amongst his four nephews, and the Priory site together with the manor of Pendleton went to Bryan Fowler, but although his descendants, who were strict adherents of the old religion, enjoyed it down to the beginning of the eighteenth century, they never resided at Pendleton. Walter Fowler, great grandson of Bryan, took the King's side in the Civil War and his estates were sequestered, but later recovered. William Fowler, the last male representative, died in 1717, leaving his estates, including Pendleton, to his niece Katherine, from whom they passed in 1726 to her daughter, wife of Thomas, 4th Earl of Fauconberg. William Fowler had, however, secretly made another will in 1715 bequeathing a moiety of the estates to a nephew, Thomas Grove. The will remained in the custody of the lawyer who drew it up, Christopher Ward of Stafford.

After his death it was discovered by his son, who communicated with Lord Aston, the principal Fowler trustee, and he in turn laid it before Richard FitzGerald, an Irish barrister, and the eldest son of Colonel Nicholas FitzGerald, who was slain at the Battle of the Boyne fighting for James II. Seeing that Rebecca Grove would inherit these estates at her father's death, Fitzgerald married her, and after an appeal to the House of Lords the manor of Pendleton passed from the Viscountess Fauconberg to Rebecca FitzGerald, whose descendants still retain possession, and formerly had their seat at Castle Irwell on the site of the present racecourse. One member of this family was Edward FitzGerald, the famous poet of Omar Khayyam.

In 1666, there were 138 hearths in Pendleton subject to tax, the largest house being that of John Hollinghurst with nine hearths, whilst there were several with five each.

A Chantry Chapel was founded at Pendleton about 1220 by Richard de Bolton, the chaplain to be approved by the monks of Stanlaw. No injury was to be done to the knights of the parish church of Eccles and no religious was to celebrate in the chapel, but any secular priest staying for a short time as guest in the Lord's house might celebrate during their visit.

BRINDLE HEATH.

Edmund, Earl of Lancaster, in 1292 granted to Adam de Prestwich a piece of moorland in the waste of Salford, whose bounds were thus described : From the corner of the ditch at Blackhow riding down to Wodarneley and Wodarneford in the Irwell ; by the Irwell up to the beginning of Pendlebury ; up to the boundary of Pendlebury to Alvenemere, and so to the ditch of Penelton ; down the ditch to the starting point. The rent was to be 6s. 8d. This appears to be what in later descent is called Brindlache and Windlehey, and in modern times Brindle Heath.

In 1437 it was leased to Robert Langley, and by the Act of Resumption of 1464, the £10 annuity then granted to Thomas Langley was secured on pastures " called Brindlache and Windlehey." These lands descended in the Langley family and formed part of the portion of Anne Dauntesy, passing in descent along with Agecroft.

BENTCLIFFE.

Where now Hope Hospital stands was formerly the lands of Beaucliffe, the manor house of which was taken down many years ago and replaced by two modern mansions called respectively Higher and Lower Bentcliffe. The capital messuage of Beaucliffe was in 1250 held of the heir of William the Clerk in socage, by rendering one pound of incense to the Church of Eccles. It was afterwards held by the Holts, from whom it passed in the reign of Henry VII. to the Valentines of Flixton. Thomas Valentine, who died in 1614, was succeeded by his son John and his grandson John. The younger John's estate was sequestered by the Parliament, because when he was High Constable of Salford in 1644 he lodged Prince Rupert at Beaucliffe. As soon as the Prince had departed, the rebel garrison at Manchester seized John Valentine, and under threat of imprisonment and loss of his estates, he was ordered to bring in £20 in money and £10 in provisions. Despite his compliance a Parliamentary Committee ordered sequestration, and he redeemed his estate in 1651 by the payment of £255 4s. 9d. John Valentine died in 1681, and his son Thomas was buried a week after his father. Richard Valentine, his grandson, who succeeded to the estate at the age of six was appointed High Sheriff of Lancashire in 1713. The family died out in the eighteenth century.

LITTLE BOLTON.

On the south side of Eccles New Road, about a mile east from Eccles village, stands an old farmhouse now incorporated in a factory. This was once the manor house of Little Bolton, a name derived in Saxon days from its being the " tun " or homestead at the foot of Buile. It was held in 1200 by William de Bolton, and assessed as six oxgangs of land held of the King in chief, in fee farm by a rent of 18s. King John, whilst Count of Mortmain, had so granted the estate to William, son of Adam, and confirmed it after he came to the throne. In 1212 William de Bolton was dead, and his heir was in ward of the King, who gave the wardship to Adam de Pendlebury. A grant was made by William de Bolton to the Canons of Cockersand of lands in Little Bolton

THE BULL'S HEAD INN, GREENGATE.

as follows : The Tanners assart from Bindley, Bradley syke, the Carr, Croshaw oak, Brandale Clough, Brendoak Clough, Rushylache, the ditch to Bradley syke ; common rights including quittance of pannage for sixty pigs."

In 1241 Richard de Bolton granted to his son Henry a messuage which Richard the Miller had held, together with half the grantor's lands in the hamlet of Bolton in the vill of Penelton, with the exception of his capital messuage (the Hall) and an acre near the Pool Bridge. About 1350 the Boltons were succeeded by the Gawens, John Gawen the Harper being a grandson of the above-mentioned Henry. The Gawens held lands in Davyhulme, and in 1357 is a record of a lease by John Gawen to Adam de Ainsworth of land in Little Bolton between Bolton Brook and Shoresworth Brook (practically the present parish of All Saints) at a rent of 24s. and the service of a reaper for one day in the year. Richard Gawen, on his marriage to Emanie, daughter of Richard de Holland, in 1390, had a grant of land in the south-west corner of the vill of Penelton, one of the boundaries of which is stated as " Bibby Lumn on Bentcliffe Brook." For two centuries Little Bolton was held by the Gawens, when two-thirds of the estate was acquired by the Valentines of Beaucliffe and the other third by the Goodens, who took up residence at Little Bolton Hall.

In 1560, Isabel Gooden, widow, and Janet and Jane her daughters, had a lease of a messuage in Broomhouse Lane (most probably the same residence as that of Richard and Emanie Gawen referred to above). In 1566 Edmund Gooden of Little Bolton complained that certain persons had made a great ditch across the way from his house to the Church at Eccles and had stopped up other ways also. In defence, Robert Barlow and Edmund Parkington said that they had allowed the tenants of Edmund Gooden to pass through their lands to the Church, but when this was claimed as right of way they withdrew it.

The Goodens were staunch Roman Catholics and sided with the King on the outbreak of the great Rebellion. One member of the family took part in the defence of Lathom House under the hero'c Countess Charlotte, and another was wounded serving with Prince Rupert. Thomas Gooden, the head of the family, who in 1631 had paid £10 as composition for declining knighthood, was suspected of having borne arms for the King and his estate of Little Bolton was sequestered. A younger brother was Peter Gooden, the Roman Catholic controversial writer who died at Little Bolton in 1695. In 1741 Little Bolton was sold by Dorothy Gooden to Thomas Worsley, who held it of the Duchy for a chief rent of 9s. 11d.

During the Great War, Little Bolton was sold to a London restaurant proprietor who, anxious to assist his native Italy, built on the site a factory for the manufacture of explosives by a new process. Unfortunately, rumour states the factory was under the influence of enemy agents, and although a fortune was spent, the war came to an end without the process being perfected.

Local feuds were not infrequent in medieval times, whole families, with their neighbours, often ranging themselves on opposing sides in disputation, and usually with fatal results. On the Monday after Low Sunday in the year 1444, there was an affray between the Booths of Barton and the Radcliffes of Ordsall, when Sir Thomas Booth, a grandson of Thos. del Bothe, Nicholas and Henry, his sons, William Gawen of Little Bolton and many others waylaid John Radcliffe and a party of his friends, killing John, his brother, Hugh Radcliffe, Ralph Oldham and Nicholas Johnson, Peter Cowopp, of the Barton faction, being shot by Peter Radcliffe. All the accused were acquitted, but at a later assize Henry and Nicholas Booth were both outlawed.

WHITTLESWICK.

South of Little Bolton, on the opposite side of the river, was the manor of Whittleswick, originally held by Adam de Pendlebury, and acquired in 1632 by Sir Cecil Trafford, who erected there the chief family seat, and so gave the manor the name which is still perpetuated in the great industrial estate of Trafford Park. The original Trafford Hall was replaced in 1762 by the present classic mansion.

CHAPTER VI

Our Own Whittington.

ONE summer morning in the year 1487, a young man set out from the house of his father at Lowton to walk the fifteen miles of white road that should lead him to a better chance of fortune in the thriving town of Salford. In the villages as he passed, all the talk was of the appearance in Ireland of young Lambert Simnel, that poor child dupe of a Yorkist plot against King Henry, but Ralph Byrom had more important thoughts of his own, ambitions that centred in that busy borough where the new industries offered far greater scope for a man's abilities than would ever be his lot as a younger son in his father's patrimony on the Lowton farm. Little, perhaps, did Ralph think that not only would he prosper to the height of his dreams, but that he was to be the founder of one of the most illustrious families in the place of his adoption.

Apprenticing himself to a merchant clothier, this Whittington of our town soon grew to be a master himself, and handing on his success to his family in such measure that his son, Adam Byrom, was accounted, with one exception, the largest merchant in all the Hundred of Salford, and in 1540 was assessed by the Commissioners of Henry the Eighth at a larger amount than even Sir Alexander Radclyffe, of Ordsall, the great magnate of the district. The Byrom wealth was invested in lands in Salford, Darcy Lever, Ardwick and Bolton-le-Moors, and ultimately Adam acquired as his chief messuage the Royal Manor House called Salford Hall, wherein he took up his residence. The feudal monopolies still in vogue found a violent opponent in this enterprising merchant, and his free-trade principles are revealed in the Kalendar of Pleadings, where he is shown prosecuting William Arram, Mayor of Preston, claiming exception from payment of all tolls and imposts in the fairs and markets of Salford and Preston. He took to wife the daughter of Hunt, of Hunt's Bank, and died on July 25, 1558, leaving two sons, George and Henry, who, strangely enough, both died within the month of their father's decease.

It was the daughter of George Byrom, Margaret, who, whilst on a visit to her friend, Margaret Starkie, of Kempnough, near Worsley, became the ill-fated victim of demoniacal possession at the hands of the wizard Hartley, that strange visitation which is one of the earliest instances of witchcraft for which Lancashire was later to become notorious.

The family litigation that afterwards widened into a complete breach is shown in a deed executed December 13, 1586, between " Raphe Byrom of Saulforde, gent, Richard Hunte of the same towne, gent, Adam Byrom of the same towne, gent, Raphe Houghton of Manchester and Lawrence Byrom of Saulforde," and witnessed by William Radcliffe and Robert Leighe."

When Adam Byrom took up his residence in Salford Hall it was in the midst of stirring times. The Bible had just been translated into English, and in the same year came the flood tide of the Reformation with its rousing of deep passions, sweeping away many abuses perhaps, but at the same time much that was vital in the lives and living of the people. The people of Salford, in common with the larger part of Lancashire, were none too partial to the new order of things, and with no little misgivings they saw the old Chapel of the Bridge, which for two centuries had enshrined their devotion and which only thirty years before had been newly rebuilt, now desecrated and turned into a dungeon in which prisoners from all the district were imprisoned without distinction. It was one of these same prisoners, a certain John Bromehead, who, about 1550, to while away the hours of his incarceration, like the Tinker in the gaol of Bedford, wrote the words of the hymn, " Jerusalem my happy home." In 1585 it was ordered that " if a man was found drunken in any alehouse in the towne he should be punished by being put in the dungeon and pay a fine of 6d., and if he could not pay this the keeper of the alehouse should pay it." When, as often happened, the river rose in flood, the unfortunate prisoners in the lower dungeon had a wretched time, and it is on record that one poor fellow had his toes eaten away by rats.

It was a time of increasing comfort of living, when glass windows came into use in the poorest of houses, when wooden bolsters began to be discarded in favour of softer pillows, and in the inns, clean linen was provided for travellers for a penny a night. Wheat was sold at 11s. 3d. a quarter ; ale, the chief beverage of all classes at all meals, was 2d. a gallon ; a horse could be bought for 44s., an ox for 35s., a cow for 15s. 6d, a sheep or a hog for 5s., and a fowl for 3d. The staple food was bread, very similar to the wheaten farls which are still made in the city, and known then as " jannock," and when unscrupulous bakers sometimes adulterated it with piecemeal, there arose our common Lancashire expression to denote something not quite above board, " It's noan jannock." Potatoes were a recent introduction, having been brought from Virginia by Sir Walter Raleigh in 1558, but were considered a great luxury and only eaten by the more wealthy burgesses, who grew them in glass-houses.

There was no public lighting in the town, and when men went abroad after nightfall they had to grope their way with the aid of a lantern of horn and run the risk of a footpad lurking in the shadows. Just as to-day there were plenty of folk to grumble and complain that the grand old days were gone for ever, that when the houses were of wattle and daub, the men were of oak, but now the houses were of oak the men were but wattle and daub. Yet Gloriana sat upon the throne to inspire Englishmen to deeds of adventure and glory yet unknown ; and the little boys " with shining morning faces," whom Adam Byrom smiled upon as they passed unwillingly on their way to Hugh Oldham's School, were contemporary with that other schoolboy in Stratford-on-Avon, the greatest poet the world has ever known.

CHAPTER VII

The Maid of the Mill.

NOTHING brings us nearer to our forbears than the realisation that despite the differences that time works in the outward visible expression of life and living, the human element in all its strength and weakness remains unchanged through every age. It is not surprising, therefore, in catching stray glimpses of certain Salfordians of the sixteenth century to find them neither saints nor devils, but just simple men and women with fallabilities like our own. When in 1592 my Lord Bishop of Chester paid a visitation, we find it recorded that " Richard Percivall of Salforde Sen., Will Bradshay of Oldfield Lane and William Battson, Tanner " were excommunicated for " talkinge in ye Churchyarde at sermontime." Sporting proclivities, too, were just as paramount then, as now, for " Peter Dudley of Salforde " was dealt with in the same drastic fashion as " a common talker in ye Churchyarde at time of Divine Service beinge an assembler of a number of them to talke of his bowlinge." Matrimony, too, was sometimes a troublous venture, for we read that " William Ratcliffe, gent., and Isabella, his wife, do not live together " and the ecclesiastical authority at York was appealed to to settle their differences, whilst " Edmond Treford and Margaret, his wife " being in a similar plight, were respited " for hearing of ye Lorde Bishop."

There is preserved an interesting document " a boke made the XXVjth daie of July of or vewing corne in Salforde, 1584," which shews how the surveyor of tithes went round the township noting in each field the number of toshers, sheaves, hattocks and riders of wheat, barley, oats, beans and pease, and inserting a branch into every tenth to denote that it was claimed for the tithe and must be left in the field. The land outside the town itself was mainly open fields cultivated in strips eventually along Oldfield Lane and Cross Lane. In 1623 Henry Keley bought a plot called the Roodlands, " containing half an acre of large measure " in the Cross Lane, in the inheritance of James Hulme, deceased. It was a narrow strip on the east side of Cross Lane, 396 yards long

and containing one acre, three roods. This was typical of
the average field holding. The names of persons and places
mentioned in the book are very interesting, and although we
have not space here to quote the whole, a few extracts will
be usefully revealing.

" Thomas Bolton, in a lytell croft, sontyn corfot . . .
(Kerfoot's or Sandy Croft).

" Mrs. Torkenton, on the back side of Clueworth . . ."

" Mr. Byron, weate shorn, in the intacke near the gret
Oldefelde."

" Wilhurst, over agenst rothwells . . ."

" James Holland, in the littell croft by the crosse . . ."

" Mrs. Trafort (Trafford) in the Oldefelde, next her
meydo . . ."

" Thos. Sorowcolde, in Golliefyld (The Gallowfield) . . ."

" Mr. Pilkington, in the Cornel Hill . . ."

" John Oldham . . . In the Checker " (near
Windsor)

" Raffe Byrom, at Brere Croft . . . apon the hawse
of Rothwell's in a dole. . . ."

" Mr. Byrom, in the nether Oldefelde, apon the backe
syde of Rothwells . . ."

" Glebe sett by the fotway yt leadeth to Ordsall, XXVij.
Ryders of otts, and lyke v tossers, in the same fylde, in the
Oldefelde."

" Edmonde Haworth, in the Claye Bancke . . ."

Walking along Oldfield Road to-day it is difficult to
conjure to mind the time when the Traffords, the Bradshaws,
the Pilkingtons, the Boltons, the Debdales, the Byroms, the
Masseys, the Holts, the Howarths, and the Hollands each
tended their fertile fields and made golden with the waving
corn that rising ground lifting from the river valley now
scarred and blackened beyond measure with smoking factory
and sordid tenement, and the silver ribbon of countless
railroad tracks.

That the tithe was not always freely rendered is seen in
the note that " Jaffraie Mr. Strangues man, and another
oulde man, and a boye lede barly forth of the Knolles (in
Broughton) and hade Lod and Lost abowt VIIJ thith and
wold not Let us be aquented woth the tithes."

Still recalling to our minds the peace and charm even
here in Salford of " sylvan slopes with corn clad fields, hung

as if with golden shields," seemingly incongruous in the heart
of a great city, stands the tower of a windmill on the river
bank in Peel Park, where even yet the name of " The Meadows"
stubbornly persists amid the overwhelming industrialisation.
Why this strange survival whose use is long past, a scarred
and lonely sentinel on the poor blackened river which in
happier days reflected in its silver depths the white sails of
the mill dancing to the wind ?   There is an old legend which
may explain it, a breath of romance from a time long past.

Once, 'tis said, a son of the Stanleys fell in love with the
daughter of the miller, and would have married her, but his
family intervened and caused him to be sent to an appointment
at Court, where, in the company of great ladies, it was thought
he would forget his passing fancy for the lowly maid on
Irwell's banks.   Vainly the girl waited for her lover's
promised return until, in broken-hearted despair, she threw
herself into the river, knowing not that even at that moment
the young noble was riding to her as fast as horse could carry
him.   Greeted with the fatal news, he too cast himself into
the swollen stream, and in death was united to her from whom
cruel circumstances had parted him in life.   Then it was that
his father, now full of contrition, commanded that the mill
which had been the lover's trysting place should stand for
ever to their memory.

Legends like this have often in them some grain of truth,
and these lands whereon the old mill stands were actually
part of the Stanley estates.   Anciently a member or hamlet
of the Royal Manor of Salford, and demesne of the Honour
of Lancaster, Broughton was granted in 1190 to Iorwerth de
Hulton, but on becoming King, John gave to Iowerth in
exchange the vill of Penelton, restoring Broughton to its
former position as a possession of the Lord of the Honour.

In 1396, Hawise de Castle Hill owned the lands of
Broughton and lived close to the site of Broughton Old Hall
on the high ground known as Castle Hill.   Eventually the
Stanleys, Lords Mounteagle, came into possession, and in
1578 the manor of Broughton was purchased by Henry,
fourth Earl of Derby, who had a son, Edward, Lord Stanley,
who died in early manhood reputedly from misadventure.
Whether the story has been woven around this young man
will perhaps never be known, but it brings into our busy
humdrum city life such a charming fragrance of old romance

that the legend deserves to be true, and perhaps when the mists rise from the river the spirits of the young lovers, the scion of a princely house and the humble maid of the mill walk abroad again at nightfall when the throbbing heart of the bustling city has sunk to rest.

The Broughton lands were given by Earl Henry to his illegitimate son, Thomas Stanley, who was succeeded by his son Ferdinando. Taken prisoner by Fairfax at Selby, Ferdinand took the National Covenant and conformed to the Parliament. Broughton Hall at that time was occupied by his sister Jane for her life, and his mother, who was still living, had married Nathaniel Atkins, physician. Because the latter had been observed during the siege of Lathom " very conversant and familiar with the officers of the garrison," his estates were also sequestered. At the Restoration, Charles II. regranted the manor of Broughton to Ferdinando, who mortgaged it to the Chethams to such an extent that his son Henry agreed to sell, in 1696, to George Chetham, who, on taking possession, pulled down the existing hall and built the Old Hall, which was demolished a few years ago. The last male of the ancient Chetham line, Edward Chetham, died a bachelor intestate in 1763, and the manor of Broughton passed to his younger sister, Mary, who married in 1769 Samuel Clowes of Chadwick, in whose family the estate has since remained. By the munificence of the present head of the Clowes family, the site of the hall has passed to the Corporation of Salford to be a notable addition to the public parks of the city.

CHAPTER VIII

Ordsall.

WHEN the wind whistles o' nights about the ancient eaves of Ordsall, what tales must it hear from the old house, fragment of a happier age, when one of the most illustrious knightly families of Lancashire gathered within its walls all the romance, the grace and the adventure of their long day. Even now, forlorn and well-nigh forgotten, it yet seems a mute rebuke to an age which has sacrificed everything to an overpreening anxiety for material enrichment. Change is not necessarily progress, and the change that Ordsall Hall has seen come over its manorial demesne from as fair a landscape as anything in this fairest of lands to the dismal desolation that has been wrought by the destructive hand of man awakens saddened reflections. No wonder ghostly traditions linger about the old place, for its history is inextricably wound in that of Salford town itself, a history of love and war, of romance and feud, of things nobly achieved and lost causes gallantly upheld. The shouts of fighting men and the sobs of grief-stricken women, prayer and praise, laughter and love, merry feet dancing to harp and madrigal through the centuries have rung about its rafters and passed into the very fabric itself.

In the Chapter House of the Cathedral in Manchester is an old brass, the headless effigies on which depict Sir Alexander Radclyffe, grandson of the Sir William, who has previously been mentioned, and Alice Booth, of Barton, his wife. This Sir Alexander, who was knighted at Lille after the Battle of the Spurs in 1513, was one of the greatest figures in the county. High Sheriff four times, and Steward of the town of Salford, he arranged, in 1543, a Salford Muster in preparation for the expedition into Scotland.

In addition to Ordsall (where there were a windmill, a water-mill, etc.), Sir Alexander held Flixton, Hope, Shoresworth, Tockholes, and Livesey, lands, etc., in Pendleton and Barton, and three parts of the manor of Newcroft in Urmston, with lands there. On his death in February, 1549, he was succeeded by his son, another Sir William, who received his knighthood in that same Scottish expedition, and in the

HATTON'S SHOP, CHAPEL STREET, SHOWING THE WATCHMAN'S BOX.

[*From a water-colour drawing by J. B. Collins.*

Military Muster of 1553 was appointed commander of the Salford contingent along with Sir Edmond Trafford of Trafford, and Sir Robert Langley of Agecroft.

After the fall of Calais, the Scots, at the instigation of their French allies, began to threaten the northern counties with invasion, and levies of men and arms were raised throughout Lancashire. Of the captains named in the Earl of Derby's despatch are " Sir William Radclyffe, his son and heir, Alexander, who is a handsome gent, and Sir John Atherton, joined with him," these three knights furnishing between them 100 men. Sir Alexander did not long survive his father, and was succeeded by Sir John Radclyffe, perhaps the most influential man of his time in these parts. He was M.P. for Wigan, 1563–67, and for Lancashire, 1571–85.

John Radclyffe succeeded to Ordsall in 1568, when his father's possessions were recorded as follows : The manor of Ordsall with two water-mills, a fulling-mill, etc., and 20 acres of land in Shoresworth—which by this time seems to have been merged in the domain—held of the Queen by the sixth part of a knight's fee and a rent of 69s. 8d. Seventeen burgages in Salford, 100 acres of land there, twenty burgages in Salford and Oldfield, and 30 acres in Salford, all held of the Queen in free burgage and socage by a rent of 12s. His holdings also included manors and lands in Flixton, Pendleton, Hope, Monton, Newcroft, Moston, Tockholes, Livesley, Oakenrod, Spotland and Radcliffe. (Duchy of Lanc. Inq. p.m. xiii. 33.)

Sir William Radclyffe in 1561 had made provision for his wife Katherine and given her the manor house at Hope for residence. At the time of his death, Sir William's brother, Alexander, was also living at Ordsall, and another brother, Edmund, at Chenies in Bucks.

These were days when Mary, having died under the weight of her accumulated disasters, the people were looking hopefully to a brighter and happier regime under the Lady Elizabeth, who assumed the sceptre she was to wield with such glory on November 17, 1558.

The Reformation had let flood upon the nation many disorders, and large bodies of men were openly scornful of all authority they could not set up and control themselves. Mary's embittered mind and bigoted persecutions had further aggravated national and local feuds, and in no part of England were these distinctions so markedly prevalent as in

Lancashire, the newly-enriched trading classes for the most part espousing the new doctrines, whilst the gentry and the common people held fast to the old traditions. It was a severe testing time for men like Sir John Radclyffe and his fellow burgesses to maintain their religious and secular loyalties in the midst of innuendo and distrust, and it speaks much for their consistency of character that they were able to show an unwavering devotion both to the faith of their fathers and in allegiance to the State.

In the General Muster of 1559, Salford supplied 394 harnessed and 649 unharnessed men. Six years later an awful sickness fell upon the town, as upon London and other parts of the country, and a great part of the population fell victims to the plague. In the midst of this came news of the Rising of the Catholics of the North under the Earls of Westmoreland and Northumberland, and again the men of Salford were summoned to arms, Sir John Radclyffe's younger brother, Richard, leading them forth to uphold their Queen even against men of his own faith. In 1574, Sir John erected at his own expense the west window in the Parish Church of Eccles, and was one of the signatories, along with John Byrom, of the Association of Lancashire Gentlemen formed to defend Queen Elizabeth from the schemes of Mary Queen of Scots. In the same year a General Muster was taken, in which Salford furnished 132 archers and 603 billmen under the leadership of Sir Edmund Trafford and Sir John Radclyffe, the latter of whom provided, at his own expense, one demilance, two light horses, three corselets, three coats of plate, three steel caps, two culivers, two morions, three pikes, three longbows and three sheaves of arrows. Notwithstanding this signal proof of his loyalty, he was included in a list of persons—" Recusants " as the Catholics were now termed—who were ill-affected to the State and as " a dangerous temporiser in religion," although he escaped the fate of many of his faith who, after the execution of the Jesuit Campion, were imprisoned in large numbers in the New Fleet Prison in Salford.

Through all the midst of plot and counter plot, when all England seemed to watch with bated breath as the Queen skilfully wove the defence of her realm against Spain, little crowds would gather in the evening dusk around the red-curtained ale-houses which clustered together in and about

Greengate and Sergeant Street, waiting for the latest of the swift rumours flying round the land, whilst on Ordsall Hill, Trafford and Radclyffe drilled their townsmen for the day when the Queen should deem the time ripe to strike.

In that grave hour of national peril, England became one people wherein all other differences were forgotten, and when the beacon fires blazed on Rivington and Holcombe, on Kersal and Buile, when the wind ran riot with clamouring bells, and the streets grew red with torches as the Salford Muster marched forth to breathe its share of defiance to Spain, Catholic and Protestant joined in the great roar of " God Save the Queen," and Walsingham's boast that when the test came the Catholic gentlemen of England would not be found wanting was echoed in that Ordsall knight who not only led his townsmen forth but headed the Salford list with £100 towards the defence of the country when the great Armada came.

Sir John Radclyffe married Anne, the daughter of Thomas Asshawe, of the Hall on the Hill, and despite the claims on him of his national and public duties, he yet found time to pursue the life of a country gentleman and to personally farm his estates both at Ordsall and Flixton, in which latter place he had increased his family holdings by his marriage. He died in 1590, and in his will expressed a desire to be buried in the Church at Manchester " betwixte the quire door and the stepps amoungst myne ancestors." His monumental brass is still preserved in the Chapter House of the Cathedral.

His younger brother, Richard, is buried in Flixton Church, where, in the porch, is still to be seen the brass to his memory.

Ordsall Hall in Sir John's time was a quadrangular building entirely in the black and white half-timbered style, of which only the Great Hall still remains. On the eastern side of the courtyard beyond where the Church of Saint Cyprian now stands was the family wing, and opposite, on the western side, was the servants' wing, the quadrangle being completed by a gatehouse and drawbridge over the moat which ran roughly along the present site of Taylorson Street.

CHAPTER IX.

Tragedy and Valour.

SIR JOHN RADCLYFFE was but fifty-three years of age
when he died, and his will reveals his concern for the
large family of tender years he was leaving behind, as
well as indicating his deep religious feeling.

"'Jesus esto mihi Jesu.' I, John Radclyffe, of
Ordsall, Knt., of good memory and health, having divers
little children both younger sons and daughters which be
unprovided for and willing God of His great mercy to
have compassion on me and trusting through the Passion
and Death of Christ to be one of the elect company of
heaven with the Blessed Virgin Mary and all the Saints
do make, etc., etc."

After his various bequests he proceeds :—

"I would have these children brought up in virtue
and learning so that after they accomplish 14 years I
would have them sent to Oxford or Cambridge there to
continue till one of them be able to go to the Inns of
Court if it be his pleasure or to tarry and reside in the
University."

Hawkins and Drake had begun to stir the minds of all
Englishmen with the vision of new lands beyond the ocean
seas, "fabl'd shores o'er the world's uncharted wastes."
And Sir John, in his ancestral home, dreamed, too, of taking
a part in forming "the large imperial legend of our race,"
for he desired

"one of mys sons to proceed in the Civil Laws within
England and when he shall be of ability to travel to go
beyond the seas . . . and not to continue in this
country for a time to come and see his mother, brothers
and friends, and not to tarry over here long."

Alas for all the dreams and planning of the gallant old
knight. His eldest son Alexander, a mere stripling of sixteen
when his father died, duly became a student of the Inner
Temple whence he was gathered into that select company of
gallant and high-spirited youth that scintillated round the
great Queen's throne. Here he formed a deep and assured
friendship with the famous Earl of Essex, whom he

accompanied to the victorious attack, when the Spanish monarch received his severest blow in the capture of Cadiz. Knighted by Elizabeth—always quick to appraise the merits of her splendid young courtiers—his chief affections were claimed and held by one of the honourable maids of her Majesty's bedchamber, the playmate of his childhood, his own cousin, Marie Radclyffe, daughter of his father's brother, Richard Radclyffe, of Newcroft, in Flixton. When Essex was appointed Lord Lieutenant of Ireland and left England at the head of the greatest expedition Elizabeth had ever sent abroad, to quell the rebellion of the Earl of Tyrone, Sir Alexander was one of the most notable of all that gallant train of nobles and gentlemen who accompanied the Earl. He left Ordsall in 1599 never to return, and Sir John Harrington has left record of the magnificent bravery shown by this heroic young man who died for his Queen in the 26th year of his age. Sir Alexander made his will, dated Ordsall, March 22, 1599, on the eve of the departure of his regiment for Ireland, settling his estates on his brother John and providing annuities for his sisters and for each of his other brothers, with bequests to his loving cousin Marie Radclyffe and his servant Thomas Gillibrand, both of whom he nominated as his executors. The will was sealed before the eminent Salford notary, Humphrey Davenport.

A few months before, the second brother, Captain William Radclyffe, serving with Montacute, had also fallen a victim to the treacheries of Tyrone, being one of the ill-fated company who fell with their general at the fort of Blackwater.

But this was not all the toll that the Irish rebellion was to extract from this great Salford family, for Thomas and Edmund, the younger twin brothers, and still only boys, both perished whilst serving with Lord Mountjoy, who succeeded where Essex had so dismally failed.

The death of Sir Alexander, to whom she was so devoted, severely affected his sister Margaret, to whom Tyrone is said to have paid his addresses during his stay at the English Court. Besides their five sons, Sir John Radclyffe and Dame Ann had three daughters—Margaret, Jane and Ann—and both of the elder of these received appointments at Court as maids of honour to the Queen's most Excellent Majesty. Her singular charm and grace commended Margaret, especially to all with whom she came in contact, and the Queen exalted

her above all the other Court ladies as her prime favourite.
Small wonder that to such a family holding so high favour in
her entourage Elizabeth should pay a visit at their ancient
manor home where, putting aside for a short hour the rigours
of her exalted state, she could join with her favourite in the
domesticities she revelled in. If the sticks and stones of
Ordsall but had tongues, they would tell, perhaps, of the
greatest of English monarchs playing on the virginal or
dancing a galliard in the homely circle of her beloved Radclyffes,
or receiving the addresses of the townsfolk of her Royal
Borough of Salford with that grace and true sympathy that
make the name of Elizabeth for ever one with that of England.
They would tell, too, of the Fair Maid of Ordsall, bereft of
her smile and lively charm, her sad heart breaking with a
great sorrow, being borne by the Queen's command from
Ordsall to her Majesty's own palace at Richmond, where she
died on November 10, 1599.

By the Queen's command, Margery Radclyffe was buried
in the Church of Saint Margaret at Westminster. Ben Jonson
writing the follòwing epitaph for the monument which the
Queen ordered to be erected over her grave —

> **M**arble weep, for thou dost cover
> **A** dead beauty underneath thee,
> **R**ich as nature could bequeath thee :
> **G**rant, then, no rude hand remove her.
> **A**ll the gazers on the skies
> **R**ead not in fair heaven's story,
> **E**xpresser truth or truer glory,
> **T**han they might in her bright eyes.
>
> **R**are as wonder was her wit ;
> **A**nd like nectar ever flowing :
> **T**ill time, strong by her bestowing,
> **C**onquered have both life and it ;
> **L**ife, whose grief was out of fashion
> **I**n these times. Few so have rued
> **F**ate in a brother. To conclude,
> **F**or wit, feature and true passion,
> **E**arth, thou hast not such another.

AGECROFT HALL FROM THE SOUTH-EAST.

The only surviving son, another Sir John, whom Sir Alexander named as his heir, married Alice, the daughter of Sir John Byron, who maintained large establishments both in Lancashire and Nottinghamshire. It was this Sir John Byron and Margery, his wife, who were celebrated in their day for the peaceful and virtuous lives and their remarkable deaths.

A deed is in existence, dated May 29, 1613, by which Sir John Radclyffe conveyed to Adam Byrom, of Salford, Gent., certain lands in Ordsall and Eccles for the term of thirteen years and eight months, for the consideration of four hundred and four score pounds. One of the witnesses is Samuel Boardman, Cl., who had been the tutor of the Radclyffes, and in the Stanley Papers is named as having accompanied Sir Alexander on his visit to Lathom in August, 1590.

His mother, Dame Ann Radclyffe, who had retired from Ordsall soon after her husband's death to the Hall on th' Hill, died there, having outlived nearly all her children, on January 10, 1627, at the age of 82.

The fame and importance of the Radclyffes, therefore, was not merely a local one, and of all the splendid company that made glorious that epic age of English history none were more distinguished than those worthy scions of that illustrious family, for centuries the leading burgesses and the dominant influence in Salford Town.

John Radclyffe, like his brothers, served with Essex, and was knighted during the Irish war, on September 24, 1600, and thereby freed from wardship. He was knight of the shire in three Parliaments, 1620 to 1625. When Buckingham, aiming to controvert Richelieu's plans for a Franco-Spanish invasion, set sail with a fleet to the relief of La Rochelle, Sir John Radclyffe was one of his company. During the engagement on the disastrous Isle of Rhe, Sir John had both his legs shot off, and died of his wounds 29th October, 1627, in the second year of Charles I.

Barritt has preserved a local story to the effect that Sir John's wife, Alice, was enamoured of Prestwich of Hulme Hall, and it was largely due to this that he joined Buckingham's expedition.

The esteem in which Sir John Radclyffe was held in the country is reflected in the laudatory ode Ben Jonson wrote on him :—

" How like a column, Radclyffe left alone
　For the great mark of virtue, those being gone
　Who did, alike with thee, thy house bear,
　Standest thou, to shew the times what you all were ?
　Two bravely in the battle fell and died,
　Upbraiding rebel's arms, and barbarous pride :
　And two that would have fall'n as great as they
　The Belgic fever ravished away.
　Thou that art all their valour, all their spirit
　And thine own greatness to increase thy merit,
　Than those I do not know a whiter soul,
　Nor could I, had I all nature's roll.
　Thou yet remain'st, unhurt in peace or war,
　Though not unproved ; which shews thy fortunes are
　Willing to expiate the fault in thee,
　Wherewith, against thy blood　they offenders be.

CHAPTER X

Guy Fawkes.

ORDSALL HALL will always, perhaps, be chiefly associated in the popular mind with the glamour that Ainsworth has thrown over it in his romance of the exploits of Guy Fawkes. Although the novelist, exercising the liberty of the craft, has not restrained his story within the strict limits of historical authenticity, it is nevertheless largely constructed on actual facts.

At the beginning of the seventeenth century, the Catholics of England were divided into two parties, the loyalists and the Jesuits, the former, comprising the old families and the majority of the secular priests, seeking only toleration for the exercise of their faith, the latter made up of the more fanatical elements, supplemented by indigent adventurers, aiming for a revengeful overthrow of the whole fabric of the State. Like all revolutionaries, what this second party lacked in numbers they made up for in vociferousness and the violence of their expressions. It will always stand to the honour and glory of the main body of English Catholics of the time that, despite indignities and the most vile persecution, they unflinchingly maintained an untrammelled fidelity to the Crown and the Realm. The Gunpowder Plot originated in the mind of one, Robert Catesby, a member of an old family in Northamptonshire, who had in turn been a bitter denouncer and a zealous supporter of the Papists, and gaining five other ruthless men to support his conspiracy, he set out to win the leading Catholic families by darkly hinting that their deliverance from persecution was at hand. Amongst his confederates was Guy Fawkes, a soldier of fortune, of Yorkshire, a man of great piety and exemplary temperance, but withal a fanatic in matters religious, an enthusiast whose understanding had been distorted by superstition until all his better feelings had become perverted.

Almost without exception, the chief families of Salford and neighbourhood clung resolutely to the old faith, and none had suffered more for recusancy than the Radclyffes of Ordsall. To win the Radclyffes to the plot would have been to have gained the support of nearly all the Catholic gentry

of Lancashire, who would have immediately responded to
such a lead. Ordsall at this time was in the possession of
Sir John Radclyffe, brother of Sir Alexander, and Catesby
would undoubtedly be well acquainted with Sir John from
the fact that they had both served with and enjoyed the
friendship of the Earl of Essex. Catesby quickly made his
way to Ordsall, hoping, by pressing his suit with Sir John's
daughter, to gain the Radclyffe support for his scheme.
Fawkes, too, was despatched to warn Sir John that a warrant
had been issued for his arrest for sheltering a Jesuit priest,
knowing nothing, however, of his confederate's amorous
instincts. Sir John was away at the time, and Catesby was
sent to warn him of his danger. Meanwhile the Hall was
raided by the messengers of the Privy Council, and Miss
Radclyffe and Guy Fawkes escaped by the secret passage
made centuries before by the monks who kept the Ordsall
Ford. Whether Miss Radclyffe did marry Fawkes thinking,
by her influence as his wife, to prevent the awful plot in which
he was engaged, we shall not know, but certain it is that
the Radclyffe family sternly refused to have part or lot in a
scheme from which their conscience and loyalty alike revolted.

Time and man's indifference have played sad havoc with
Ordsall Hall, but thanks to the public-spirited generosity of
the late Earl Egerton of Tatton (who was also Viscount Salford)
an extensive restoration of the fabric was carried out in
1896–8, so that the Great Hall, the Star Chamber and Ann
Radclyffe's bedroom are still to be seen very largely as they
appeared to the eyes of Guy Fawkes and Catesby. It is a
thousand pities that greater perception was not shewn when
Ordsall Park was made, and a site chosen for the park that
would have enabled the hall to have been preserved within
something of its natural setting.

The Hall was originally a great mansion of exceptional
beauty, and a notable example of a medieval half-timbered
house. Leland remarks on the beauty of its surroundings
when he passed by on his journey through Lancashire. To the
south-west it commanded a lovely outlook over the winding
course of the river, with Hulme Hall, the seat of the Prestwich
family on the opposite bank, and in the near distance,
Trafford Hall, beyond which were the wooded uplands of
Cheshire stretching away to the distant Peckforton Hills.
The house stood within a moated enclosure, the sloping land

to the north draining into the Ordsall Brook supplying the moat with water. The gardens were laid out in the formal style of Elizabeth's day, and beyond were orchards and detached buildings for shippons, barns and so forth. The main approach was by way of Ordsall Lane, which ran from Chapel Street following the course of the modern street as far as the present junction with New Oldfield Road, and thence in a south-westerly direction, through a noble avenue of sycamores to the main gates of the Hall, a drawbridge affording access over the moat to the entrance by a corbelled gateway into the quadrangle.

As it stands to-day, the Hall consists of a central block standing east and west, forming the main portion of the original fourteenth century house, and a west wing rebuilt in brick about 1639. In the latter year the east wing was pulled down, together with the buildings on the north side, part of the foundations of which were unearthed in 1898. From this it is possible to reconstruct the earlier appearance of the house, with buildings surrounding the four sides of a quadrangle, about 64 ft. by 75 ft. The still existing older part of the Hall is of timber construction on a stone base, the main beams being of 10 in. scantling.

The chief feature is the Great Hall, undoubtedly one of the largest and finest of its kind in the North of England, and dates from the time when it was the custom for the lord and his retainers to dine together in patriarchal fashion. Living history is incorporated in those noble timbers, that have heard first-hand the stories of Creci and Agincourt from warriors freshly returned from those memorable fields ; that have heard the sound of Gloriana's voice, and listened to converse and discussion that has helped to mould the destiny of England.

The old walls are framed in square panels in quatrefoils formed by the insertion of oak struts and angle pieces, framed with mortices and oak pegs—a rigid and splendid ornamental piece of construction. The east wall shews traces of the remains of a still older house. The high-pitched, open-timbered roof rising to a height of 32 ft. is carried on three principal trusses, forming two wide bays of 14 ft. each and two narrow bays of 7 ft. each. The middle truss springs from wooden moulded responds set against the side walls, with moulded octagonal capitals and large arched braces below a cambered and embattled tie-beam. The space over the tie-beam is filled in with a series of fourteen arched openings with traceried spandrels. The tie-beam of the western truss is cambered over a central arched opening 15 ft. wide, but runs horizontally over the narrow screens which flank the opening, and are made of two tiers of solid square-headed panels, two in each tier. These screens were fitted for warmth, and across the centre was formerly a movable screen sheltering the hall from the draughts of the main entrance and shutting off the entrance to the butteries and kitchens. At the opposite end of the hall stood the dais, whereon was the " high table." The panelled cove over the dais has been replaced with a flat ceiling, and the truss at this end of the hall is closed in with quatrefoiled panels.

A notable feature is the great bay of unusual character. Its plan is a seven-sided decagon, with pairs of square-headed lights on each side, and a transom at half-height carved with a low relief design of grapes and vine leaves similar to that on the tomb of St. Frideswide in Oxford Cathedral, indicating fifteenth century workmanship. The bay opens to the hall by a four-centred arch of wood, and the upper portion of the bay forms a Minstrel Gallery, presumably made in the sixteenth century.

Between the bay and the dais is the entrance to the Lord's Chamber, and also, formerly, a newel staircase to the Chapel. Here, too, are traces of a cellar, where a stone closes the entrance to an underground passage. The hall is lighted on the north side by a continuous line of narrow lights, six between each pair of uprights, along the upper portion of the wall, forming a sort of " clerestory." Originally the south wall was of similar character, but unfortunate restoration has caused it to be rebuilt in brick with utterly unsuitable and unattractive four-light perpendicular windows.

In the bay was formerly some fine stained glass inserted by Sir Alexander Radclyffe, the armourial bearings of his wife's father, Robert Radclyffe, 5th Earl of Sussex, and also some bearing the Three Legs of Man, the Stanley Badge; another crest of that family, the Eagle's Claw, being carved on a shield outside the hall just west of the bay. There is no record of the Stanleys being connected with Ordsall except as friends of the Radclyffes. The south windows of the hall contain some fragments of glass of Our Lady and Saint Katherine, recovered from the Chapel.

The Lord's Chamber, or, as it is generally known, the Star Chamber, from the ceiling being ornamented with gilded leaden stars, was originally 25 ft. by 18 ft., but it has grievously suffered from unsympathetic restoration. This is the room that Ainsworth so minutely describes as the scene of the interview with Catesby. It still retains a portion of the frieze with its beautiful cresting of Tudor roses exactly the same as on St. Frideswide's shrine. At the south end of the chamber was a remarkable and very beautiful arrangement of " vis-a-vis " bay windows of six lights, divided by an entrance to the garden. The room has been marred by modern alterations, but it is easy to detect the former recesses where the luckless priest of the household hid when pursued. The room over the Star Chamber is also panelled, but with seventeenth century work, and retains above its canted plaster ceiling the medieval roof with cambered tie-beam and braced arches beneath. This room was originally lighted by a continuation of the bay window, ending under a rectangular projecting gable filled in with wooden studding. In the floor is a spy hole, through which it was possible to look down on whoever was being received in the audience chamber below. Adjoining the Star Chamber on the eastern side is a block of two low stories and an attic erected in the sixteenth century. The lower room is of no particular interest, but the first-floor room is reputed to be Ann Radclyffe's bedroom. Its walls are panelled and the ceiling has a geometrical pattern of moulded ribs. Over the Gothic fireplace are four oak panels carved in linen-folds. The attic fireplace is surmounted with a representation in late Gothic plaster work of a crest, helm mantling, and shield of arms showing Radclyffe of Ordsall quartering Legh of the Booths, Arderne, and Sandbach, the latter estates coming to the Radclyffes by the marriage of Robert Radclyffe, who was drowned in Rossendale Water in 1380, with Matilda, heiress of John Legh of the Booths. The plaster is most probably a reproduction of earlier work, and was perhaps placed in the room during the extensive alterations of the seventeenth century.

The buildings at the west end of the hall retain on the north side their picturesque original frontage, with a two-storied bay set against a Gothic front with quatrefoil panels.

To the east of the bay was formerly the entrance to the Great Hall, the passage between the screens being on the axial line of the former courtyard. In the early days of the house these rooms would form the kitchens, pantries and buttery with chambers over, but were reorganised when the west wing was rebuilt in 1639. This latter wing is in brick with square-headed mullion windows, with a projecting bay to the courtyard. The roof of this wing preserves its stone slates and one of the original brick chimney stacks, with single bricks set herring-bone fashion between the shafts. Near the north end of the wing, the east wall sets back on a line nearly coinciding with that of a foundation discovered in 1896, running westward from the old east wing, that it may be taken as marking the width of an original north wing, and suggests that this wing was in existence when the seventeenth century work was begun.

Naturally, Ordsall has its ghost, and within recent years quite a number of people claim to have seen a diaphanous female figure wandering about the corridors of the west wing.

One of the principal buildings was the Great Barn, with nave and aisles divided by great oak posts. This was perhaps older than the hall, and, tradition asserts, was in the long-ago used as a church, perhaps by the monks who kept the near-by ford. Humphrey Chetham rebuilt the barn at Ordsall in 1646 and it was pulled down in or about 1898. The chancel beam of the Church of St. Cyprian is one of the timbers of the ancient barn, inserted by the architect to preserve the link between old and new.

No trace remains nowadays of the small building beyond the moat, where the fugitives rested on escaping from the pursuivant, but across from Taylorson Street is an old farmhouse, part of the old farm buildings of the hall, where traces still remain of the entrances to the secret passages, and a stone is still pointed out in the yard as marking the place whence Guy Faukes escaped. In the grounds of the hall stood, as late as 1890, an acacia tree, reputed as old as the hall itself, and one of the finest of its kind in the country.

The later descent of Ordsall has been through the Egerton family. Samuel Egerton, in 1756, purchased the manor from a near relative, Samuel Hill. On the death, without issue, of Samuel Egerton's only daughter, his estates, in 1780, passed to his sister Hester, widow of William Tatton of

Wythenshaw, who resumed her maiden name of Egerton. She was succeeded by her only son William, who died in 1806, his son Wilbraham, the beloved Squire Egerton, inheriting. He died in 1856, and was succeeded by his son, William, who was created Lord Egerton of Tatton in 1859. Wilbraham, his son, was created Earl Egerton of Tatton and Viscount Salford in 1897, at which time he was engaged in restoring Ordsall Hall. He died without issue and was succeeded by his brother, from whom his son, Maurice, the present Lord Egerton of Tatton, inherits.

For a place of its historic importance, Salford has singularly enough few relics of its glorious past. Should we not be therefore all the more eager to preserve for posterity so priceless a survival as Ordsall Hall. Hemmed in at present by incongruous surroundings, it is safe to say that only a fraction of the citizens know of its existence or whereabouts. With its interior refurnished to something suggestive of its former state, and its precincts cleared and laid out with trees and shrubs to provide a worthy setting, the Old Hall would be a showplace that would attract hundreds of people to Salford. There was a great outburst when we lost Agecroft Hall. Ought we not to make a real effort to show our pride in the preservation of what is still left to us ?

CHAPTER XI

A Prince of Benefactors.

IN the same year that Francis Drake returned from his
memorable voyage to the Pacific there was born in Salford
a child who was destined to be, in many respects, its
greatest son, and through the centuries that have passed
thousands of toil-worn hands have been raised towards
heaven to bless the name of Humphrey Booth. The second
son of Robert Booth and Isabel, his wife, the great benefactor
was descended from the same family that loomed so illustriously
in Salford two and a half centuries before,* and in him the strain
of noble beneficence that characterised his ancestor, Thomas
del Bothe, blossomed forth into a bequest of whose splendour
perhaps no other town in all the world can show the like.

Robert Booth, like all his line, was a yeoman merchant who
owned considerable freehold property in the town, and young
Humphrey, on being taken into partnership, immediately
showed the nobility of soul that dominated his whole life.
Salford had been visited about that time with a great plague,
supposed to have been introduced from the East in bales of
cotton imported from Smyrna, and a large proportion of the
population was carried off. Moved to compassion, doubtless
by the plight of his townsmen, and particularly by the old
people deprived of their supports, Humphrey was seized with
a great resolve. With the first profits he received from his
share in the business he bought certain lands, to which he
added every alternate parcel of land he acquired, and in
February, 1630, calling around him his friends, Adam Byrom,

---

* In 1454, William Booth, Archbishop of York, and Sir Robert
Booth, sons of John Booth, as surviving feoffees, granted to Thomas,
son and heir of Sir Thomas Booth, various lands in Salford, Flixton,
Hulme and Croft, with ultimate remainders to the heirs male of John
Booth, eldest son of Thos. del Bothe. (De Trafford Deeds No. 132.).

At the Heralds' visitation in 1613, the Booths recorded their
pedigree as beginning with Robert Booth, who in 1563 purchased
messuages and lands from John Booth of Barton and Ellen his wife.

The will of Robert Booth, Esq., of Salford (dated 1707), who
married Frances, daughter of William Assheton, of Salford, gent., is
sealed with a shield containing the three boars' heads of the Booths
of Dunham and Barton surmounted with a lion rampant, crown and
knight's helmet as crest, exactly the same as the seals of the Booths
of Dunham Massey.

Thomas Mort, Adam Pilkington, John Lownds, George Crannage and John Whitworth, whom he appointed trustees, he executed a deed of feoffment granting this estate in fee simple the income to be " for ever, justly, truly, carefully, faithfully and wholly disposed of for the succour, aid or relief of such poor, aged, needy or impotent people as for the time being should dwell within the Borough or Town of Salford."

To-day this income is over £20,000, which is distributed in grants of 2s. 6d. to 10s. weekly to the respectable poor of the city who have attained the age of 65, and so for nearly three centuries before the State realised its responsibility in the matter, by the thoughtful generosity of a simple merchant, Salford was able to rejoice in being the only town in the world to have the benefit of old age pensions.

But this was not the only service that Humphrey Booth rendered to his native town. For long enough there had been great dissatisfaction amongst the burgesses that, despite its commercial importance and ancient status, Salford suffered the strange anomaly of having no ecclesiastical centre to enshrine the religious devotions of its inhabitants, and for public worship they were obliged to endure the indignity of crossing into another town. A petition was, therefore, prepared and presented to the Lord Bishop of Chester to remedy matters. Fearful of prejudicing the position and revenues of the parish church of Manchester, his Lordship and his advisers would only issue a faculty for a Chapel-at-Ease. In 1634, therefore, Humphrey Booth laid the foundation stone of the new church, the cost of which erection, with the exception of two hundred pounds given jointly by Sir Alexander Radclyffe of Ordsall, Henry Quigley, Robert Pendleton, Charles Haworth, John Hartley, John Gaskell, George Scholes and Ralph Bayley, he defrayed himself, and, further, set aside certain lands to provide the endowment. On May 20, 1635, the Chapel of the Sacred Trinity, the dedication perpetuating the ancient patronal significance of the Kersal Monastery and the Salford Chantry in the Parish Church, was consecrated by the Bishop of Chester. Humphrey was too ill to attend this ceremony, but was recovered sufficiently to fulfil his great desire to receive the Blessed Sacrament in the chapel some weeks later, after which he never left his house again until his death on July 23 of that year.

His deed of gift delivered to the Bishop eloquently illustrates the pious devotion of this Salfordian who took the first steps to deliver his town from a position that, more than anything else, has placed it in the background whilst places of far less eminence and status have been accorded a greater fame. For, however little religion may operate to-day in commercial progress, it was, in past days, the supreme motive force in the common life when men sought to develop their businesses and prosper their towns to the glory and honour of God. Salford owes much to old Earl Ranulph, but in depriving the town of a parish church in its early days as a Free Borough he, unconsciously, was responsible for its identity being largely merged in that of the newer and far less important neighbouring town which was fortunate enough to give its name to the parochial jurisdiction in which Salford was consequently obliged to be situate. The sincere piety of the medieval merchants who laid the moral foundations on which, more than anything, the greatness of England has been built, shone forth anew in many places in the early seventeenth century, but never was there a more worthy exemplar of that noble tradition than Humphrey Booth.

Richard Hollingworth, the first minister of Salford Chapel, has left on record an impressive tribute to the founder as follows :—

" Anno 1634, Humfrey Booth of Salford laid the foundation of Trinity Chapell, in Salford, and of his oune cost (save about £200 was given by severall persons) did finish it and endow it with £20 lands per annum : the sayd Humfrey Booth, being by God's blessing on his trading made rich, gave allso to the poore of Saulford, the first lands that he bought, to the value of £20 per ann. and payd it duely all his lifetime. Hee beinge in greate weakness, earnestly desired that he might live to see the Chappell finished, which hee did, but immediately after the solemn dedication of it by the Lord Bishop of Chester, hee more apparently weakened ; then hee earnestly begged that hee might partake of the Lord's Supper there, and then hee would not wish to live longer. It pleased God to revive him in such measure, as that hee was able to goe to the Chappell constantly till hee was partaker of the Supper (which could not be done of some months after the consecration) in the Chappell, and was never able to goe forth after, nor scarce to get home. Hee was a man just in his trading, generous in his entertainment of any gentlemen of qualitye that came to the towne, though mere strangers to hym, bountifull to the Church and Poore, faithfull to his friend, and wee hope God gave hym both repentance for, and remission of his sins, in the blood of Jesus."

The tombstone of the founder (now affixed to the interior wall in the tower of the Church) records : " Hee committed hys deeds not to the fayth of hys Executors, butt finished and perfected them in hys own lyfe."

We, his fellow-townsmen, who are so profoundly his debtors, should be proud to obey the injunction of his epitaph :—

> " Love his memory,
> Imitate his devotion."

In 1650 the Commissioners reported of the Church, " this is fit to be made a parish, and not to be united to Manchester, though within a quarter of a mile of it, because it hath a competency of inhabitants and communicants within itself." An allowance of £35 10s. was to be paid to the minister. The right of nomination had been given to Mr. Booth and his heirs by the Bishop of Chester without any mention of the consent of the wardens of Manchester.*

Only two of Humphrey the Elder's five children outlived infancy. Robert married Anne Mosley, of Ancoats, and died a few months before his father, leaving a son of his name who became the Rt. Hon. Sir Robert Booth, Kt., Chief Justice of the Common Pleas and of the King's Bench in Ireland† ; and another son, Humphrey, from whom the Gore Booths, the present representatives of the family, are descended. Humphrey, the older surviving son of the Elder, was in business partnership with his father and took over the family responsibilities in the town, becoming a captain in the

---

*Gastrell, Notitia Cestr, (Chetham Socy.), ii, 92.

†In Newcombe's " Diary " is a notice of the interment at the chapel of Sir Robert Booth. " Wed., March 2nd, 1686, Sir Robert Booth buried at Salford, y day. Mr. Hyde preached on Isai. lvii, 1."

Royalist Forces when the Civil War broke out.*   It was his
son, Humphrey the Grandson who, dying unmarried at the
age of 36, bequeathed his estates, including " my house and
croft in the Gravall Hole within Sallford and those ffoure
closes. and barne lyeing and being neare the Broken Bank
together with one roode land which hath a well in it commonly
called Oldfields Well within Sallford now in the occupation
of George Richardson," to " the maintenance of the Chappell
of Sallford, and the remainder to be distributed amongst the
poore of Sallford as ye monies left by my grandfather is."
A sister of Humphrey the Grandson married Samuel Dickanson,
linen draper, and their son, Thomas, by his will in 1711,
founded the Dickanson's Charity which now distributes
something like £1,000 a year in clothing to the aged poor of
Salford.

Another sister, Mary, was the mother of Humphrey
Oldfield, who left his books and £5 to form the Trinity Church
library, the nucleus which gave Salford a further distinction
as the home of the first public free library in the country.

In the quaint diction of the time, this Humphrey's will
runs : " . . . I give and bequeath the Interest, Proffitt or
Improvement of ffifty pounds unto and amongst the Poore of
Salford . . . I give and bequeath the sume of ffive pounds
more to buy a Silver Solver or plate to lay the Communion
bread on att Salford Chappell which Solver or plate when
bought I give and bequeath to the use of the said Chappell
for Ever . . . I give and bequeath the sum of twenty pounds
more to bee laid out in Practicall bookes of Divinity which
bookes when bought, Togather with soe many bookes of my
owne, which I now have as shall bee thought fitt or convenient
I order shall bee placed in a Desk or Cupboard to bee made
for that purpose att the charge of my said Executor in Salford
Chappell aforesaid and there to remaine to bee for Ever
hereafter publickly made use of and read therein by any
person or persons Euery Sunday in the yeare . . ."

---

*His widow married the Rev. Thos. Case, M.A., one of the Assembly
of Divines and a zealous upholder of the League and Covenant, who
often preached before the Parliament.   He was severely censured
for his fiery advice in a sermon preached before a Court Martial in 1644
which earned him the name of the " Presbyterian Hildebrand."
" Noble Sirs," he said, " imitate God and be merciful to none
that have sinned of malicious wickedness," meaning the Royalists,
who were styled Malignants.

It is a strange thing that we have neither sculptured stone nor storied urn to tell to those who pass by of our Prince of Benefactors who, in himself and through his descendants, showed forth such unexcelled devotion to the interests of his town and its people. But he has a memorial more enduring than marble or brass in the hundreds of aged hearts which brighten week by week at the receipt of his bounty, and we cannot honour his memory more than by fanning into a living flame the embers of that civic pride he kindled three centuries ago here in the town he loved and served so well.*

---

*In 1882 the east window of Sacred Trinity Church was filled with stained glass as a memorial to Humphrey Booth the Elder and Humphrey the Grandson, the subjects depicted being, " The Good Samaritan " and " Peter and John healing the lame man."

CHAPTER XII

The Draper Astronomer.

WHEN in far-away Italy Galileo languished as a victim of the Inquisition, gazing out through his prison bars, searching still the mystery of the starry abyss, a young tradesman of Salford was diligently applying himself to the same studies, earning a reputation that was to place him as one of the most brilliant of that small band of astronomers whose labours have revealed to the world what knowledge it now has of the wonders of the heavens.

In our day, the name of William Crabtree has been well-nigh forgotten, typical of that extraordinary attitude which Salford has adopted towards many of the brightest and best of her sons until their very name and fame has become lost in the mists of indifference and apathetic neglect.

The Crabtree family had been settled in Broughton for many generations and were prosperous merchant clothiers and woollen drapers. They were closely intermarried with another local family of importance, the Pendletons. William Crabtree was born in 1610 and, being sent to Cambridge to complete his education, there made the acquaintance of Jeremiah Horrox, whose devoted friend he became. The association of these two young men in their ardent pursuit of astronomy at so early an age led the science being for the first time established on a mathematical basis, and in his writings Horrox frequently refers to his friend in terms of praise and compliment. Leaving Cambridge, Crabtree became engaged in trade with no small measure of success, and his prosperous circumstances, in striking contrast to his friend, enabled him to become a buyer of books, to visit his astronomical acquaintances, and generally to enlarge his knowledge of his favourite study. In September, 1633, he married Elizabeth Pendleton, and built himself a house at Broughton Spout on the slopes of the Cliff, the upper chamber of which he fitted as an observatory. Crabtree was an expert calculator and had industriously investigated the motions of the planets and found out serious defects in the tables of Continental astronomers, despite the fact that he

SCARR WHEEL COTTAGES, BROUGHTON SPOUT. THE HOME OF WM. CRABTREE, THE DRAPER-ASTRONOMER.

had to work under serious drawbacks, including the lack of good instruments. He and Horrox were in constant co-operation by correspondence and visits of the latter to the house at Broughton. In a letter dated April 29, 1637, Horrox pays tribute to Crabtree's better knowledge of a point under discussion, and urges his friend to publish his astronomical observations, of which he speaks very highly.

In the autumn of 1639, from studying the tables they had drawn up together, Horrox had his first intimation that a rare spectacle was imminent in the conjunction of the sun with Venus. He thereupon wrote to his friend, whom, in the *"Venus in Sole Visa,"* he terms "my learned friend, William Crabtree, who has few superiors in mathematical learning," advising him of the remarkable phenomenon, and Crabtree carefully made his preparations for the great event. The plan adopted was to let the sun's image through a telescope into a darkened room. The critical day, November 24th., fell that year on a Sunday, and throughout the day Crabtree watched by his telescope. But the sky was unfavourable, obscured during the larger part of the day with thick clouds, and, unable to obtain a view of the sun, he despaired of making any observation, and was on the point of resolving to take no further trouble in the matter when a little before sunset, about half-past three in the afternoon, the sun burst forth from behind the clouds. Rapt in contemplation, he stood for some time motionless, scarcely trusting his own senses through excess of joy, and thus Crabtree, in his house at Broughton Spout, and Horrox, in his rectory at Hoole, were the only two men in England who then witnessed the transit of Venus, a phenomenon that was not to occur again for 122 years. From their joint observation the friends were able to prove to the scientific world that the planet was only about one-eighth of the size previously supposed. In a letter to Gascoigne, the inventor of the micrometer, Crabtree writes, after discussing the theories of the ancients : " . . . So that had not our own observation and study taught us a better theory than any of these, we had never attended at that time for that rare spectacle . . . The clouds deprived me of part of the observation, but my friend and second self, Mr. Jeremiah Horrox, observed it clearly from the time of its coming into the sun until the sun's setting ; and both our observations agreed most precisely."

Horrox was intending to visit his friend in the Christmas of 1640, and in the last letter he ever wrote, had fixed Monday, January 4, 1641, as the day of his visit to Salford, but on the day before he took ill and died suddenly. His death greatly affected Crabtree, who, on the back of the letter he received from his friend has written, " Thus God puts an end to all worldly affairs. I have lost, alas, my most dear Horrox. *Hinc illae lachrimae.* Irreparable loss." The date of Crabtree's death has never truly been ascertained, owing to the confusion which ensued on the outbreak of the Civil War. In the protestation taken before Richard Hollinworth, Curate of Salford, in February, 1641, John Crabtree and William Crabtree are named among the Protestors of Broughton, Kersal and Tetlow, and although it is believed in some quarters that Crabtree lived until about 1652, it is generally held that he only survived his friend, to whom he was so much attached, and with whom he held so much in common, by a few weeks.

William Crabtree left a son and two daughters, one of whom married Benjamin Brooks and inherited the house at Broughton Spout. Henry Newcombe, Minister of Manchester during the Commonwealth, recording a visit paid to the house in July, 1658, described Mrs. Brooke as " a woman well disposed and of sorrowful spirit. Her father was that famous mathematician and built the house."

Crabtree's observations are included in Horrox's " *Opera Posthuma,*" but these are only a tenth part of what he made. But for the Civil War, which is the most probable explanation of the loss of the remainder, the science of astronomy would, without doubt, have been further advanced by the labours of this Salford woollen draper, who, whilst conducting a successful business, could also apply himself to, and gain so distinguished a place in the realm of scientific study.

A great philanthropist and a great scientist. A town which in one generation produced Humphrey Booth and William Crabtree has, indeed, just cause to hold high its head with pride.

CHAPTER XIII.

In the Seventeenth Century.

N O period of English history has been so wilfully and deliberately misrepresented as the unfortunate years of the reign of King Charles the First. Never did a more virtuous and able monarch ascend a throne. Yet, to serve an ulterior political motive, his heroic memory has been most foully traduced and the greatest national crime of all times officially justified through the energies of political pamphleteers. Here is not the place to enter into a dissertation on the political events of the time, but if we are to understand the devotion that led our forefathers in Salford to suffer so gladly and freely for the Royal Cause, it is necessary to state the naked facts that lay behind the struggle.

It was the end of an epoch. The faith and traditions of yester-year were confronted with the growing influence of a new order which recognised no authority it could not set up and control itself. Intolerance, that dark stain which blots every page of history, forced its determined way, and ever since the Reformation had been arming itself into a tyranny more ruthless and unreasoning than even the former papal oppression. Religion, as the seat of authority, had to go, and, as the Defender of the Church, the attack was centred on the person of the King. Parliament began its relations by a deliberate breach with precedent, hoping thereby to put the King in its power by denying him the financial necessities for the carrying on of the Government unless he would agree to terms that no self-respecting monarch could possibly accept. The King strove valiantly for peace, but the dissimulating artfulness of such men as Pym and Hampden was too much for him.

In May, 1641, the Long Parliament issued a Protestation to defend the Church from Romish innovation ; to protect the King's person and power ; the freedom of the Parliament and the rights and liberties of the subject. From the Protestation taken in Salford before Richard Hollinworth, Curate of Salford, we get a valuable record of our townsmen then living. The list is not a complete one, inasmuch as no

E

Roman Catholic took the Protestation, and the members of this communion formed a very large proportion of the population. Later, when the open rupture came, the document became invalid, of course, to all Royalists. But the list of names does supply valuable genealogical information about the forefathers of modern Salford.

The leading inhabitants of the town were, almost entirely, well-to-do clothworkers or clothiers, who gave employment to websters or weavers, spinners, throwers and fullers. There were also linen drapers and chapmen, and in each household was included workmen and apprentices, whilst every family had women servants. The wealth of the town may be inferred from a collection made to alleviate distress in Bolton, when the large sum of £140 was contributed. There was a school in the town kept by William Hodshon and his wife, Isabel, but the schoolmaster did not take the Protestation. It has been calculated that there were at the time in Salford, with its environs of Ordsall, Ouldfield, Cross Lane, Broughton, Kersal and Tetlow, 900 households, which will convey an idea of the entire population.

The town proper was comprised within a great triangle, the main street known as Salford Street with Sergeant Street, Salford Bridge, Gravel Lane and Back Salford. Trinity Church stood at the apex of the triangle, beyond which was Higher End leading to Ordsall, Ouldfield, Cross Lane and Broken Bank. Higher End was the scene of a tragedy referred to in the parish register when William Barlow, of ffosterwood, was slain on January 21, 1580, and his body was not recovered until two days later. On one side of the Green stood the Courthouse, and facing it at the other side was the Town Cross and the Exchange.

The Byroms still lived at Salford Hall, and Mr. Adam Byrom, then in possession, named in the list, was a person of position expending in the town annually £100. He served with the Royalist Forces on the outbreak of war and was quartermaster to Knype. He died at Chester on January 31, 1644. His son, Adam, died on the same day of the same month three years earlier. A brother, John, became sergeant-major in Colonel Roger Nowell's Regiment of Foot, the Lancashire Militia. His estates were seized by the Committee of Sequestration and he was obliged to compound them for the sum of £201 16s. 6d.

Another brother, Edward, was living at Kersal Cell, which the Byroms had purchased in 1613, from George Siddall who, owing to his spendthrift habits, had been obliged to alienate the property.

Ordsall was in the possession of Sir Alexander Radclyffe, who succeeded his father, Sir John, after the latter's death at La Rochelle, when he was barely twenty years of age. Four years earlier he had been made a Knight of the Most Honourable Order of the Bath, a notable distinction for one so young, and in 1625 he attended King Charles at his coronation. He married the Lady Jane Radclyffe, daughter of Robert, fifth Earl of Sussex, and was elected to represent Lancashire in the Parliament of 1628. The Radclyffes at this time, owing to repeated fines for recusancy and other causes, had become sadly impoverished, and Sir Alexander was obliged to dispose of large portions of his estate to his friends, Humphrey Booth and Humphrey and Edward Chetham. This decline in the family wealth made it difficult to maintain so large a mansion as Ordsall, and the abolition of the military retinue further reduced the necessity for so large a house. Sir Alexander, therefore, largely rebuilt the Hall, pulling down completely the family wing and rebuilding the westerly or servants' wing on a smaller scale in brick as it exists to-day, where is still to be seen the stone he placed in position, bearing within the garter a shield with single bend engrailed, his initials, "A.R." and the date 1639. A staunch Roman Catholic, in common with all others of his faith, he placed himself devotedly at the service of the King, and in 1642 was appointed one of the Commissioners of Array. After the momentous meeting on Preston Moor, when the two parties of Cavaliers and Roundheads first came into being in Lancashire, it was to Ordsall that Lord Strange and Lord Molyneux came to hold council with the Royalist leaders in the county, and from whence Lord Strange went forth to demand from the burgesses of Manchester the arms and munitions belonging to the King that they had illegally seized. Sir Alexander was wounded and taken prisoner at the Battle of Edgehill and committed to the Tower by special resolution of Parliament. His eldest son, William, then a boy of fifteen, was wounded and taken prisoner in the fight at Ribble Bridge in 1648, and died in London. Worn out with suffering and privation, Sir Alexander returned to

Ordsall a dying man in the spring of 1654, and on April 14 his spirit fled to join the King in whose cause his body had been so gladly broken. Thus ended the connection of this gallant but ill-starr'd family with the place that had been their ancestral home for over three centuries, for Lady Jane, his widow, and John Radclyffe, his son, in 1658, conveyed to Edward Chetham the Manor of Ordsall, with the hall, water, corn-mill and lands in Ordsall, Salford, Pendleton and Pendlebury, on mortgage for £3,600, and in 1670 Edward Chetham assigned his interest to the celebrated Colonel John Birch, who, originally a Bristol trader, entered the Parliamentary army and was elected to Parliament for Leominster and afterwards for Penryn. A moderate Presbyterian, he was excluded by " Pride's Purge " in 1648 and imprisoned. Thereafter he became one of Cromwell's most strenuous opponents, and took a considerable part in securing the restoration of Charles II. He represented Weobley in Parliament until his death in 1691, just prior to which he conveyed Ordsall Hall to Leftwich Oldfield, together with the rights of the manor and the chapel of Saint George in Manchester Church.

One son of Sir Alexander Radclyffe was killed in a duel on Bowdon Downs at a spot long known as Radclyffe's Hollow, and in a deed of 1663, another son, Humphrey Radclyffe is described as " late of Ordsall and now of Oldfield within Salford, gent." Humphrey married Margaret Radley, of the Hall upon the Hill.

The Great Barn of Ordsall, with nave and aisles divided by great oak posts, reputed to have been an early church building, was rebuilt by Humphrey Chetham in 1646, and in the following year he also paid half the chief rent due for the manor, so deeply had the Radclyffes fallen on evil times. The Shoresworth portion of the Ordsall demesne passed to the Clowes family.

At Broughton lived another prominent Royalist family in Henry Stanley, his wife Jane, and his son Ferdinando, who has been referred to in a previous chapter and who married as his first wife the daughter of William Lever of Kersal Hall. The Lever estates ran alongside those of the Ravalds, a considerable yeoman family who, besides farming considerable lands on the south side of Kersal Moor, also occupied a burgage on one side of Garden Lane, giving their name to present-day " Ravald Street."

Another knightly family living in the town, also Roman Catholics, were the Barlows, whose seat was Barlow Hall, at Chorlton, but who had a mansion on Broken Bank (now The Crescent) where, in 1641, were in residence Sir Alexander Barlow, his wife known and esteemed in Salford as Lady Dorothy, their three daughters, Elizabeth, Mary and Ann, and their son, Thomas, with a number of female servants and attendants. Sir Alexander died in 1612.

A cousin of the Barlows was Father Ambrose Barlow, who, after being educated at Douai,* was sent to South Lancashire, where he laboured for twenty-five years, and was held in high esteem. On Easter Day, 1641, he was apprehended whilst celebrating Mass in Morleys Hall by the Puritan Vicar of Eccles at the head of a mob of 400, armed with clubs and swords. He was tried at Lancaster and executed, but his head was secured by the Tyldesleys, whose family priest he had been, and carefully secreted at Wardleys Hall, Worsley, where the grinning skull in a glazed niche on the stairway still looks out to remind us of the curious ideas of religious toleration that our forefathers held.

Amongst other leading burgesses are to be noted Mr. Alexander Johnson, who owned, amongst other properties in the town, the Hanging Meadow, the Three Legs of Man, the Beancrofte and land near Broken Bank. Mr. Henry Butler was the town physician, and an interesting name is that of the Cuthbertsons, of whom Robert in 1683, gave £100 to the poor inhabitants of Salford, the Cuthbertson's Charity, which is still disbursed at Christmas every year.

The Masseys were a long-established family in the town. In 1420 a messuage in Salford was granted to Thomas, son of William Massey of Salford, and Beatrice his wife, with reversion to William, the father, and Joan his wife. (Harl. M.S. 2077, fol.216g.) Adam Massey died in 1559 leaving as heir his sister Isabel, about sixteen years of age, who is noted in the Court Records as having paid relief. Another Adam Massey, who died in 1604, held four burgages, etc., of the king in socage by a rent of 17s. 1d. His heir was his grandson, John Olive, son of Joan, daughter of Adam. John Olive

---

* The English Colleges at Douai and Rome were founded by Cardinal William Allen for the training of priests to serve in England. Allen (who was created Cardinal in 1587 and died in 1594) was a descendant of an old Salford family, who, prior to removing to Rossall Grange, were settled in Greengate.

(or Clive) died in 1620, holding the same estate and leaving
a widow, Margaret, and an infant son, Roger. The latter
died without issue in December, 1640, his uncle Roger Olive
being the heir, and age fifty. In the Duchy Inquisition
which records this (p.m. xxix., 60) a settlement of 1599 made
by Adam Massey, " late of Oldfield," is recited.

Another family of old standing was the Pilkingtons. The
Duchy Pleadings record a complaint made in 1533 by Adam
Pilkington regarding the seizure of lands. A later Adam, with
his wife Margaret, made a settlement of five messuages in
1574. His son, another Adam, died in 1605, holding ten
messuages or burgages, with 10 acres of land, etc., the Pinfold,
land called the Oatfield and Checkers (improved from the
waste), and " the Island " by the Irwell, in Salford. These
were held of the king—the burgages in socage by 17s. rent,
the Oatfield and Checkers by the hundredth part of a knight's
fee, and the Island by knight's service and 6s. 8d. rent.

This reference to " the Island " is interesting. The extent
made in 1346 shews that Henry de Pilkington then held
" three islands of land by the bank of the Irwell by charter
of William de Ferrars to Robert, son of Thomas de Salford,
at 6s. 8d. rent. Consideration of the whereabouts of this
holding raises the surmise that at one time the river at the
Crescent Bend completely encircled what we now term " the
Meadows," a not unlikely assumption when it is remembered
that prior to the raising of the land level there, the river
running high regularly submerged the larger portion of these
meadows.

The Pendletons and the Bibbys were other old families
whose holdings date back to sixteenth century records. A
portion of the Pendleton's holdings passed to the Rodleys on
the death of Robt. Pendleton in 1641, his heir being his
daughter Margaret, wife of William Rodley, descendant of a
long line of Salford burgesses.

In 1662 the old Anglo-Saxon Hearth Tax was revived,
when a tax of two shillings per hearth was levied on all houses
except cottages. From the return made in connection with
this, we find there were 312 hearths in Salford proper liable
to tax. The largest was Ordsall Hall with nineteen hearths,
and other considerable mansions were those of Dr. Chadwick
(12 hearths) ; Robert Birch and Alexander Davie (10 hearths
each) ; Major John Byrom (9) ; Richard Pennington and

Hugh Johnson (8 each) ; William Tassle (7) ; Joshua Wilson, William Higginbotham, James Johnson, Mr. Hewitt and Dr. Davenport (6 each). There were four houses with five hearths, ten with four, and fourteen with three. In Broughton were 95 hearths liable, of which William Allen's house had 12 hearths, Elizabeth Lever's (Kersal Hall), nine, and George Kenyon's (Kersal Cell), eight. Pendleton had 138 hearths liable, the largest house being that of John Hollinpriest with nine hearths, and several others with five hearths each. The only large house in Pendlebury was Agecroft Hall with 11 hearths, and twenty-four others were liable, making a total of 35 hearths. This return gives a significant picture of the social state of the town at the period immediately following the Civil War.

CHAPTER XIV

Kersal.

A T the Reformation, the manor and cell of Kersal, with 20 messuages, a water mill, 1,000 acres of land and 20s. rent, became confiscate to the Crown, and Henry VIII. sold it to Baldwin Willoughby for the sum of £155 6s. 8d. In 1548 it was purchased from Phillipa daughter and heiress of Baldwin, by Ralph Kenyon, who immediately sold two-thirds of the estate to James Chetham and Richard Siddall, each of whom paid Kenyon the sum of £132. In November of the same year Kenyon died, and the King granted the third part of a third part of the Kersal Manor, including the monastic buildings, to Sir John Byron in custody for George, Ralph Kenyon's young son and heir. The other two-thirds of Kenyon's portion had been sold to Richard Radclyffe of Langley, and Robert Ravald of Kersal. George Kenyon and Robert Ravald were, in 1582, charged by Ralph Byrom and Adam Pilkington with depriving the Queen's tenants of Salford of their common pasture in the 100 acres of Kersal Wood.

In 1548, William Ravald purchased a messuage and 22 acres of land in Kersal from Baldwin Willoughby, Joan his wife, and Ralph Sacheverell and Phillipa his wife (daughter and heiress apparent of Baldwin). (Pal. of Lancs. F. of F., bundle 13, m.158). He was succeeded in 1560 by his son, William. This was apparently an adjoining holding to that of his brother Robert Ravald mentioned above, the Duchy records showing evidence of two distinct estates, each held of the Queen, the one by the hundredth part of a knight's fee, passing through successive Williams, and the other, held by the two-hundredth part of a knight's fee, which passed through a line of Roberts. The Protestators of Kersal include William Ravald, Wm. Ravald, jun., Richard Ravald, Robert Ravald, William Ravald. (Pal. N.B. iv. 125). According to the Clowes Deeds, the portion of William Ravald was in 1619 acquired by James Chetham of Crumpsall.

The remainder of the Kenyon's lands was about 1660 alienated to the Byroms. No record of the transfer is in existence, but Edward Byrom, on his death in 1668, is described as " of Kersal." This was the grandfather of Dr. John Byrom, who was born at Kersal Cell in 1691.

The Siddall third was alienated in 1616 to William Lever of Darcy Lever, whose son married a daughter of George Kenyon. Their grandson, Rawsthorne Lever married Alice, daughter of Edward Chetham of Smedley, and dying without heir in 1689 bequeathed his lands to Thomas Greenhalgh of Brandlesholme in Bury. This portion came later to the Hopwoods of Hopwood by a foreclosure, and in 1775 was purchased by Samuel Clowes for £4,260 as " one undivided third part of the manor or lordship of Kersal, and the whole of the capital messuage called Kersal Hall, with the appurtenances belonging, " with third parts of the moor and mill." Samuel Clowes at the same time conveyed a moiety of an undivided third part of the manor to Elizabeth, widow of John Byrom, M.A.

The Chetham portion, on the death of Edward Chetham in 1772, passed to Mary Chetham, the wife of Samuel Clowes, and the Clowes family still retain the larger portion of Kersal manor as well as Broughton and Shoresworth.

The older portion of the existing house still known as Kersal Cell was built most probably by Baldwin Willoughby, and is a fragment of a much larger house. The whole fabric has been very severely modernised at various times, to its extreme disadvantage, but the interior still retains some good oak and plaster work. Its exterior is very picturesque despite the modern brick additions, the roof of which rises above the older building. The site of the house has apparently sunk, being considerably below the level of the garden.

The plan retains a central apartment about 18 ft. long with an oak panelled settle along one wall, and an ornamental plaster frieze. Opening from this is a room on the east side, oak panelled to a height of 7 ft., and in one of the windows an heraldic device and the name " Aunesworth." The room on the west side has a fine bay window, in one of the upper lights of which is an interesting glass sundial so fixed that the shadow is visible from inside. Over this room is a chamber known as the " Priest's Room," and to the rear of this what is known as " The Chapel," containing a five-light window with fragments of sixteenth-century glass. In the centre light is a small square of glass depicting the Crucifixion, presumably a relic of the monastic days. The heraldic devices repeat the arms of the Aunesworths, and are perhaps those of a benefactor to the monastery in the sixteenth century. A beam in front of the window bears three shields of arms in plaster enrichment. In the centre is the Royal Arms (England quartered with France). The left-hand shield is that of Ratcliffe, Earl of Sussex, and the right-hand shield of Stanley, Earl of Derby. Ordsall Hall also had the arms of both these families ornamenting the interior and exterior of the hall. Is there some significance in this connecting both these manor houses and two of the greatest families of Lancashire ?

North of Kersal Cell, on the opposite side of Littleton Road is Kersal Hall, a half-timbered, two-storey building, the front of which has been rebuilt in brick painted to represent the original half-timbering. Like the Cell, this house is also built on the principle of a central hall, with north and south wings, the interior rooms in the latter of which retain some excellent oak panelling. It is likely that this house was erected at the same time as Kersal Cell, towards the end of the reign of Henry VIII. Some ghostly traditions attach to it.

CHAPTER XV

The End of an Epoch.

HENRY WRIGLEY, Borough Reeve of Salford, gazed out through the window of his counting house with a troubled mind, as the Constables of the Watch, Peter Bowker and Thomas Blamore, withdrew. As High Constable of the Hundred he had received the Royal messages regarding the Commission of Array, yet, like many another, suspense hung heavily on his heart, and his whole soul, nourished in a strict, if narrow piety, revolted from the threat of civil war that now seemed so imminent. Eager groups clustered about the Town Cross and the steps of the Exchange, and the Reeve knew that, almost to a man, when the call came, they would stand for the King, just as across the river, whose width was as nothing to the broad stream of prejudice that divided the two towns, their neighbours would be as zealous for the Parliament, and were even now throwing up barricades on the far side of Salford Bridge.

Wrigley combined his business as a linen draper with a flourishing connection as a money-lender. He was, in fact, the banker of the town, and his well-stocked warehouse, through the open door of which he could see his apprentices, John Wells and William Plungeon, busy among the fustians and jeans, did not represent the whole of his wealth, for away in London he had two further well-plenished stores.

Whilst the Reeve stood trying to make up his mind, a distinguished company was gathered in earnest council in another part of the town, where Lord Strange and his noble wife, the Lady Charlotte de Tremouille, were come with some of the most illustrious names in Lancashire and Cheshire to the house of Sir Alexander Radclyffe at Ordsall.

There was a sudden rush of the crowds towards the Bridge. Lord Strange was coming to demand, in the name of the King, the surrender of the magazine which the burgesses of Manchester had seized. Excitement grew intense. There was a sudden skirmish as the rival factions came to blows, and when order was restored, two men of Salford lay dead upon the Bridge, the first victims of that holocaust that for seven years was to sweep through the land. Blood had been spilled, and when the King's standard was raised at Nottingham on that cloudy, windy August day in 1642, Henry Wrigley was not left to decide. True to its ancient traditions, though standing alone in what was almost an enemy land, the Royal Borough of Salford echoed with the clarion call, " To the King—To the King ! ! ! "

Manchester, the Puritan stronghold, became the centre of the rebel activities in Lancashire, and early in September Lord Strange marched his troops into Salford, where the people received them with joy. Wrigley thought it best to secrete his goods and papers, and fled to London.

The Burgesses of Manchester refusing compliance to his Lordship's demands, it was decided to besiege the town, and on Monday, September 26, was commenced the Battle of Salford Bridge, an inconclusive action which was maintained until the following Friday, when, realising the strength of the defences erected by the German engineer Rosworm, Lord Strange (now, through the death of his father, seventh Earl of Derby), withdrew his forces and joined the King at Shrewsbury.

Salford was left to the mercy of the Parliamentarians who, rejoicing in their seeming victory, sought to possess the now defenceless town, and skirmishes and looting became rampant. Infected by the Parliamentary fervour in London, Wrigley bought there two brass pieces for the use of Manchester, and, returning himself, enlisted in the rebel forces, lending large sums to the Parliament. His warehouse, left unoccupied on his flight, had been pillaged and burnt in the course of hostilities, but, worse than this, he found himself called upon to answer a serious charge. The Borough Charter, entrusted to his keeping as the Reeve, was lost. How seriously this was regarded is seen in that the loss was described as being " to the great danger of the disinheriting of the free tenants and freeholders of the town and borough of the said free tenure, for want of which grant and charter they are in danger to be reduced to the bondage or perilous tenure of Knyght's service ' in capite.' " Fortunately, the old Charter was recovered, but how many other precious records did the Reeve mislay that would have shed invaluable light on the town's past, and for lack of which Salford has suffered so complete an eclipse and had scant justice at the hands of the historians ?

His zeal amongst his new friends did not remove Wrigley above suspicion. An embargo was laid upon the goods in his London warehouses by the Committee of Sequestration, and he himself was placed under restraint. In a letter to his wife he urges her to bestir herself in his behalf and " to raise upp all the friends you can. I doe request you to make it your whole marke." In his distress, the poor merchant advances a curious plea : " I suppose ye gentlemen of Saullford will not looke upon itt as any advantage to the Co. of Lanc'r to have my whole estate sequestered heare (in London)." At last, however, he secured his discharge, and once again a wealthy man, in 1646 he bought the ancient inheritance of the Tetlows, Chamber Hall, near Werneth, where he took up his residence. His domestic affairs were no happier than his public office. One of his Puritan friends, after describing him as " a great tradesman," and " a knowing man," informs us that husband and wife " could not hit it to live quietly and comfortably together, but lived a secret perpetual unkindness." After one of those matrimonial squalls Wrigley had occasion to go to London, leaving his wife ill. She died, and on receiving news of her demise he was taken suddenly ill in his warehouse, and within a few days he, too, was dead. Such was the man who was lifted into prominence by having the guidance of the town's affairs at the most critical period of its long history.

God bless the King ! God guard the Parliament ! For seven long and weary years the conflicting elements raised their cries in the streets of Salford. Its trade was stagnant, its prosperity fled, its ruin a symbol of an age that had come to an end. When workmen unearthed in Greengate, some years ago, a hoard of coins of the period, they were revealing one of the minor tragedies of the time, of the townsman who had hidden his all and never returned to recover it. From being a virile, thriving community, Salford became a little obscure town. The Court Leet ceased to be held except at irregular intervals. Dancing and games were prohibited, the Book of Sports was, as in other towns, publicly burned in the market place. A gloom as of death lay over the place, and in 1646 death itself in the form of a violent pestilence came to add further devastation.

The Chapel of the Sacred Trinity, whose erection only a few short years before had given such joy to the town, was outraged by Parliamentary edict, the Town Cross destroyed. In this excess of fanatical fury, Humphrey Booth's grave was apparently not even respected, for only last century his tombstone was found by accident covering another grave in the Collegiate churchyard, the great founder's name and inscription face downwards and the reverse side used for a family named Holt.

The Church was made to conform to a Presbyterian constitution, the accustomed forms of worship were abolished, and when " elders " were appointed for the Salford congregation it was none of the old townsmen who were elected, but members of new families in the town, Philip Stamp and William Higginbottom.

In those days no one dared to remain neutral, and although both sides had their due proportion of noble-minded men forced by the stress of events to assume one party or the other when they would gladly have chosen a middle course, none could moderate the merciless despotism of the military autocracy who dominated the nation's affairs, and who finally, in defiance of public opinion, hounded an innocent king to an execrable death.

On the day following the King's execution a great storm broke over the land and the Irwell rose in a great flood, more threatening even than the extraordinary flood of 1616, when " men stood on Salford Bridge and laded up water with a little piggin." A new terror fell on the long-suffering town as the swollen river rose higher and higher, sweeping all before its torrential onrush, and such was the feeling of awe throughout the land the dreadful deed had inspired in all classes of men that zealous Parliamentarians hereabouts equally with Royalists were prone to regard the flood as evidence of the Divine resentment of the murder of King Charles.

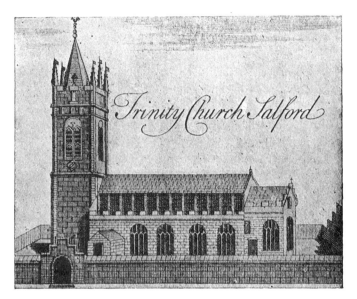

TRINITY CHURCH, 1635.

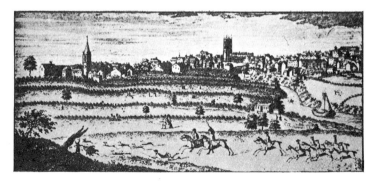

VIEW OF SALFORD ABOUT 1690.

CHAPTER XVI.

The Port Mote Records.

THE real history of a nation lies not so much in the rolling thunder of the great events as in the simple lives of the common people, those unknown generations of dead men and women who, century after century, have spent their spirit, been moved by the throb of heartfelt things, lived and loved and sinned, building unconsciously and with but dim understanding " milestones upon Time." So it is that the most interesting of all ancient annals are the records of the old Townmotes, for although the shallow-minded may look on them just as curios, they are indeed a breath " from those dead hearts, so passionate once, so truly kind . . . a muttering from behind the veils of death from long-dead men," who, like ourselves, held those stones and streets inestimably dear.

In May of 1894 a gentleman of Nottingham wrote to the Town Clerk of Salford advising him of an important discovery he had made in going through the library of a deceased cleric, a quarto book of MS. in a vellum cover which proved to be a record of the Presentments of Juries for the Town of Salford from 1597 to 1669. By the public spirit of this gentleman, there thus came into the possession of the Corporation a valuable portion of the missing records of the town, and our knowledge of our ancestors has been enriched by documents of unusual interest. Strangely enough, such is the apathy that has typified our regard for priceless relics of the past, the Corporation took no steps to make the records available to the public, but left entirely the printing and publishing of these records to the generosity and public spirit of a private society ; the late Alderman Mandley undertaking the valuable task of transcription.*

It will be recalled that the Portmote was a Court of Record held before the Steward of the Leet, being a King's Court granted by charter to the head of the manor. Its original intent was to view the frank pledges, that is, the freemen within the liberty who, by the institution of Alfred, were all mutual pledges for the good behaviour of each other.

---

*Salford Port Mote Records (Chetham Society).

It was annually the custom to summon all the King's subjects as they came to years of discretion and strength to come to the Court and take there the oath of allegiance to the King. The other business was to present by jury all crimes that happened within the jurisdiction and to punish all misdemeanours. At the time now under review the business of the Court may be summarised as :—

(1) The selection of the jury.

(2) The appointment of Borough Reeve and Constables.

(3) The presentment in court of the property owners and burgesses whose duty it was to do fealty, suit and service to the Lord of the Manor.

(4) To hear and determine disputes and differences, to record the ownership and devolution of landed property, to enforce the duty of every inhabitant to keep clean and in good repair pavements, watercourses, hedges, ditches and so forth.

(5) To prevent the influx and settlement of strangers and persons likely to become chargeable on the town.

(6) To inflict fines for misconduct, for Breaches of the Assize of Bread and Ale, and for trespass of cattle and swine and unmuzzled dogs.

(7) To provide the watch of police and fire protection.

(8) To furnish a water supply through the medium of the parish pump.

The Salford Port Mote Court was far more than a manorial court Leet, for it was a Hundred Court possessing a wider and superior jurisdiction. Burgesses were summoned to the Court from all parts of the Hundred and under the head of " Nomina Burgensium," or Roll Call of the Burgesses are found such distinguished names as William, Earl of Derby ; Sir Alex. Radcliffe, K.B. ; Sir Ralphe Assheton, Bart. ; Sir Humphrey Davenport, Lord Chief Baron of the King's Exchequer ; and others styled variously " generosus " (gentlemen) and " inhabitants." This Roll Call was made every half-year, at Eastertide and Michaelmas.

Immediately after the Roll Call the Jury was elected, and at the Michaelmas Court the Officers of the Borough were appointed. The titles of the latter were quaint and various. Besides the Borough Reeve and the two Constables, there were two Mise (rate)-layers, two Misegatherers, two Ale-founders, two Praysers (valuers), two Afferers (assessors),

two Birlemen (bylawmen), two Scavengers for Greengate and
Gravelhole, two scavengers for Lowergate, two Officers of the
Pump, Overseers for the suppressing of abuse at Wedding
Dinners, Overseers to see "yt the Syes of Bread be kept
accordinge to the Statute in yt cause pvyded." Officers
were also assigned to the duty of seeing " yt Bad Dogges be
kept tyed upp or mussiled lawfullye." A further office was
an Overseer for measuring cloth. The Hereditary Stewards
of the Court were the Molyneaux, of Sefton ; this position
having been granted by the King in 1436 to Sir Richard
Molyneaux to descend by hereditary right.

The Richard Molyneaux named in the opening entry of
the Records as " Steward of our said Lady the Queen "
at the " Port Mote Court of the Borough, Town and Manor
of Salford, holden for our Lady the Queen at Salford
aforesaid," was one of the earliest to receive the then novel
dignity of a baronetcy. His son, who succeeded him in the
office was the first Viscount Molyneaux. From 1644 to 1660
the office was held by Edwarde Holte and others of the local
gentry favourable to the Parliament. At the Restoration,
Caryll, Viscount Molyneaux, was installed in the family
office.*

The Salford we glimpse from these old documents wherein
our forefathers have left rude record of the zeal with which,
without fear or favour, they pursued the tasks of local
government is a pleasant enough town, where the very place
names breathe a fragrance all their own. Substantial half-
timbered buildings and low white-washed thatched cottages
stood cheek by jowl within the ancient walls, whose gates were
closed at nightfall. Red-curtained alehouses were numerous
enough, and more imposing inns, of which The Bull's Head,
The Shears, The King's Head, and The Old Ship still survive
in name if not in form, dispensed hospitality beneath their
overhanging eaves. Orchards and garden plots lay between
the backs of the buildings that clustered the highways
intersecting the town, although it is difficult to locate the

*The Earl of Sefton is the present High Steward, and used to have
the right of appointing the Registrar. Prior to 1868, the Court Leet
of the Hundred of Salford was held twice a year at the Salford Town
Hall, but in the latter year a Court of Record for Manchester (founded
in 1838) was amalgamated with the Salford Court and the sittings
transferred from Salford to Manchester. The judge of the Court is
now appointed through the Duchy of Lancaster.

buildings named in the records with the exception of Rodley Houses, which Robert Rodley built in Greengate, and afterwards sold to John Hyde. Of street names beside Greengate, Sergeant Street, and Gravel Lane, we find Galley Lane, High Lane, Lowergate and Lowergate Hill, Sandywell and Georgecroft, Shawfoot Stile and Goodstile. There were The Shaw Fields, Galleyfields, Duckett Fields, Middlefield and High Oldfield, Barrow Brook Acre, The Checkers and Hanging Meadow.

Amongst the occupations of the inhabitants we glean : alehouse keepers, brewers, innkeepers, blacksmiths, carpenters, chapmen, cobblers, clothworkers, clothiers, cooks, colliers, dyers, joiners, mercers, poyntmakers, ropemakers, shearmen, silkweavers, tailors, websters (weavers), and whittaners (bleachers). Others there were, no doubt, but no occasion arose to mention them.

When the Lord High Steward attended the Town Fair or other public ceremony he was supported by all the burgesses within the town, each bringing with him a man with Bill or Halberd, and every night the watch, similarly armed, patrolled the town. It is told, though with what degree of truth is not vouched for, that nightly the officers of the watch would assemble in one of the hostelries about Greengate and, at the call from the Constable, " Gentlemen, let us make our rounds ! " would solemnly rise and march round the table once and then sit to resume their merry quaffing.

The period comprised within this Book of Records is one of the most momentous in all our land. It begins in the latter days of the golden Elizabethan age, through the reigns of James I. and Charles I., the Protectorate of Cromwell, and ends in 1669, the ninth year of the Restoration of Charles II. Those were the days when, from a yeoman's house at Stratford-on-Avon, William Shakespeare was pouring out the genius of an art that was to " show, sustain and nourish the world " for all time ; when Spenser and Ben Jonson and the joyous company of the Mermaid Tavern were " strengthening poetry for her noblest flights " ; the days when Milton and Bacon and Bunyan were each bearing their quota of literary wealth to enrich our English heritage. They cover the times of the Gunpowder Plot, of the Great Rebellion, of the Plague and the Great Fire of London. Yet, strange to say, in all the records there is no mention of any of these great events, and beyond the change in the title of the headship of the Court, Salford might have been remote from and in ignorance of all the mighty happenings in the outer national world.

Salford was declared by its Charter to be a " Free Borough," but it was a freedom which extended only to its own kith and kin, and one of the most striking entries in the transactions of the court, occurring with frequency, was the preservation of the exclusiveness of its inhabitants. No " foreigner " (the accepted term for all strangers) was permitted to reside within its boundaries, and all such found within the town without the sanction of the authorities were ordered to depart or were summarily ejected, except in cases where the host was prepared to assume responsibility that they should not be "burthensome to the towne." In 1669 John Balye, of Salford, whitster, was removing to Bolton, and, being in special favour, it was decided that he and his family should have " free liberty to come and inhabit our towne of Salford . . . as likewise the Burroreve and Minister and Constables of our towne do consent to this order."

In 1654, " Joane, the wife of John Ashton, hath lived out of this towne for the space of five years . . . and she is now lately crept into this towne, being removed by Sir Cecil Trafford from his house wherein she lived for many misdemeanours, as we are given to understand, and doth now begin to brew without licence, and if she go on it may be prejudicial to the burgesses and inhabitants we doe therefore order . . . that she shall remove out of the towne within a month upon paine of five pounds."

Amongst numerous similar entries at the Michaelmas Court in 1653 : " The Jury doe order Mr. John Byrom for entertaining a stranger Thomas Wharmbie th' elder that if hee doe not remove within a month hee shall stay upon the paine of payinge ffiftie shillings and so much for every month as hee shall stay longer." Inhospitable it may seem, yet it was a wise provision to prevent the settlement of dubious people and to provide against the abuse of the great privileges that residence in the Salford of those days carried with it.

That there were plenty of ladies of spirit in the town is shown in the many entries that occur of female assaults. " Martha, wife of Peter Ffarrant did most disorderly abuse Mr. Adam Warmingham, Constable of this towne, by most uncivell language in the execution of his assize." For which offence the lady was ordered to have the bridle put upon her and to bear it for one whole hour. In 1608, " Jane, the wife of Ralph Romage, made an assault and afraye upon Anne, the wife of Robert Hygenson, at which tyme the sayde Jane dyd draw bloode by scratchinge her by the face, and the sayd Anne drew bloode upon the sayd Jane in breakinge her head in her one defence." At the same court " The wiffe of James Corner " was fined " for washing clothes under the pumpe." Indeed, the women of Salford in those days must have been a severe trial to the authorities, for in April, 1608, is the cheerful entry, " The Jurye doth find there is no Cuckestoole, but a payre of stocks and the dungeons to punishe unreasonable women in."

But if the womenfolk were troublesome the men were none the less sanguinary. In October, 1597, amongst other cases of assault and tusselement " George Sherrate of Blackrod, drover, gave unto James Compton a bloodye nose.' In 1641, " John Kay for drawinge bloode and stabbinge . . . the bodies of Samuel Parcivall and Ester his wife for hurtinge and drawinge bloode in the bodies of Charlotte Tiddler, Nathaniel Benton and James Snowden." In 1607, " Wee doe present theis persons followinge for a fraye made the fyrst of Maye by James Blakeley, George Hampson, Raphe Hunt in which fraye there was bloode drawne upon Robert Rodwell but by whom wee knowe not."

Then, even as now, our townsmen sometimes imbibed more well than wisely, for at the October Court in 1631 " Robert Smith of the Cross Lane for tipplinge and night walkinge " was fined 6d., as was also Thomas Ouldham " for keepinge, tipplinge and drinkinge in his house at eleven of the clock on the night the 7th of December," whilst James Cottrell was one of the many alas, who were publicly proclaimed " for a common drunkard."

In 1608 the jury order that " whereas drovers of the towne of Manchester do dryve their swyne into the wash of Salford there to depasture to the great annoyance of the inhabitants of the towne of Salford " officers are appointed to impound these foreign and intrusive porkers.

There is an inquiry in 1610 as to the right to use a footway to Ordsall. This had been stopped, but is claimed to have been the original footpath until more or less superseded by a new road made by Sir John Radclyffe that " his lyttell babes " might go over Georgecroft to School at William Debdall's.

Some of the entries have a rather ludicrous aspect, particularly those which show a rather careless sanitary knowledge on the part of numerous inhabitants who " lefte midinge very noisome in the stretes."

They had a summary way of dealing with dishonest traders, for in 1646 it is recorded that, complaint having been made of those who bring milk to the town to sell and do not sell it by measure, it is ordered that if they still are at fault the constables are empowered to take their milk from them and give it to the poor. Four years later a similar record occurs of " the great abuse committed by divers persons who bring coals to be sold in Salford by gelding and robbing their loads before they come to the towne," such offenders were also dealt with by having their loads seized by the assessors appointed for the purpose, and the same distributed amongst the poor.

In 1658, the jury finding that " nine and twenty shillings for the relief of poor Protestants behynde seas " being still in the officers' hands, that twenty shillings " bee given to young Samuell Smethurst towards byndeinge him apprentice and the rest to Elizabeth his sister beine both of them fatherlesse and motherlesse to help her in her wants."

To peruse these ancient records is more fascinating than any novel. They are a mirror of real life, revealing to us not the airy creations of fancy, but the life and living of our own people (It is interesting to note how over and over again are repeated the familiar household names of to-day), showing that though times may change, the human soul is much akin throughout all ages, even though the simplicity of living in those days contrasts welcomely with the complexities of to-day.

Further records belonging rightly to Salford are actually in the possession of the Duchy of Lancaster Record Office in London, and others in the muniment room at the Manchester Town Hall. Surely these ought to be handed over to our own Corporation, and when collected and transcribed, would serve to illumine even more clearly our knowledge of our city's glorious past.

CHAPTER XVII

The Records of the Wapentake.

IT is not generally known that in addition to the Port Mote Records, there are also in existence, in the Public Record Office in London, five rolls containing the records of the Court of the Wapentake of Salford for five separate years during the reign of Henry VIII.

It has been previously pointed out that the jurisdiction of the Wapentake of Salford and of the Sheriff's tourn continued in force throughout the Hundred of Salford, and that where a Manorial Court was established, its judicial privileges were limited, and the supreme authority retained by the lord of the Wapentake. The one exception to this was the Free Borough of Salford itself. Thus we find in Salford, as distinct from other towns, the working of two separate courts, one the Court of the Free Portmanmote wherein the burgesses of Salford transacted their affairs free entirely from all exterior authority, and the other, the Court of the Wapentake, whose jurisdiction extended over the whole of the Hundred, and which survives to-day in the Court of Record for the Hundred of Salford.

The Wapentake Court met every four weeks—thirteen to the year—and concerned itself only with questions of debt, false detention of chattels and such like. There was no jury sworn, there were no presentments, and its proclamations were made with a single " Oyez ! " as distinct from the triple " Oyez ! " of the Court Leet.

These records are written on parchment rolls in law Latin with very abbreviated forms, and contain the records of twelve Wapentake Courts and one or two Portmotes for the year. In the first of these rolls, which covers the twelve months of the second year of Henry VIII., there are twelve Wapentakes and only one Portmote. At the end of each court the scribe is careful to add up the total of fines, also at the end of the roll to give the complete total of all the courts, namely, the twelve Wapentakes and the single Portmote. In the case of the Wapentakes the majority of the fines are levied from the bailiffs of the court for not procuring the defendant to answer in court to the plaintiff, and the same fines for the same cases occur over and over again, sometimes through the whole twelve Wapentakes. Doubtless the bailiffs recouped themselves by levying the fine on one or other of the defaulters, so that the thing resolved itself into a rough and ready method of adjournment of the suit. Should the disputants wish to make a settlement between themselves, a "love-day" was appointed, notice of the settlement recorded at the next court, and the fine (for there had to be always a fine for the lord) levied from one or the other as they happened to have agreed upon between themselves. This was termed "Licence of Concord Made," when the parties would come before the Steward and confess that they had made peace and concord in the plea which was between them, one of them being in mercy ("*misericordium*," or fine) for his false claim or because he had not prosecuted his suit.

At the opening of the Court a conversation such as this would occur : "Bailiff," saith the Steward, "cause to come before us . . . those who took and received love-days from this court, and the distresses, if any there be."

"By my faith, sir," saith the Bailiff, "see here all that for which thou askest written in this roll."

"Bailiff, what hast thou done as to John att Wells ? "

"Sir, he is distrained to come."

"Have him better distrained."

"That I will, sir."

There is given below a translation of a typical record of the Wapentakes, and also of the earliest dated Portmote of Salford of which there is any trace.

The Pleas of the "Wappintake" of Salfordshire, held there on the Thursday before the Feast of St. Edward the King and Confessor, in the second year of the reign of Henry VIII.

John Forster complains of William Brown, of Salford, on a plaint of debt of xxs.

The same John complains of the same William on a plaint of debt of xxvis.

A fine of 3d. from the bailiffs because they have not procured Richard Jaks, of Middleton, to reply to John Gee.

A fine of 3d. from the same because they have not procured the executrix of William Radclif, of Salford, to proceed against John Birkenhead.

A fine of 3d. from the same because they have not procured William Lynay, of Rochdale, to answer to John Hardware.

A fine of 3d. from the same because they have not procured Robert Dunster, of Halgh, to reply to Richard Hodgkinson.

A fine of 3d. from the same because they have not procured Thomas Turnor, of Salford, superior, to answer to Hugh Leech.

A fine of 3d. from the same because they have not procured Thomas Hope, of Slodigh, to reply to Henry Holt.

A fine of 3d. from the same because they have not procured Arthur Isherwood, of Bury, to reply to Robert Heynson.

A fine of 3d. from the same because they have not procured Cecilia, late the wife of Oliver Bradshaw, of Oldfield, to reply to John Burdsell.

A fine of 3d. from the same because they have not procured Richard Draper, of Barton, to reply to Thomas Birches.

A fine of 6d. from the same because they have not procured Robert Gregory, of Hulton, to reply to Alfred Sheryngton, twice.

Total of fines, 2s. 9d.

The Portmoot of Salford, held there on the Friday before the Feast of St. Edward King and Confessor, in the second year of Henry VIII., before Sir William Molyneux, Steward there.

Inquisition taken there for the Lord the King by the oath of Edward Pilkington, Richard Hunt, William Radcliffe, John Forster, Adam Byrom, Edmund Thomlinson, Laurence Chadkirk, Ralph Bibby, John Randles, Richard Mosly, Hugh Leech, James Taylor, Peter Mosty, and Robert Walker, jurors, who say on their oath.

Election of Officers—Reeve, John Forster, sworn ; constables, Adam Byrom, Thomas Barlow, sworn ; myselayers, Richard Hunt, Edward Pilkington, sworn ; byelawman, John Oldham, sworn ; tasters of ale, John Knott, Peter Mosty, sworn ; mysegatherers, William Bolton, Edward Pendleton, sworn.

The jury say upon their oath that John Whalley, burgess of Salford, died seised of all the burgages, lands, and tenements which lately descended to the said John after the death of John Whalley, his father, and Agnes, his mother, in Salford aforesaid, and who is the heir they do not at all know.

Fine of 2s. because George Watson, pedler, broke into a certain house and made an assault and affray upon Nicholas Tinker, and struck him and wounded him, &c. (witnessed, &c.), by pled of Robert Redilstone.

Also a fine of 2s. because Nicholas Tinker made an assault and affray upon a certain stranger (outdweller), whose name is unknown, and struck him, &c. (witnessed), by the pledge of George Birom.

Fine of 3d. because John Bradshaw stopped up the water in his tenure at the Wallis Stile.

Also a fine of 3d. because John Forster kept his pigs unyoked and did not remedy this in them by the day given him, viz., one pig.

A fine of 3d., Thomas Turner, for ditto, viz., one pig.

A fine of 3d., John White, for ditto, viz., one pig.

A fine of 1s. 4d., John Cannok, for ditto, viz., 12 pigs.

A fine of 4d., Thomas Birom, for ditto, viz., two pigs.

A fine of 2d., Joanna Mosly, for ditto, viz., one pig.

A fine of 4d., Thomas Thomlynson, for ditto, viz., two pigs.

A fine of 4d. (because) William Young did not ring his pigs before the day given him, viz., two pigs.

A fine of 4d., Thomas Wolstoncroft, for ditto, viz., two pigs.

A fine of 2d., Martha Chetham, for ditto, viz., one pig. Total of fines, 7s. 9d.

Sum total of the said 12 Wappintakes 29s. 6d., and of one Portmoot 7s. 9d. ; total, 37s. 3d.

Thus by these quaint and curious sidelights are we able to peep out on the stream of life as it flowed through the narrow ways and by the hedgerows of this Royal Manor three hundred years ago.

BOOK THREE
1700 to 1800.

CONTENTS

BOOK THREE.—1700–1800.

CHAPTER I..............................In Wesley's Days.

CHAPTER II.....................When Salford was a Spa.

CHAPTER III..................................Oak Hall.

CHAPTER IV. ....John Byrom.

CHAPTER V...........................The " Forty-five."

CHAPTER VI. ....An Old Salford Plan.

CHAPTER VII. ....The New Bayley.

CHAPTER VIII. ....An Amazing Woman.

CHAPTER IX......................The Cripple Factory.

CHAPTER X.............A Centre of Culture and Fashion.

CHAPTER XI..........................Legends of Kersal.

CHAPTER I

In Wesley's Days.

THERE is no period of English history so eventful as the eighteenth century, that age of mighty figures sustaining their tremendous roles against a background of world-changing events. England's valour was gaining the mastery of the high seas. Her trading companies were consolidating the achievements of the early merchant adventurers ; new sources of wealth were bringing to an increasing population an even more rapidly increasing prosperity, and a more gracious expression of living. Knowledge increased with comfort, and with a deeper appreciation of the elegancies of life went a new realisation of building on the ancient free institutions of the land a new sense of individual freedom making for the greater security of society.

And in Salford, during that time, we see an epitome of the larger national life shaping itself on our local stage. The lassitude of a century past was fading before a new phase in which the town was coming to be regarded by the fashionable world of the day as a desirable place of residence.

In 1733, there came to visit Salford one who, though then but little known, was to exercise a powerful influence upon the life of the nation—the Rev. John Wesley. He stayed for some time, preaching several times in Trinity Church. The merits and demerits of political differences which urged men into bitter factions concerned Wesley not at all, but with all the enthusiasm of a sincere man, he pleaded with all classes for a deeper religious life, and from what we can gather he was not unfavourably heard by the burghers of Salford. Fourteen years later he came once again, this time as an itinerant preacher, though still a priest of the English Church, but who was now looked upon as the leader of a Schismatic movement, a role which did not assist to commend him to the people who had once regarded him so kindly. He records in his " Journal " under date of May, 1747 : " I walked to Salford Cross ; a crowd of people partly ran before and partly after me. I thought it best not to sing, but looking round asked abruptly, ' Why do you look as though you have never seen me before ? Many of you have seen me in the neighbouring church both preaching and administering the Sacraments.' I then began . . . As I was drawing to a conclusion, a big man thrust in with three or four more unbroken spirits and bade them bring out the engine. Our friends desired me to remove into a yard just by, which I did, and concluded in peace.''

Wesley had been a fellow-collegian with the Rev. John Clayton, the Jacobite schoolmaster of Salford, who publicly blessed the Young Chevalier at Salford Cross. He was a friend, too, of Dr. John Byrom, who taught Wesley shorthand. It is said that the three friends were the joint authors of Byrom's tract against the races on Kersal Moor, published in 1761 at a time when a violent controversy raged in, the town and district over the renewal of this sport.

Our ancestors of these days were not much addicted to the use of carriages, for in 1720 the only carriage in Salford belonged to Madam Drake. This lady was the leader of the fashionable society of the town and the chief hostess of the Tories and of the High Church Party, as Lady Bland on the other side of the river, was for the Whigs and Hanoverians.

In moving about the somewhat circumscribed area of the locality, the Sedan chair, with the nimble link-boy in attendance, was the general method of progression apart from nature's own. Amusement facilities were very little behind those of the capital itself. In 1769 the Riding School in Water Street (now Blackfriars) was taken over for use as a theatre by a company of players from Dublin, who were known as " H.M. Servants." These " comedians," as they were called—a term applied in those days without distinction to everyone associated with the playhouse—built a bridge of wood across the river, the original Blackfriars Bridge, to enable their patrons from the Manchester side to reach the theatre. In June, 1761, a very respectable part of the combined companies of Drury Lane and Covent Garden took possession of the Salford theatre and acted for several months. The town, considering the population, must have been highly theatrical in those days, for one play, " The Jealous Wife," was acted four times during the season ; and the company was so well satisfied that in the summer of 1762 they again

NOTE.—The earliest record of horse-racing at Kersal is contained in a notice in the *London Gazette* of 2–5 May, 1687.

F

returned to Salford, a practice that they repeated for several years. With the exception of Mr. Garrick and Mr. Barry, the company performing at the Salford theatre contained all the most eminent talent of which both the London theatres could at that time boast.

Until 1776, the only means of communication between the towns of Salford and Manchester was, with the exception of the wooden Blackfriars Bridge, the old Salford Bridge, and it was highly dangerous for foot passengers to cross in view of the growing volume of wheeled traffic, especially on market day. It was practically impossible for persons who were not very active to get over the bridge, and to escape their imminent danger, the pedestrians were obliged to take refuge in the angular recesses on both sides of the bridge. In this year it was decided to widen the old bridge and extend the piers and arches. Even this did not suffice to accommodate the ever-increasing traffic, and seven years later a new bridge was built—the present New Bayley Bridge. This was opened under toll for passengers and carriages in 1785.

The Church of the Sacred Trinity, (the only known dedication of this name in the world, and believed to be derived from a Latin psalm), which Humphrey Booth had built in 1635, had now become unsafe, and in 1752 it was decided to rebuild it. The Gothic tower is all that remains of the earlier edifice,* the body of the church being entirely rebuilt in the Doric style, as it still exists. The necessity for rebuilding was caused by the vast number of burials which took place in the churchyard making the ground unstable and shifting.

The Rector of the church during the rebuilding was the Rev. Thomas Barker, who, in October, 1766, was appointed the Principal of Brazenose College, Oxford. There is in existence an old wardens' account book which gives some interesting glimpses of the town in the latter half of the eighteenth century. Umbrellas, for instance, in those days

---

* The tower, which originally had a short steeple, was largely rebuilt in 1859, when a large four-light mullioned and transomed window with ogie head was inserted on the west side in the lower stage. Under the west clock-face are singular decorations of a gilt crown surmounting a rose, circled by a garter, with the usual inscription, and beneath are a harp and a thistle. At the east end of the Church is a niche intended for a statue of King Charles the First, a carved wooden statue of this monarch occupying a similar position in the old building.—(Joseph Aston.)

KERSAL CELL.

were communal property, and expensive. Two of these were bought, presumably for use in the churchyard at funerals, and cost £1 11s. 6d. each, the second being paid for in two instalments. One entry reads : " Paid to James Ashton for washing surpels (surplice) and Him Self, 2 shillings," whilst no less ambiguous is the further entry : " For washing Surpels and Sextons, etc., 5 shillings."

The Church had apparently several useful sources of income. There was, for instance, " loitering money," a survival of the time when the churchwardens exercised a lawful authority over the parishioners, exacting a fine of one shilling from all who did not attend their parish church on Sundays. What would not many a harassed churchwarden give for a revival of " loitering money " to-day ?

In 1766 is a note : " Paid by Henry Collinge, Landlord of the Bull's Head, Salford, for suffering gaming in his house." Part of this fine was remitted because (as the book says) " it appeared on the examining the parties that Collinge was not at all to blame." In 1782 one shilling was received " from a person tipling in the King's Head on Sunday." There is quite a long entry regarding one Josh Addison : " May 29th, 1786. To cash received from Josh Addison for loitering (1s.) with expenses of summoning him (1s. 6d.). He being a very ill-behaved, refractory person."

The Town Bellman of the period was named Jepson, and he appears to have been paid quite a number of sixpences for " going about to decry the practice of breaking the church windows." The one who benefited most from this most reprehensible practice was the sexton, James Berry, who appears to have been a regular handyman who made a nice little sum from extras such as the church repairs. He would hardly be begrudged some of his jobs, however, as, for instance, one entry of payment to him runs : " For taking up a body which was become offensive from not being buried at a sufficient depth, 2s." He certainly deserved it.

List of the Curates and Rectors of Sacred Trinity Church from its foundation as Salford Chapel :—

1636.—Richd. Hollinworth, M.A.
1648.—Wm. Meek (described by the Commonwealth Commissioners as " an able and sufficient minister.")

1658.—Robt. Brown. (He conformed at the Restoration and was presented to Hoole).

1667.—John Hyde (afterward Vicar of Bowden).

1694—Robt. Assheton (buried at Salford in 1731—an ardent Jacobite).

1731.—Richd. Assheton (son of the above).

1764.—Thos Barker.

1766.—Robt. Oldfield.
Robt. Kenyon.

1787.—John Clowes (also Vicar of Eccles).

1818.—Saml. Booth.

1859.—Joseph Nelsey Pocklington.

1861.—Edward Allen.

1876.—Capel Wolseley.

1885.—Hy. Francis Gore-Booth.

1902.—Peter Green.

1911.—Albert Edwd. Cornibeer.

1920.—J. Rideout.

1923.—Jos. H. Kidd.

The Church has a complete ring of six bells by Abel Rudhall of Gloucester, hung in 1748. The tenor was recast in 1901 by John Taylor & Co., of Loughborough. The bells are inscribed as follows :—

(1) WILLM. BARLOW & RICHD. WHITEHEAD
Gentlemen
PEACE AND GOOD NEIGHBOURHOOD.
A.R. 1748. (29 in. diam.)

(2) PROSPERITY TO THE TOWN OF SALFORD.
A.R. 1748. (31 in. diam.)

(3) FEAR GOD. HONOUR THE KING.
A.R. 1748. (32 in. diam.)

(4) ABEL RUDHALL, FOUNDER, 1748.
SAMUEL WORTHINGTON, CH. WARDEN. (33 in. diam.)

(5) THE GIFT OF JAMES CHETHAM OF SMEDLEY, ESQR.
A.R. 1748. (36 in. diam.)

(6) LAUDATE DOMINUM.
THE GIFT OF ROBERT BOOTH, ESQR.
PATRON OF THIS CHAPEL. A.R. 1748.
First hung A.D. 1748. Re-cast 1901.

The following rules are cut in "lower case" letters on a stone in the north wall of the ringing chamber :—

> You that are Ringers or would learn to Ring
> Observe these orders well in every thing.
> He that for want of care o'er turns a Bell
> Shall 2d. pay in Money not in Ale.
> And he that Rings with either Spur or Hat
> Shall pay His 6d. certainly for that.
> He that presumes to Ring and spoils a Peal
> Shall 6d. pay in Money or in Ale.
> These orders well observe and then you may
> With Pleasure spend with us this joyful day.

CHAPTER II

When Salford was a Spa.

A NY suggestion that Salford was a health resort would nowadays be greeted with loud guffaws, although, strange as it may seem, we have heard of quite a number of people, not at all natives and therefore liable to fantastic prejudices, who stoutly aver that they are healthier in Salford than elsewhere. This is not at all surprising when it is remembered that our prevailing wind comes to us unpolluted from the Irish Sea, over the Welsh mountains and the verdant Cheshire plain. But it is scarcely more than a century ago since people came deliberately to Salford for the healing virtues of the waters of the Pirle Spring.

An entry in the Portmote Records in 1611 mentions an order made " concerninge one foot waye leadinge from the Halle of Ordsall alongside the river to a springe called the Pirle." In 1636, Edward Walker, of Ashton-under-Lyne, purchased four messuages in Salford and " one little crofte called the Penny Meadow, lyinge neeare the Ladye Pearle, of Mr. John Holcroft and his wife." Amongst the Manchester Grammar School grants is one of " a burgage next the Pirle-wall-gate," which Roger, son of Richard de Manchester, gave to Richard del Crosseshagh and Dyota his wife.

In his introduction to Vol. II. of the Portmote Records, Alderman Mandley calls attention to items in the Salford Constable accounts for " carrying a creple to the powl." In some cases, he said, " the creples were carried on horseback, in other on a barrow (stretcher). By the ' powl,' or ' pool,' I take it, is meant the Pirle or Lady Pearle Spring . . . credited, like Holywell, in North Wales, and other such places, with miraculous healing properties."

In medieval times wells, as the chief water supply, were treated with respect, and particularly so when they were revealed as having medicinal properties, in which case they were placed under the special protection of a Patron Saint, usually Our Blessed Lady herself. So it was with this spring here in Salford, " a broket or pirle of water running out of a hill neare the toun and cumming through a peace of the toun withyn the wall," ; the term " pirle " being an English dialect word meaning to gush, bubble or well forth. The natural waters of Salford were anciently famed for their purity, hence the long establishment of the brewing industry in the town, and from Sandywell the burgesses anciently derived their main supplies, as the residents of Eccles did until comparatively recent times, from the " Lady Well " on the Gilda Brook, where the Sanatorium now stands. To the Pirle Spring, however, were attributed special properties of healing, and doubtless at one time it was enwrapped in the glamour of legendary lore, of which, alas, no echo has survived.

The spring was reached by a footpath that followed the course of the river from the Old Bridge to where Ralli's warehouse now is. Another path led from Higher End to the spring, the present Spaw Street, and the riverside path continued, as mentioned in the Portmote Records, to Ordsall. It was along this path that Guy Fawkes is traditionally supposed to have come after he rescued Mad Meg from the river. There is little of romance suggested in the present surroundings of the place, but here in the centuries agone came the halt, the lame and the sick to bathe and to drink the healing waters of Our Lady's Spring, which still is in existence, most people will be surprised to know, some feet below the basement of the mighty concrete building that now occupies the site.

When the age of faith came to an end the fame of the healing spring still went on, though shorn of its holy character. In the eighteenth century it became a fashionable bathing establishment, to which the beaux and belles of the period resorted, and in the gardens of the Spa these exquisites would sip their glasses after their bathe and recount the spicy tit-bits of the day as their modern prototypes do nowadays at Harrogate and elsewhere. In 1747 " Whitworth's Magazine " advertised for sale " three houses opposite the Spaw Stile in Salford," and in March, 1793, appears an advertisement in " Harrop's Newspaper " of " The Bath Inn, in Salford, situate on the bank of the River Irwell, near the new stone bridge (New Bayley) and near the intended junction of the Bolton and Bury Canal with the said river. There is also a celebrated Cold Bath well frequented, and supplied with spring water, in a convenient part of the house." On July 5, 1796, appears the following advertisement :—

> " PUBLICK COLD BATH at the lying-in Hospital, Stanley Street, Salford. The ancient cold bath called the Spaw, so well known for its coldness and for the plentiful supply of spring water which is constantly running through it is now fitted up for the use of the publick. Terms of bathing, sixpence per time, or ten shillings and sixpence per quarter. Towels included."

On Green's Map of 1787 the Bath Inn is shown at the river end of Bolton Street, and Spaw Street then, as now, ran from Chapel Street towards the river parallel with the north side of New Bayley Street.

In the famous engraving, " South-west Prospect of Manchester and Salford, 1710," where Salford is described as " a populous, beautiful town," there is a building shown in the foreground which is described as " The Boat House, in which is a curious Bath." Proctor, writing in 1874, says : " The bath, long ago fallen out of public use, is now but faintly remembered ; yet Spaw Street retains the name, while marking the site where it flourished.

CHAPTER III.

Oak Hall.

TOWARDS the end of the seventeenth century, when the nation was stirred with indignation at the Rye House Plot, there came to Salford a man named Haigh, from the township of the same name near Wigan, who, purchasing a messuage in the Cross Lane, built thereon a house which he called Oak Hall. Salford at that time had sunk beneath its many disasters from a thriving, busy borough into the langour of a semi-rural somnolence, and Cross Lane was quite an isolated outpost of the town. At its northern end, where, through the centuries, the feet of countless travellers had paused by the wayside cross, destroyed during the fury of the late troublous times, along with the similar crosses at Pendleton Green and White Cross Bank, now stood the gibbet, from the rusty chains of which, clanking in the wind, hung the mouldering remains of footpad and murderer.

The last grisly occupant of this gibbet was a man named John Grindrod, a resident of Greengate (where a close of land for long bore his name), who, in September, 1758, in a fit of madness, murdered his wife and their four children by poisoning, and in March of the following year was hanged and gibbeted for the crime*. So fearsome was Grindrod's memory that it was long a popular belief in Salford and district—

" That the wretch in his chains each night took the pains
  To come down from the gibbet and walk."

Harrison Ainsworth has told of a traveller staying at one of the inns in the town who laughed to scorn the prevailing belief, and laid a wager with the tavern-keeper that he would visit the gibbet at midnight.

" To the gibbet I'll go, and this I will do
  As sure as I stand in my shoes ;
  Some address I'll devise, and if Grinny replies,
  My wager, of course, I shall lose."

---

* In 1807, James Massey, a prisoner in the New Bayley, charged with an unnatural crime, hung himself, and the same evening was conveyed away and buried near the distance chair on Kersal Moor. A few days afterwards his body was removed and buried in the ditch where old Grindrod was gibbeted, but after lying there two days it was again taken up and buried near the town weighing machine.

With a bold front the scoffer set out in the dark and dismal night to Cross Lane and stood beneath the gruesome structure and its fearsome burden.

" Though dark as could be, yet he thought he could see
 The skeleton hanging on high ;
The gibbet it creaked ; and the rusty chains squeaked ;
 And a screech-owl flew solemnly by.
The heavy rain pattered, the hollow bones clattered,
 The travellers' teeth chattered with cold, not with fright :
The wind it blew hastily, piercingly, gustily ;
 Certainly not an agreeable night !
' Ho ! Grindrod, old fellow,' thus loudly did bellow
 The traveller mellow, ' how are ye, my blade ? '
' I'm cold and I'm dreary ; I'm wet and I'm weary ;
 But soon I'll be near ye ! ' the skeleton said.
The grisly bones rattled, and with the chains battled ;
 The gibbet appallingly shook ;
On the ground something stirred, but no more the man heard,
 To his heels on the instant he took.
Over moorland he dashed, and through quagmire he splashed,
 His pace never daring to slack ;
Till the hostel he neared, for greatly he feared
 Old Grindrod would leap on his back.
His wager he lost, and a trifle it cost ;
 But that which annoyed him the most
Was to find out, too late, that certain as fate
 The landlord had acted the ghost."

Passing into Cross Lane, then a muddy, rutted track, but half its present breadth, was reached a stile leading to a footpath across the fields, past the ancient fold of the Land o' Nod to Eccles, whose massive square church tower was just visible in the distance. Hard by this stile was the house of Mr. Haigh, not a mansion, but the roomy, comfortable abode of a prosperous farmer. A short distance from the house were the stables, dairy and outhouses, and where now the Cattle Market Hotel stands was the orchard, a very fruitful plot of ground which, it is recorded, in one season yielded eight cartloads of pears. Here for many years lived the Haighs in undisturbed seclusion tending their orchards, their cattle and their hayfields, whilst a succession of monarchs filled the throne of Britain.

But already to the sleepy town was coming the first faint stirrings of a new industrial activity that was to break forth in all its vigour over a century later. The mind of the people was slowly turning aside from worrying over forms of government to the wider sphere of science, wherein, disdainful of the conflicts of the time, many wise heads had long been labouring to extend the power of man over matter. The draper-astronomer of Salford of half a century before now had many counterparts—men who directed their inquiring thoughts delving into experimental science, seeking the key to those secrets of human happiness which the philosophy of Francis Bacon had taught his countrymen Providence had filled the world with if only they would arise and find. All the arts of life were stimulated by this new application, and in industrial pursuits chemical discoveries came to revolutionise the ancient processes. This was not the least marked in the bleaching and dyeing of cotton and woollen goods.

Bleaching and dyeing need a good and plentiful water supply, and in Salford it was to be had in abundance. Hither came, in 1745, a calico printer from Carlisle, a man with a canny mind and a broad Scots tongue, named Jordan, with a cousin, Blacklock, and set up the first calico printing works in this district. Soon after his arrival, William Jordan purchased from the Haighs the estate in Cross Lane and took up his residence at Oak Hall. By the marriage of his son, William, with Miss Astley, of Stakes, he acquired connections with many of the oldest families in Lancashire, including the Stanleys ; and the then Earl of Derby frequently dined with him.

The Jordans were very industrious people, and painstaking in research in connection with their business, and along with their friend, Mr. Jonathan Varley, of Strangeways Hall, they were instrumental in introducing the chemical mode of bleaching into this district as well as making many improvements in the so-called " blue printing " of the time. At the Seedley end of the estate they erected a new bleach works to carry out the process on the most up-to-date lines.

There is in existence a view of Oak Hall (with a plan of the estate) made for the Jordan family in 1771 by Henry Clarke, a noted schoolmaster of Salford, and a skilled mathematician. At one time tutor to George IV., when Prince of Wales, and later Professor in the Military

Academy, Clarke eventually returned and established a school in his native town, to which most of the leading burgesses sent their sons.

The cousin of William Jordan, who came with him from Carlisle, also settled here, and became the ancestor of the Blacklock family of rail-guide printing fame.

Early in the nineteenth century, when the attractiveness of Salford was making a strong residential appeal to the wealthy merchant and manufacturing classes, a man named Jones was seized with the idea of creating in Salford a fashionable West End, as in the capital. He therefore commenced to build in Cross Lane a number of fine stone houses, which were rapidly occupied by most desirable tenants. The Jordan who then was occupying Oak Hall was attracted by the possibilities of the scheme, and he decided to develop the Oak Hall Estate on similar lines. To this end he sought to make an arrangement with Jones to join in one drainage system. Unable to come to terms, Jordan deferred his plans until there presented itself the opportunity for getting his revenge on the unwilling Mr. Jones. The Salford Corporation advertised for some land for the purpose of a cattle market and Jordan made them an offer of a portion of the Oak Hall estate, which was accepted. Naturally, this had the effect of driving out all Jones' tenants and utterly ruining the prospects of the district as a fashionable residential quarter.

To-day, gaunt and incongruous, Mr. Jones' great houses raise themselves above the squalor of their surroundings in Park Place, a monument alike to an enterprise which, had it succeeded, would have left us a more desirable heritage in Cross Lane than we have to-day, and to the jealousy of a rival and the shortsightedness of a municipal policy that ruined the enterprise.

CHAPTER IV.

John Byrom.

O F all the long line of illustrious Salfordians whose names
we cherish, none, perhaps, has achieved a wider fame
than that extraordinary genius who gave to the
Christian world its best-known hymn, and who has been
described as " one of our most distinguished British classics ;
one with neither precursor nor successor in his particular line
of composition ; whose learning was equal to his originality ;
and whose mental powers and personal character were alike
an honour to the English nation "—the Laureate of the
Jacobites, John Byrom, of Kersal Cell.

It would be difficult to picture a more delightful spot
than the quiet retreat on the banks of the Irwell where Hugo
de Burun and his Cluniac brethren founded their sanctuary.
Even in these days urbanisation has not taken quite all the
charm from the vale of Kersal, but in days long agone,
nestling at the foot of the breezy moor, sheltered by low-
wooded hills, the wide shimmering river gliding swiftly by,
and noble oaks and stately beech forming forest groves almost
to the water's edge, it was, indeed, a place to touch the soul
and lift the heart. When, after the Reformation, it passed
into lay hands, Baldwin Willoughby built on the site of Hugo's
cell the present picturesque half-timbered house, with its
mullions and oriels and projecting gables, and here, in 1680,
Edward Byrom brought home his beautiful bride, Dorothy
Allen. Here, too, first saw the light his seven daughters,
and Edward and John, his sons, the latter in February, 1691.
After a preparatory course at Chester, John was admitted into
the Merchant Taylors' School, where his progress in the
classics was so satisfactory that at the age of eighteen he
passed as a pensioner to Trinity College, Cambridge. Two
years later, his father having died in the meantime, he
exchanged the blue undergraduate's gown for the black one
of Bachelor of Arts and came home to spend a happy vacation
in his beloved Kersal home, where, his sister Sarah tells, " he
would go night and morning down to the waterside and bawl

out a Latin oration so loudly that he could be heard a mile off, till all the neighbourhood thought him mad ; or sometimes he went threshing corn with John Rigby's men, working as hard as any of them."

In 1714 he was admitted a fellow of his college, and published his pastorale " Colin and Phœbe," which Bishop Monk described as " one of the most exquisite specimens in existence." Previously he had earned the commendation of Addison, and a year later he achieved his master's degree. This was the golden age of literary and scientific advancement, and the brilliant young Byrom walked and talked as an equal with the giants of the day. And a giant he was, physically as well as mentally. It is recorded that he only once met a man taller than himself.

Queen Anne died in 1714, and within a few months the nation was in a foment consequent upon the Hanoverian succession. Young Byrom was an ardent Jacobite, as his correspondence at that time reveals ; so much so that, unable to accept the obligation towards George I. that ordination would have entailed, he put aside his great aspirations to enter Holy Orders, and for two years his movements were shrouded in mystery as he moved about Europe actively associated with planning a Jacobite insurrection. In 1718, however, he returned to Kersal and fell head over ears in love with the lovely daughter of his uncle, Joseph. The hard-headed merchant was loth to accept for a son-in-law a dreamy philosopher with no prospects, but John and Beppy got their way and were married on St. Valentine's Day in 1721.

Byrom now applied himself to perfecting his system of shorthand which he had invented while at Cambridge, the principle of which was to denote the different sounds of language by strokes of the shortest and simplest form. Stenography was greatly in vogue then amongst students and the better-educated people, but Byrom was the first to introduce a system based on a clearly-defined principle, and his is, indeed, the parent of all subsequent systems. He had as pupils the most distinguished men of the day, and in 1724 he was admitted a Fellow of the Royal Society. His great intellectual ability, ceaseless industry, and a high religious feeling caused him to be held in the highest esteem by Sir Isaac Newton and Sir Hans Sloane, amongst others, but even in the midst of his fame and glory in London he still could sigh for his dearly-loved haunt at Kersal, and in one of his letters he says : " I long to jump into Kersall river." In 1725 he published his famous epigram on the merits of Handel and Bononcini, which created a literary sensation, and later became embroiled in the political tumults of the time, earning the fierce hatred of the Whigs for the ridicule he poured upon them, and the playful wit and good-humoured satire with which he refuted the coarse and angry invectives with which he was assailed.

At the age of forty-nine he succeeded to the family estate at Kersal through the death of his elder brother, and in 1742 his good fortune was crowned by the passing of an Act securing to him for a period of twenty-one years the exclusive rights in his " Art and method of Shorthand "—the nation's testimony to the merits of his system.

If his political sympathies, with increasing years, had become less demonstrative, they burned none the less fervently, and when events thickened and excitement grew apace in Salford, as in many other parts of the North country, there was no more thorough-going Church and King-man, no more ardent supporter of the Stuart cause than John Byrom. He was foremost amongst those who paid court to the Young Chevalier in the disastrous rising of '45, and many interesting glimpses of the Prince's stay in these parts are found in the sprightly chatter of his daughter Beppy's diary. When the rising was suppressed and the fickle mob flaunted the orange ribbons of Brunswick as gaily as they had erstwhile displayed the white cockade, the Byroms were not spared the insults and attacks that were meted out to the adherents of the exiled dynasty, and in his Journal Dr. John writes : " We ourselves were many of us fugitives : and had we not met with some kind asylum towns might have wandered among the inhospitable hills, like the present mountaineer rebels."

But at last things settled down, and in his pleasant home at Kersal, surrounded by domestic comforts and the joyous company of many friends, Byrom whiled away the days poetising on subjects grave and gay, ridiculing without malice his political opponents in some *jeu d'esprit* or sparkling epigram, and in deeper vein pouring out his strong religious feelings in poems that breathe his piety and firm belief in the great truths of Christianity. Religion to such a man could not be gloomy. His was a creed of habitual cheerfulness tinged with an air of mysticism, and in all his utterances he showed forth a true manliness and the happy facility of the man of genius. He was the first writer to employ as a literary vehicle the racy vernacular of his native shire, and for one of the speech days at the Grammar School he wrote the famous " Three Black Crows."

It was whilst he was living at Kersal Cell that he wrote, as a birthday present for his second daughter, Dorothy, what will always be his most famous composition, " Christians, awake ! " John Wainwright set it to music, and before the old house, wrapped in a mantle of snow, the choristers of the Old Church greeted the author on the Christmas morning of 1747 with the strains of the hymn whose melody echoes around the globe as year by year the Feast of The Nativity comes round.

The private journal of Dr. Byrom is a literary treasure which, in its simple narrative of the daily doings of an amazing genius and the vivid picture of the life of his day is not surpassed even by the Diary of Pepys.

Scholar, critic, gentleman, never has there been a deeper student of literary and scientific subjects ; never was there a question agitated by the scholars of his day into which he did not enter ; never did " an idle man " accomplish such wonderful industry or exercise so energetic, manly and intellectual influence on the politics and learning of his day. On September 26, 1763, at the ripe age of 72, this great ornament of his native Salford passed forward to a higher service, leaving behind him a memory and a tradition to inspire his townsmen for ever.

It is worthy of note that Dr. Byrom's niece, Sarah Brearcliffe, was the founder of Brearcliffe's Charity, by her will dated December 1, 1792, bequeathing £3,000, the income to be applied to the maintenance or relief of fifteen old housekeepers of good character, inhabitants of Salford or Manchester, for seven successive years who did not severally possess an income of 40s. per year, the oldest persons always to be preferred.

CHAPTER V

The "Forty-five."

THE cold grey chill of a November day hung over Salford Town, but a fierce flame of excitement burned in its narrow clamorous streets. Ardent souls were stirred, ancient loyalties revived ; men women and children, surrendered ready hearts to the princely hero who moved in their midst, Charles Edward, the Young Chevalier. The clean, courageous heart of youth will always win adherents, and in this old Jacobite town 'twas small wonder the people were in raptures as he whom they regarded as their rightful Prince came by his noble and high-hearted presence to rouse them to a glorious adventure.

The boys of St. Cyprian's School in Gravel Lane were as enthusiastic as boys will always be, and particularly as became the pupils of so noteworthy a Jacobite as the Rev. John Clayton. Prominent among them were young Charlie Deacon, the 15-year old son of Dr. Deacon, the non-juring Bishop, as eagerly he made his way along Sergeant Street to where his friend, William Brettargh stood awaiting him at the door of his uncle, Mr. Banks, the attorney, to whom he was apprenticed. An hour or two later these boys received their commissions, the youngest ensigns in the Army of the Prince, and were busily engaged entering the names of recruits and making up blue and white cockades.

The next day, Saturday, was the Feast of Saint Andrew. The populace packed the Church of the Sacred Trinity to lift up their hearts and pray for the triumph of the Cause, then flocked to the Town Cross to await the coming of the Prince, who rode thence in procession acclaimed by the deafening plaudits of the great crowd. In tartan short coat, blue bonnet and sash, and breeches of red velvet, his fair hair tossed back over a peruke, revealing the fine Stuart forehead, with all the grace and beauty of his Royal line, greeting his people with a gesture of his hand or with a gay smile never to be forgotten, Bonnie Prince Charlie was indeed a hero of romance. A hush fell as he arrived at the Cross ; King James III. was proclaimed the rightful King of Britain ; then Parson Clayton stepped forward and, falling on his knees, made homage to the Prince ere stretching forth his hands to bless him, and from the assembled crowds rose a mighty echoing shout, " God bless the Prince of Wales."

Early on Sunday morning the Salford contingent marched away through Stretford and over the newly-made Crossford Bridge, through Altrincham to Wilmslow and Macclesfield. Alas for the gallant hearts and high hopes, the march to Derby is too well known, and its disastrous sequel in the retreat to Carlisle. The shadow of Culloden Moor already was falling on the brief hour of glory of the Young Chevalier.

Let us take up again the fortunes of our two young Salford boys. Valiantly they played their parts in the defence of Carlisle, and when the Scots surrendered the town to " Butcher " Cumberland they were taken prisoners. Charles Deacon's brother Robert had fallen ill of fever, but despite this he was dragged along to Kendal and left there to die under guard in the Town Hall. Four weeks and two days after leaving Carlisle, the hapless boys arrived in London, and here the friends were separated for the first time. Charles was sent with his eldest brother, Thomas, to Newgate, and William Brettargh with the other ensigns to the New Prison, and here they languished for four and a half months whilst the Government decided their place of trial. On June 25 the Grand Jury found a true bill against the Deacon boys and the following day against Brettargh. The trials began in July and each of the boys were found guilty of high treason. From pulpit after pulpit, and throughout the Press, the feelings of the people were incited against the luckless prisoners that they had sought to relight the Smithfield fires and impose the Roman yoke on the English Church. Yet no one ever thought it worth while to comment on the absurdity of such a charge or to point to the support in arms and money that the Roman Catholics were giving to the Hanoverians. It is a striking commentary on the falsity of the religious outcry that whilst the Prince's officers who were Roman Catholics were treated with comparative leniency, those like the Deacons, who were not, were sent to their deaths, or even worse. Thomas Deacon was executed at Kennington Common on Wednesday, July 30, and by the express orders of Duke William, " who loved blood like a leech " and was " untouch'd with pity and with shame unaw'd," the poor child, Charlie Deacon, was taken out under a detachment of soldiers to see his beloved and heroic brother die and forced to watch the ghastly and obscene operation performed afterwards on the still breathing body. Small wonder that the lad lay for weeks in Southwark Gaol between life and death. Great efforts were made to secure his reprieve, but without avail. Slowly he recovered, but with an unconquerable soul he faced whatever fate was in store for him unflinchingly and without recantation. At last, in January, 1749, after nearly three years' imprisonment, both Charlie Deacon and William Brettargh were ordered to be transported for life. On the eve of his departure Charles wrote to his younger brother, Humphrey, a letter which reveals what his martyrdom had taught his constant heart and that he still looked forward to a fresh rising in which Humphrey was to take up the Cause in which the three elder brothers had sacrificed their lives. In April, at Kingston, in Jamaica, this heroic young soul was called to his Maker at the age of 19.

Nevertheless, he was more fortunate than his friend. Sold into slavery in Antigua, William Brettargh drew out his life through years of nightmare until, in 1771, sick and neglected, we find him writing to his brother Peter in Salford a piteous note of appeal for news and help.

Thus ends the story of two gallant Salford boys, and it is difficult to understand the severity meted out to them or why it was that although they were the youngest they were treated as the two principal rebel prisoners in Southwark New Gaol. But across the bridge of time their heroic souls march in the van of those who, in the drama of our city's life achieved true greatness, for " this heroism of other days shines like a star across the sky of history and passes on its splendid radiance down an infinity of time."

CHAPTER VI

An Old Salford Plan.

A N interesting glimpse of Salford in the eighteenth century is provided by a plan which was discovered some years ago in an old deed box. It is drawn on parchment and inscribed : " A new and very accurate plan of the whole township of Salford, wherein most of the publick and private ways and roads thereof are planely sett forth, with the most remarkable matters and places therein, and likewise those on the River Irwell, which chiefly abounds the same, occularly taken on the seventh day of August, 1740, by Joseph Hill."

This plan was presumably prepared in view of certain litigation about the repair of the highways, which was rendered more necessary by the increased traffic and the expansion of the town, and it states further that it was designed " to give those who must be concerned in judgment and counsel a right geographical notion of the places or lanes in question, which are herein marked Old Field Lane, Back Lane, Cross Lane." The dispute, as shown by a Salford highway surveyor's book of the time, was concerning Oldfield Lane, for the non-repair of which the inhabitants were being indicted. Although styled " a very accurate plan," there are some notable omissions, and it is apparent that the author was more particularly concerned with showing the roads, and only mentions the houses whose occupants were to be cited as witnesses in the proceedings. For instance, the Court House in Greengate is not shown, though it was then standing, and in Cross Lane, Oak Hall, which still belonged to the Haigh family, is not distinguished at all from the rest of the houses, although the most important residence.

The town proper is grouped around a triangle formed by Greengate, Gravel Lane and Sergeant Street. The former is continued by Green Lane to a point approximately where the Church of St. Matthias now stands, where it divided into two paths running to the fords at Broughton Bridge and the Adelphi. In Green Lane is marked the house of Lady Dukenfield, close to the spot where the first Salford poorhouse was afterwards built. Sergeant Street continues beyond

KERSAL HALL.

Trinity Church by present-day Chapel Street to the commencement of Ordsall Lane, from which point a road is shown leading to the Pirle Spring along the line of the existing Bolton Street. From this point the roadway widens out and was known as White Cross Bank, from the ancient wayside cross which formerly stood there. In Mrs. Raffald's Directory of 1772 it is called Top Salford. Later the south side was known as Bank Parade, by which name it is still referred to by old townspeople. The Port Mote Records show that formerly wide strips of waste land lined this part of the roadway, and on these grassy margins the burgesses allowed their pigs to roam. From time to time burgesses were presented to the Court for encroachments by enclosing plots of considerable dimension. In recent times the Duchy of Lancaster have made grants of these waste strips to the frontagers along the road, and an interesting survival of these is the narrow triangular plot between the footpath and the houses from the corner of George Street. Fortunately some portions of these waste strips have been preserved for perpetuity, and are represented for us in the garden spaces that line the north side of Broad Street. Two such enclosures are shown on the plan. On the site of Bexley Square was the house of Mr. Richard Bury, and adjoining this at the corner of Ford Street stood the Town Pinfold. Mr. Richard Bury was of ancient Salford descent. In 1650 " Anne, wife of Richard Burie, of Oldfield Lane, was presented for a common scould," and in 1668 Richard Bury was fined 3d. " for not keeping the assize of Ale and Beare." They were not the same family as the Burys of Adelphi, who originated from Oswaldtwistle. Hill's plan shows a gate by the present Royal Hospital, but no road nothwards is indicated, although Green's map of 1793 shows the house of Mr. Holland Ackers at the Bank (the name by which the Adelphi was then known) and a road along the present Adelphi Street to the Bank Mill.

The top portion of the town is comprised around a huge square formed by Oldfield Lane, Back Lane (now Regent Road), Cross Lane and Broken Bank (now The Crescent). This, it will be recalled, was suggested in an earlier chapter as the site of the Saxon Houldfield. From Back Lane, along the line approximately of Oxford Street, a lane ran towards Ordsall Mill with its great dam and its kilns, where the tenants' corn was ground and the barley malted, and on further to

Ordsall Hall. Goodiers Lane is still in existence, of course, and led from Back Lane to New Barnes Farm at Shoresworth, tenanted by Mr. John Goodier, whose memorial tablet is in Eccles Church. Broad Street is shown as Warrington Road, although Hill, in his description, states that " Hodge Lane is said to be an uninterrupted highway leading to Warrington." This is the survival of the old Roman Road which ran from Campfield along present-day Regent Road, branching at Cross Lane corner, one branch going via Eccles and Warrington and the other along Hodge Lane by Hope and Worsley to Wigan—(the course of this road is still preserved through the grounds of the New Hall at Worsley). The New Barns Estate, lying between Ordsall Hall and Mode Wheel, belonged to the Clowes family of Broughton.

Ordsall Hall, shown with its grange adjacent (now a lodging-house at the eastern end of Smith-street), and an avenue of trees leading to the river was, in 1740, in the possession of Mr. John Stock, whose father had acquired the estate from Leftwich Oldfield in 1704. On his death in 1755, Samuel Hill bought the property, and in 1756 sold it to Samuel Egerton, from whom it has descended to its present owner, Lord Egerton of Tatton.

A very substantial house in Oldfield Lane is shown as the residence of George Britland, Esq., and directly opposite are shown " Mr. Fletcher's " and " Mr. Warmingham's." In 1708, John Fletcher, of Oldfield Lane, gentleman, married the daughter of Otho Holland, of New Hall at Pendleton. He died in 1741, when his will was proved at Chester. Another important resident of Oldfield Lane was Mr. Richard Stringer. In Back Lane is shown " Mr. William Alred's," a member of an old Salford family whose name is preserved in Aldred Street, off The Crescent. Nathaniel Bolton, of Ordsall Hill, was also of old Salford stock. On the site of Regent Road Library was the house of Mr. John Roylance, whose brother, Sam, farmed part of the New Barns lands and had his house in Goodiers Lane.

It is interesting to note that two of the houses shown on this plan are still standing, that of Nathaniel Bolton at the junction of New Oldfield Road and Regent Road, and the house at the corner of Hampson Street formerly owned by the noted " Oldfield Lane Doctor," Edmund Taylor.

Old inhabitants relate how in Dr. Taylor's time, every Christmas, he would gather his neighbours of all classes into the courtyard of this house, where they were regaled with food and drink to their hearts' content, whilst the local brass band played popular selections of music.

There is in the attic of the house what appears to be a " cock-loft," where the old bonesetter and his friends gathered for the popular sport.

About 1830 Dr. Taylor purchased Booth Hall in Blackley, built in 1639 by Humphrey Booth the Elder for his son.

There is another link between the township of Blackley and Salford, inasmuch as Blackley Chapel, in 1720, was endowed with an estate in Salford called " Ringspiggott Hall." It has not been possible to establish the exact location of this estate, which was later sold to the Bridgewater Trustees.

What changes have come over Salford since this old cartographer made his plan less than two centuries ago. Could he have dreamed, as he sketched the peaceful farmsteads of New Barns, that in the days to come great ocean liners would there deposit the merchandise of all the world on the quays of the Port of Salford ; that secluded Back Lane would become the throbbing highway of commerce ; or that over the golden grain lands whispering in the summer breeze was falling even then the shadow of industry and of a thousandfold population huddled away in drab, dark streets, shut off alike from the vision of the countryside and the melody of the wind on the heath. What greater changes still will have to be recorded in the days to come ? May they be more joyous ones, more redolent in spirit—since it may not be in form— with Salford as it was when the First George was King.

CHAPTER VII

The New Bayley.

WHEN the Old Bridge was widened and rebuilt in 1776 it necessitated the pulling down of the Old Dungeon. This, it will be recalled, was the ancient Guild Chapel which Thomas del Bothe had built and endowed in 1368, but which at the Reformation had been converted to serve as the town prison. Herein debtors, malefactors and political prisoners had been indiscriminately herded during two centuries. The growth of population during the eighteenth century made incumbent the provision of extended facilities for the treatment of offenders, and in 1782 an Act was obtained for building the New Bayley Prison for the Hundred of Salford. The site chosen was adjacent to the Lady Pirle Spring, where the Bath Hotel had now been converted into a lying-in hospital.

The prime mover in the scheme for building the prison was the chairman of the Salford Quarter Sessions (Thomas Butterworth Bayley, Esq., of Hope Hall). One of the most prominent figures in the life of Salford at that time, and a keen student of social conditions, Mr. Bayley was an earnest disciple of John Howard, the famous prison reformer, and being convinced of the necessity for a prison on a modern plan, with characteristic energy he overcame all opposition to his project and, in 1787, laid the first stone of the new prison. In 1790 the place was finished, and opened for the reception of prisoners in April of that year—the first prison in England constructed entirely in accordance with the ideas of Howard, who had unfortunately died only a few weeks before the completion. The name of the prison has excited some discussion, many people believing that it was called after the Old Bailey in London. As a matter of fact, its name is derived from the man to whom it owed its existence, Mr. Butterworth Bayley, during whose lifetime it was always spelled as he spelled his own name. The next chairman of quarter sessions, who did not share Mr. Bayley's political views, was, however, disinclined to allow the honour of the name of his predecessor, and always insisted that the gaol was named after the London prison. Into such unfairness does political prejudice lead many worthy men.

The following is a copy of the Inscription on the Foundation Stone of the New Gaol :—

" On the 22nd May, 1787, and in the 27th year of the reign of George III., King of Great Britain, France and Ireland, this Gaol and Penitentiary House (at the expense of the Hundred of Salford, in the County Palatine of Lancaster) was begun to be erected, and the first stone laid by Thomas Butterworth Bayley : and that there may remain to posterity a monument of the affection and gratitude of this County to that most excellent person, who hath so fully proved the wisdom and humanity of separate and solitary confinement of Offenders, this Prison is inscribed with the name of John Howard."

The New Bayley Prison continued to be the chief prison of the Hundred of Salford for many years, and it was considerably enlarged in 1816. It was the scene of some memorable executions, including that of the Fenians who murdered Sergeant Brett in 1867, one of the last public executions in England. The prison was eventually pulled down in 1871 when the New Prison at Strangeways was built, and the site is now, of course, occupied by the Lancashire and Yorkshire Goods Station.

Thomas Butterworth Bayley was typical of the high-minded and public-spirited citizenship of his day. He was born at Hope Hall in June, 1744, and at the early age of 24 was appointed High Sheriff. For many years he acted as Chairman of Quarter Sessions for Salford and as Receiver of Duchy Rents. He was elected F.R.S. in February, 1773. and a year later was a candidate for the Borough of Liverpool, but he did not go to the poll. Bayley took a leading part in all the patriotic efforts in the neighbourhood, and no scheme for the amelioration of the condition of the people was carried out without his whole-hearted assistance. When in the later days of the century the American War of Independence roused the martial fervour of the nation, and volunteer corps sprang up in every town, Bayley took a prominent part. In 1782 he was Lieut.-Colonel of the local Military Association, and in 1797 was one of the prime movers in raising the Manchester and Salford Volunteers, subscribing twenty guineas towards the initial expenses and becoming Colonel of the Regiment of its embodiment. The Board of Health, the

Literary and Philosophical Society, the Humane Society and the Abolition of the Slave Trade each found in this magistrate of wide sympathies one of their strongest upholders, and as early as 1788 Mr. Bayley was advocating the substitution of paid constables for the then universal honorary constables.

The chief interest of his leisure time was devoted to agriculture, and to him we owe the elms at Hope Hall. It was largely owing to his efforts that the Royal Lancashire Agricultural Society came into being in Salford in 1796. The Bayleys were a staunch Dissenting family and were connected by marriage with the family of Mrs. Gaskell, the novelist, and also with the Clives of Styche. Robert Clive, the maker of modern India, as a young boy, lived for a long time with his uncle and aunt, Mr. and Mrs. Daniel Bayley, attending Stand Grammar School, and later, as a young man, often stayed with them at Hope Hall. To the care and influence of this Salford home is due much of the moulding of that imperious character, the uncle Bayley in one of his letters saying : " . . . I do what I can to suppress the hero . . . It is a matter of concern to us, as it is of importance to himself, that he may be a good and virtuous man, to which no care of ours shall be wanting." Long afterwards, in far-away India, the great empire-builder would look back longingly and sigh in his letters for the pleasant Lancashire home where so many of his happiest days had been spent. Mr. Daniel Bayley married for his second wife, Anne Butterworth, granddaughter of Sir Robert and Lady Duckinfield, whose house in Garden Lane is shown on Hill's Plan of Salford in 1740. Of this marriage Thomas Bradshaw Bayley was the second and only surviving son. Harrison Ainsworth, the novelist, was also a descendant of the Bayley family. Thomas Bradshaw Bayley was a man of broad religious sympathies, and despite his Presbyterian upbringing, was a regular attender at Eccles Church, where his body still lies, and a marble tablet extols his virtues.

CHAPTER VIII

An Amazing Woman.

A NOTHER eminent family of those days was that of the Drinkwaters, one of whom built Irwell House, Prestwich (now a Municipal Hospital), about 1760. John Drinkwater was a surgeon in Greengate. His eldest son joined the Army at the age of sixteen, receiving a commission in the 72nd Regiment, largely raised in Salford. He took part in the defence of Gibraltar, and kept a faithful account of every particular connected with the famous siege. From these memoranda he was enabled to publish the graphic " History of the Siege of Gibraltar," which is the official record, and full of interesting information alike to the military and general reader. At the request of the King, a vote of thanks and a grant of money to Drinkwater were to have been moved in the House of Commons by Percival, the Prime Minister, the same night that he was shot in the lobby of the House by Bellingham. Colonel Drinkwater was also present at the Battle of St. Vincent, and published, amongst other literary works, " Anecdotes of Nelson." He subsequently was appointed Military Secretary to the Governor of Toulon, to the Commander of the Forces in the Mediterranean, and to the Viceroy of Corsica. He was also Commissary General of Accounts with the Army in Holland, Commissioner of Military Enquiry, and Comptroller of Army Accounts, completing a total service under the Crown of fifty-seven years. He assumed the name of Bethune from his relatives of Balfour in the County of Fife. Almost the last survivor of the Siege of Gibraltar, the gallant Colonel passed forward in 1844 at the age of 81. His memory is perpetuated by a monument in Trinity Church, together with that of his eldest son, John Elliott Drinkwater Bethune, a member of the Supreme Council of India, who died in 1851. A neat marble monument in the same Church was erected by Colonel Drinkwater to the memory of his brother, and bears the following inscription :—

" Sacred to the memory of Thos. Drinkwater, Major of His Majesty's 62nd Regiment of Foot, who perished at sea, on his return from the West Indies, April 22nd, 1797, aged 32 years.

> " Thrice had his foot Domingo's island prest,
> 　　'Midst horrid war and fierce barbarian wiles ;
> Thrice had his blood repelled the yellow pest
> 　　That stalks, gigantic, through the Western Isles :
> Returning to his native shores again
> 　　In hopes t' embrace a father, brother, friends—
> 　　　　Alas ! the faithless ratlin snaps in twain,
> 　　He falls, and to a wat'ry grave descends."

" Major Drinkwater was the second son of John Drinkwater, M.D., and Eliz. Andrews his wife, who are buried in the centre isle of this chapel ; and this Monument was erected by his only surviving brother, Lieut.-Colonel Drinkwater, as an affectionate tribute to his memory."

But it is a woman who fills perhaps the most distinguished place in the local history of these times. The King's Head was one of the most ancient of Salford's hostelries, and, tradition states, sheltered Henry VII. during his visits to his mother at Lathom. It rose to its chief glory, however, when, about 1770, it passed into the hands of Mrs. Elizabeth Raffald, the author of the first English cookery book, entitled " The Experienced English Housekeeper." Mrs. Raffald had been housekeeper to Lady Elizabeth Warburton, of Arley Hall, Cheshire, and after her marriage at Great Budworth, she established a confectionery business in Manchester, where she rapidly established a high reputation, and eventually moved to Salford, to the King's Head. Under her regime the inn became a sort of superior hotel, and included a whole range of buildings, with extensive stabling. It was the chief posting house, and from here started the London stage. The house made a special appeal to foreigners, who could communicate with the landlady through their own language, and who found better accommodation, greater comforts, and a French cuisine. At the King's Head, officers of the Regiment stationed in the locality had their mess table.

The first Masonic Lodge of which there is record in Lancashire met at the King's Head, and was in existence before 1727, in which year it applied to and was entered in the Grand Lodge Register as No. 48. It was one of the four original Lodges comprised within the Masonic Province of Lancashire, founded in 1734.

As a matter of fact, Mrs. Raffald set a new standard entirely for English cookery, and embodied her conceptions and ideas in the book which is the source from which all later experts have derived their knowledge.

Mrs. Raffald's was the first English Cookery Book ever published, and the rights of which she sold for £600 to a London firm of publishers.

In Salford she was looked upon as a Lady Bountiful who daily dispensed to the poor victuals, clothing and simple medicines. With her amazing energy and gifted attainments she took up the question of female education, and established a normal school in which young ladies were grounded in all the attributes of the English gentlewoman ; not merely the making of puddings and pies, but all the sterling family duties of good wives, good mothers and good Christians, as well as the elegant accomplishments cultivated at that time. But the labours of this amazing woman did not end here She gave a new impetus to local trade and commerce by doing for the commercial community what they had not thought to do for themselves, when she published the earliest-known Directory of Manchester and Salford. Mrs. Raffald died of spasms after only an hour's illness on April 19, 1781. Her husband was an able botanist, and together with his brother, who lived in a large detached house at the end of Greengate, cultivated very extensive gardens which occupied the area now covered by present-day King Street, Queen Street and Bury Street. Garden Lane divided these nursery gardens from those of Mr. Ravald, a totally distinct family of yeoman origin, anciently settled in Salford, and from whom Ravald Street is named.

In those days every man was to some extent his own banker, and Mr. Raffald was wont to conceal his cash by hiding it at the bottom of a sack which he filled up with peas or beans. His favourite servant man discovered his expedient, and one day absconded with a hundred guineas. He was caught, tried and hung, and this so preyed on his employer that he was often heard to say he would never have any luck again. His son ran away to sea shortly afterwards.

G

One day his mother was in the gardens about noon when the youth appeared to her in an apparition. News was later received that at that very day and hour the boy had been drowned at sea. The poor father never looked up again, and the mother became an imbecile. Having no heir, their house was annexed to the poorhouse adjoining, and the old lady was looked after there in a private apartment until she died, being buried beside her husband and brother-in-law in Trinity Churchyard.

CHAPTER IX

New Hall and the Cripple Factory.

O N the site of the present Priory of Saint Sebastian formerly stood an ancient house known as New Hall, which was demolished in 1872. It was an irregular low range of brick buildings with many rooms, dimly lighted by green lozenge-shaped panes, and oak stair flights to nearly every room. Not a very pretentious place when first erected in 1640, but, like Oak Hall, which belonged to the same period, the substantial home of a comfortably-circumstanced family who, to display their ancestral dignity, placed a carved escutcheon of the family arms on the front of the Hall facing on to the spacious courtyard.

In 1319 Thomas, Earl of Lancaster, granted land and tenements in le Hope, together with the Bailiwick of Salford-shire to Robert de Holland and Matilda, his wife, a branch of an ancient Lancashire family deriving their ancestry from one Robertus de Holland, of Holland, near Wigan, who lived in the reign of John. The local Hollands presumably had their seat at Hope Hall, removing perhaps in the fifteenth century to New Hall, then just erected. In the Vestry Orders of the Parish Church of Eccles in 1595, the churchwardens were empowered to appoint places in the church for the gentlemen of the parish, and amongst others, for " Otho Holland of Pendleton." The register of the Collegiate Church of Manchester, 1619–20, records : " Buried, Othes Holland, of New Hall, gent., Jan. 26th." George Holland, son and heir of Otho, is recorded amongst the gentlemen of the best standing in the Salford Hundred who, in January, 1588, were willing to find money for Queen Elizabeth to help to defray the cost of resistance to the Spanish Armada. In 1622, during the reign of James I., Thomas Holland, of New Hall, brother of George, married at Eccles Parish Church, Joan Irlam, and five years later another brother, James, had conveyed to him by George Holland the New Hall estate. It was this James who, in 1640, pulled down the original house and reconstructed the New Hall.

At the visitation of Sir William Dugdale, Garter King at Arms, in 1677, divers persons within the Hundred of Salford were warned to appear before him at the King's Head in Salford, to justify their titles to Esquire and Gentleman, and in the list appears the name of James Holland, of Pendleton.

According to the MS. heraldic scroll, the due authorisation of the King-at-Arms was obtained at this visitation, and James Holland then placed the carved shield, bearing his initials, on the front of New Hall. The son of James Holland married Alice, daughter of Edward and Joan Stanley, of Broughton Hall, of the illustrious family of the Stanleys, Earls of Derby, and a daughter of this marriage, Mary, married in 1699, Robert Cooke of Worsley, when the New Hall estate passed into the hands of the Cookes. In 1743, Otho Cooke married Elizabeth, daughter of John Kay, of Salford, gentleman, a descendant of James, brother of the famous Humphrey Chetham. A James Holland was a Borough Reeve of Salford in 1772.

New Hall was occupied by the Cooke family until 1781, during which time a more imposing mansion was built on to the old building, and the carved escutcheon removed from the front of the hall to a position over the fireplace of one of the old rooms, where it remained until the building was demolished. The Cookes let the hall to a Mr. Daniel Whittaker, and in 1788 to the Barrow family, who lived there for many years, and finally left in 1841 in consequence of a joke by Captain Fitzgerald, whose father held the lease of the coal mines under the New Hall estates. Paying a visit one day to the benevolent " Lady " Barrow and her sisters, he was asked to inspect the old cellars for some purpose or other, and jokingly said : " Why, I have been right under the old house and grounds a hundred yards below, and seen the cellars through the cracks in the mines." The old ladies were so alarmed, as there had been a crack in the stone staircase a short time before, that they left the house until a strong support was placed under the stairs. When New Hall was pulled down, this interior staircase was still intact, and was removed to and set up at Barningham's Foundry.

Looking over Charlestown to-day, it is difficult to picture that less than a century ago New Hall reposed in the midst of waving trees in whose tall elms the rooks swarmed, and the villagers gathered flowers and blackberry in the hedge backings. Where Whit Lane follows its tortuous paved way

OLD BUILDINGS, ON RIVERSIDE, NEAR GREENGATE.
[*From a drawing by Thomas Girtin.*

was then a sort of occupation road, with a few folds of back-to-back whitewashed cottages, making a steep descent from the side of a large and fruitful orchard, where now stand Armitage's Mills, and beyond which was the " Pendleton Pow," the ancient maypole. There was a maypole on Pendleton Green as far back as 1373, as is shown in the bequest of Thomas del Bothe of " 30s. towards making ye Causeway neare le Poll at Pendleton." During the Cromwellian era the maypole was thrown down, but it was re-erected at the Restoration, and on the building of the Church of St. Thomas it was moved further down Ford Lane, nearly opposite where an old house called the Priory then stood. By the pole stood a low white-washed building called " The May Pole Inn," then styled an " October House." Ale was not allowed to be consumed on the premises, customers being served in pots through a small shuttered square opening in the wall of the side entry, where they were told to " soop up an' goo." It is from such ale-houses that is derived the quaint inn sign of " Th' Hole i' th' Wall." The maypole was the scene of great revelries every year at the annual wakes, including the popular sport of bull-baiting ; the bull being fastened to a ring driven in the pole. Across the top of the hill, in Seedley, even so late as 1830, there would be seen, during the hunting season, the red-coated huntsmen and packs of harriers in full cry after Reynard the fox.

Beyond the orchard, on the north-easterly side, stood, until quite recently, a group of buildings of great age, constructed of wattle and daub in oak framing, with a great barn built of solid oak posts and pegs, and known as New Hall Fold. It is hard to realise that even half a century ago this was one of the model farms of Lancashire.

Returning to Whit Lane, just past New Hall, was Pendleton Old Hall, standing within very extensive grounds whose area is shown on a plan of 1856 as 17,070 square yards. The early history of Pendleton Hall is lost entirely, but the original house was demolished and an entirely new one erected on its site about 1770, by William Douglas, owner of the Douglas Green Mills. Of all the sinister figures which blacken that abortive period known as the Industrial Revolution, William Douglas stands out as one of the worst characters, and his mills were a monument to that system of appalling cruelty which marks the transition during which the factory system was slowly but unmercifully crushing out the domestic spinner and hand loom weaver.

To provide cheap labour for the factories, it was the custom to take orphan children from the parish and apprentice them at a tender age to the mills. These children were vilely ill-used, and the girls were subjected to gross indecencies. If suspected of an attempt to escape, they were fettered with rings and links like common felons, and compelled to sleep in the irons. Suicides were common, and those who worked out their time became stunted, crooked and crippled in body and in mind. The Douglas Mills were notorious even in that time, and were known as the " Cripple Factory " and the " White Slave Mills." Up to a comparatively recent period there was still standing in Whit Lane a long three-storied, weather-worn, barrack-like building, with low windows, one of the two Apprentice Houses. A steep stone staircase gave access to the rooms, left and right, on each flat, and up to this almost perpendicular ascent the tired-out limbs of these martyred children had to drag themselves at the end of a long, hard day in the mills.

In 1810 the power to oppress the defenceless was taken away from William Douglas for ever. Never one single act of kindness, never a single generous gesture was this man known ever to perform, and for nearly half a century after his death children and old folk were afraid to go at night by the river bank lest they should see " Owd Billy " on his grey mare galloping past. The Hall acquired the reputation of being haunted, and remained for long unoccupied, successive tenants being alarmed by unaccountable noises at night. The last occupier declared that he had suffered such a fright that he would not pass another night under its roof for worlds.

In the old churchyard of St. Anne, Brindleheath, is a remarkably massive and ugly stone, and peering through the rails of this repulsive tomb it is possible to decipher the inscription that records the dates of the birth and death of " William Douglas, of the Old Hall, in this parish, esquire."

CHAPTER X

A Centre of Fashion and Culture.

THOSE who chatter so blithely of joining Salford and Manchester into one community should be interested to know that this proposal is as devoid of originality as it is of practicability. In the thirty-second year of George III., Parliament itself refused to consider the two towns as other than one, and passed an Act appointing one body of Police Commissioners for both boroughs. Parliament may decree, but when it refuses to contemplate essential local considerations it has only itself to blame if its edicts " gang agley." No sooner had the Act been passed than it was apparent that though the body was one, it was not indivisible, and the Commissioners immediately found it necessary to divide themselves into two bodies, one for Salford and the other for Manchester, each administering the Act separately within what it regarded as its own jurisdiction. This was an arrangement that the Act had certainly never contemplated, but Parliament was eventually obliged to recognise it. In 1830 a further Act * was passed, declaring that the two boroughs could not " conveniently " be regulated by one body of Commissioners acting separately as aforesaid." Accordingly, two separate bodies of Commissioners were appointed, and law was harmonised with practice. So by a strange coincidence just six centuries to the very year after Earl Ranulph's Charter founded its medieval fame, the ancient town of Salford had its modern re-birth, a renaissance that has taken a full century to mature. One hundred years of struggling through the pains of gigantic development to a new phase of existence, labouring under amazing difficulties, depressed and distressed by contrary circumstances, yet losing never its native individuality, showing ever in its young old age the inveterate pioneer spirit of its youth.

Probably in no other town did the full meaning of the term " Industrial Revolution " apply in such measure as in Salford. Picture the place in Georgian days, a little town

* The Salford Improvement Act, 1830, provided that Salford should be governed by Commissioners of Police, consisting of a Borough Reeve, Constables " and 120 male persons who shall have attained the age of 21." According to official records, these numbers were, in 1835, reduced to a Borough Reeve, 2 Constables and 26 Burgesses, of whom one-third retired every year.

of fashion and culture ; its quiet English beauty set like a jewel in the encircling bends of its enfolding river ; its coffee houses the resorts of wit ; its streets and dwellings reflecting the subtle grace of an elegant communal life. On Broken Bank had arisen a notable example of eighteenth century town planning. Whether or no tradition speaks true in ascribing the laying-out of the Crescent to the brothers Adam, it is a feature that would distinguish any town, and we can well understand the delight that prompted one of its earliest residents to write :—

> '' The inhabitants of this charming elevation
> will always be sure of rich rural scenery in
> view of their front windows, however crowded
> and confined the back part of their dwellings
> may become. The fertile valley, the meander-
> ing of the River Irwell approaching to and
> receding from the Crescent, the rural cots,
> the pleasant villas, the rising hills and the
> distant mountains, never fail to create admira-
> tion as often as the eye looks over this
> fascinating picture.''

Top Salford had become a fashionable residential district, and what Salford might have been like had not the force of events altered its destiny can be glimpsed in the streets and squares and substantial houses that industrial one-sidedness has not quite obliterated in the parishes of St. Stephen and St. Philip. The former church was built in 1793 by the Rev. Nicholas Mosley Cheek at his own expense to provide for the spiritual needs of the new district,* and

---

* The Register of the Church bears on its fly-leaf the following inscription :—

"This Sacred Edifice was erected by the Rev. Nicholas Mosley Cheek, Clerk, and is named after the first Christian martyr. The first stone of this Church was laid by Rev. James Bayley, M.A., and Fellow of the Collegiate Church of Manchester, the 25th day of April, Anno Domini 1793. The founder of the Church, Rev. N. M. Cheek was appointed the first Minister by Dr. Cleaver, Lord Bishop of Chester, July 24, 1794, on which date the Church was consecrated.

The first stone was laid in prayer, and the second stone was laid in praise.

" The former stone is inscribed "Glory to God on high, and on earth, peace, goodwill towards men."

The cost of building the Church was nearly £6,000, and an architect recently estimated that to build a similar edifice to-day would cost more than £25,000. The founder is buried in a vault immediately beneath the High Altar.

in 1825 the classic tower of St. Philip's arose from designs by Barry, one of the churches erected by Parliamentary grant as a thankoffering for the nation's deliverance from the Napoleonic terror.

A century and a half ago one of the institutions of Salford, known far beyond its borders, was " The Cockpit," in Bridgewater Street, whence came the nobility, and even Royalty, to enjoy the fashionable sport of cock-fighting. Whitsuntide was the chief occasion of the year for this recreation, and the leading patron of the Salford Pit was the twelfth Earl of Derby, who, year after year, would drive hither in his four-horsed barouche with the gentry of the neighbouring counties to match their game-birds in the sanguinary honours of the pit. The sight of the celebrated Derby main bag, we are told, was alone worth the five shillings admission fee.

The lower part of the town still retained something of its ancient character in the high-gabled, quaintly-pinnacled houses of aforetime substantial burgesses, and low, simple cottages with roofs of rustic thatch fronting the expanse of the Old Orchard. In Nightingale Square was the Salford Lyceum, the local home of the Arts and Sciences, and in Bury Street, Mr. John Hampson, for half a century, conducted the Salford Academy, where the youth of the town were trained in " superior educational courses." There was no lack of old-fashioned inns, with their quaint signboards. Blue Lions and fabled Griffins and Unicorns ; the Bridge Tavern by Paradise Hill ; the Quiet Woman (whose sign displayed a comely but headless lady) in Queen Street ; the Blue Cap, the Legs of Man, the Shears, and the Bull's Head in Greengate ; the Fisherman's Hut in Chapel Street ; and away up on the edge of the Crescent, the ancient Black Horse, whilst, of course, the King's Head fulfilled the functions of a superior hotel.

The working people of the town, we are told, were " as industrious as in any parts of the Kingdom," and if they worked hard, they knew how to play hard, too. The chroniclers tell that one day in July, 1792, the morris dancers of Pendleton paid their annual visit to Salford, and that they were " adorned with all the variety of colours that a profusion of ribbons could give them, and had a very showy garland."

There was little demand for indoor amusements then, for the Irwell was as yet unpolluted ; the green fields afforded space for healthy sports, and, although the " hays " in the woods and the " hawk's aery " had disappeared, Salford was still a country town in which one could

> " Lounge i' th' market-place
> An' see the meadows mown."

CHAPTER XI

Legends of Kersal.

THE Celtic strain that runs through our Lancashire character reveals itself in the quaint legends that have grown up around many of the ancient halls and manors in all parts of the county, in which the storied happenings of bygone days have been invested with a wealth of mysticism and superstitious awe, of traffickings with the Evil One, and the pranks of mischievous boggarts. Perhaps more than most places, the Manor of Kersal is rich in this legendary lore, and though told in many forms, the attached traditions form three separate stories of different periods, interesting examples of local folk-lore based on half-historical truths.

In that early day " when Saxon felt the Norman sway " Kersal was held by a Saxon family named Peveril, whom the Norman invaders sought to oust from the domain. Richard Peveril made a valiant defence, but was overcome, and his slaughtered body thrown into the Irwell. The Norman knight took immediate possession of the hall, and held a high feast in celebration of his victory. Short was his hour of triumph. He retired to rest at midnight, and next morning his lifeless body was discovered stretched across the threshold of his chamber. A parchment was bound to his brow, written in blood, and proclaiming that the same fate would attend any other who dared to emulate his usurping hand. One, by the name of Bold Avaranches, coveted the fair domain sufficiently to disregard the deadly threat. Passionately he swore to hold the lands by his good blade against any assassin. Calling together a great and gallant company, he made a splendid feast. Joyously the cup was passed around amidst noisy revelry and mirth, and in their merry quaffing the guests failed to notice how their host had grown gloomy and abstracted. As the hour of midnight drew on, they rose to drink the toast of " Avaranches," when suddenly " his terrored eye glared wildly on a pillar nigh," and, springing from his seat, his drawn sword in his hand, he gave a frenzied shout : " Friends, 'tis here, but Avaranches knows no fear ! " The goblets were flung down, the company drew their blades, and screaming wild oaths made a cordon around the hall and searched its every nook and cranny to find the Saxon who had dared their might. Out into the surrounding grounds they poured to continue their search—without result. Returning to the hall they found the brilliant lights all extinguished, and but a single taper to illumine the gloom. A low groan of anguish came from a corner of the hall, and fearfully drawing near they discovered the mangled body of Avaranches breathing its last.

Undaunted, another Norman took possession. A strong guard was set nightly around the lord's chamber, but without avail. The Saxon vengeance claimed another victim in the same manner as before. Twice more the Normans took the risk, only to meet with the same fate, until believing, quite naturally, the place to be accursed, they left it to the rightful lords to re-assume possession.

A beautiful legend is woven around the founding of Kersal Cell. Sir Hugh le Biron was a valiant knight, and, attended by a hundred stout followers, went off to join in the Crusades, leaving his lady at Kersal. In the Holy Land his fame spread, through the fierceness of his onslaughts on the pagan forces, until he was hailed as one of the most redoubtable champions of Christendom. One night, whilst resting in his tent, he grew sore troubled in mind—phantoms of his slain foes passed endlessly before him, and the wailing of their widows and orphans haunted his ears. Amidst it all he saw the vision of his dear lady's face in sorrowful reproach. Contrition and remorse grew upon him, and with troubled mind he hastened back from the Holy Land, with deep-stirring doubts as to what had seemed his most righteous cause. As he neared the English home, whence he had so long been absent, he met a funeral cortege bearing the body of his lady to her last resting-place. Long had she awaited his return, pining through the years for his dear presence, until at last a sickness had come upon her, and not knowing whether he was living or dead, she gradually passed away in hopelessness. Sir Hugh became as one distraught, renounced all the glory of the world, handed over his lands and wealth to Holy Church, and retired a solitary recluse to that sequestered spot in the vale of Kersal where once he had wandered with his lady in the happiness of their love. Here, in prayer and good works, he sought repentance, toiling in the woods or wandering in lonely meditation on the high moor of Kersal and in the cloughs of Prestwich. Eventually he was joined by the monks from Ordsall, and old in years, more honoured in his piety than even he had been as a warrior, the gallant knight ended his days.

The third legend concerns one Eustace Dauntessey. There is no record of anyone of this name having held the Kersal lands, although the Daunteseys of Agecroft had large holdings in the district. As a youth, Eustace had dabbled in the black arts—not an unusual practise in those days. Light enough in his affections, he at length fell overwhelmingly in love with a beautiful maid, the ward of a neighbouring lord. Her troth was, however, plighted elsewhere, and her wedding day fixed. Before the happy event could take place the successful suitor was found in the woods stabbed to death. Grief-striken, the maid fled to a convent and decided to renounce the world. Eustace would not let the prize slip so easily from him, and sought the aid of the demon master he had served. The usual bargain was made, the man's soul was bartered for the coveted body of the maid. To the terror of the servants, a new resident came to keep their lord company at the hall, a sable-clothed elegant—" Strange was his mien, stranger than e'er was stranger seen ; whene'er he trod the spacious hall, they might not hear his footstep fall ; his name, or yet from whence he came, the vassals knew not." There formerly stood on the banks of the river nigh to Kersal, the story tells, a chapel or hermitage, and hither one stormy night came Eustace and his attendant demon with the beautiful weeping nun. The old priest was roused and commanded to perform the marriage ceremony. The old man was bold, and met the demands of Eustace with firm reproof of his impiety. Loudly the lord swore and threatened, without avail, until at length the hermit led the way into the chapel and bade them kneel.

> " A solemn sight—the father kneeling,
> And thunder o'er him loudly pealing.
>
> . . . Between each echoing crash
> Its messenger, in lightning's flash.
>
> He spoke of hell, of fiendish power,
> Of those who lived to curse the hour
> When first they left the righteous path
> To brave a mighty Maker's wrath."

In the flash of the lightning Eustace's gaze beheld the Cross and the faint glow that seemed to illuminate it. Turning, he saw a similar holy light like a sunny beam hovering about the head of the girl. Terror seized him, as gradually like as in a fleecy cloud the maid was enveloped and borne upwards from his sight. Eustace fled out into the night, where his demon companion awaited him, a fiery wand in his hand. " Bend, Eustace, bend ! Thy mortal days for ever end ! " the demon cried, then " laughed in fearful, fiendish glee " as from his victim came the deep moan of a broken heart. At their feet yawned a great gulf, and seizing the unhappy man in his arms the demon leapt with him into the chasm.

Another version declares that Eustace, repenting of his bargain, sought a priest to rid him from the demon agency, and with fervent prayer knelt reverently before the altar until the fiend was banished.

Even yet at nightfall about this district there is a peculiar sense of remoteness, and it is not difficult to imagine in less enlightened days how the quiet ripple of the river, the mist forms which linger perpetually about, the wind sighing through the cloughs would awaken in the fanciful minds of our ancestors strange notions of supernatural intervention in any unusual happenings amongst the families hereabouts, and conjure up in their minds a sincere belief that—

> " A pining spirit ever dwells
> To mourn—aye, mourn—for ever bound,
> The hour which made it cursed ground ;
> That it will grieve on Irwell's shore
> Till Time itself shall be no more."

BOOK   FOUR
1800 to 1930.

CONTENTS

BOOK FOUR.—1800–1930.

CHAPTER I. ....Metamorphosis.

CHAPTER II....................The Road of Seven M.P.'s.

CHAPTER III..............................Down South.

CHAPTER IV. ....The Religious Revival.

CHAPTER V............Social and Political Developments.

CHAPTER VI. ....Peel Park and the Irwell Floods.

CHAPTER VII. ....A City of Achievement.

CHAPTER VIII. ....Literary and Scientific Associations.

CHAPTER IX. ....Incorporation.

CHAPTER X..........................The Town in 1844.

CHAPTER XI..........................These Later Days.

EPILOGUE.

CHAPTER I

Metamorphosis.

IN 1780 Samuel Crompton gave to the world his invention of the mule, which made cotton spinning independent of steam and water power. Probably the world has never seen in a short period of time such changes as were wrought in Lancashire by the introduction of this and other new machines in the textile trade, and the extraordinary demand that grew up for Lancashire goods during this period. Mills were erected all along the banks of the Irwell ; the new mule was introduced into garrets and out-buildings. High wages were earned by spinners and weavers, and to supply the demands for labour came a rush of new population from all over the country. Boatloads of persons from the London workhouses were imported into the county. Old buildings were hastily converted into lodgings to accommodate the newcomers. New erections, ill-constructed and badly ven- tilated were literally thrown up. The same rooms were used for eating, sleeping and working ; and even damp, dark cellars were utilised as dwellings. The population of Salford was doubled within a very short time, and the pleasant, spacious town became a maze of dark, narrow courts and alleys and mean little houses. A poet of the time thus depicts the effect of the metamorphosis on the culture of the town :—

" Deep in a den concealed from Phœbus' beams,
Where neighb'ring Irwell leads his sable streams,
Where misty dye-rooms fragrant scents bestow,
And fires more fierce than love for ever glow,
Damætas sate."

If, therefore, we would look for the real source of the many social ills our city suffers from to-day, we shall find it—and a significant lesson, too—in those years when Salford, and, indeed, South Lancashire as a whole, was suffering so hasty and complete a transformation.

Let us see what an actual inhabitant of Salford of those days has left on record : " Born in Paradise Vale, at the foot of Green Bank, near Broughton Bridge, and dating our existence from the sixteenth year of the present century

(1815), we have seen more than the usual amount of change come over our birthplace. The small town, with its twenty thousand inhabitants, has grown into a borough of importance with a population exceeding one hundred and twenty-four thousand souls. . . . Our earliest impressions of Salford embrace a cluster of gardens adjacent to our home ; beyond these appeared meadowland, which, in turn, was bounded by the river as it flowed brightly through an abundance of marginal flowers. Shaw Brows was a sort of enclosed common where the juvenile Waltons angled for jack-sharps with thread and worm. One night the storm king, in a convivial humour, played at ninepins with the gates and rails and trees of the garden, and daylight revealed a heap of ruins which no one cared to restore. To increase the disaster, the river had overflowed its banks, covering the meadows almost to the cottage door. This was an event of frequent occurrence, although the deposits of the Irwell were neither so rich nor so desirable as those of the Egyptian Nile. No such wild pranks are permitted to the Irwell now ; utilitarians have confined it with stones, and embanked it with earth. But sometimes the river chafes under these restraints, fretting unsafely within its now narrowed channel. Springfield Lane was bounded with meadows stretching to the river and to Sandywells, with nothing intervening save two or three isolated dwellings. How densely that neighbourhood has become packed with dwellings until the hungriest feaster upon bricks and mortar may there satiate his appetite. In Springfield Lane was Collier's Printworks, one of the oldest linen dyers in the district, and between the works and the house was Mr. Collier's private pond abounding in choice fish. Broster Street, approaching Broughton Bridge, derives its name from one Charles Broster, " gentleman, of Salford," who, at the close of the seventeenth century, bequeathed £100, " one-half thereof to be distributed in coals among poor widows and housekeepers of the township not receiving alms, and the other half to be applied in clothing poor children."

Houses have now displaced the verdure in all directions, and the pellucid character of the river has been destroyed by chemical refuse, and although the old localities still retain their favourite names—names suggestive of " Flora and the countrie green "—they form so odd an amalgamation with the new streets to which they are wedded that the contrast raises our mirth along with our melancholy. Wheat Hill has not an ear of corn to bless itself withal ; Springfield has lost every trace of the vernal season ; Garden Lane, Posy Street, Blossom Street, and the Old Orchard lead to anything rather than fruit and flowers. Even Paradise and Paradise Hill are shorn of their primeval attractions ; and as to the Green Gate that once guarded the Salford pastures—where shall we look for that ? Our taste in this matter is confessedly behind the ages and the fashion." (R. W. Proctor's " Memorials.")

In the *City News* of January 20, 1906, a further picture is given of the Broughton district as the correspondent saw it seventy years before : " At the Strangeways end of Broughton Lane were a few residences, whilst in the near fields was a nest of working-men's lock-up gardens, wherein many a rare pink and picotee, and many a swelling stalk of celery were nourished with fond and jealous care. The lane was knee-deep in sand, and the resort of numerous red and brown butterflies, till it joined the lower road from Broughton Bridge near the Suspension Bridge. So by a few cottages to the Griffin Inn, the Cheetham Arms and its opposite ford—a noted bathing place for Salford youths. Round about this locality were several farms. One especially (now covered by Albert Park) lives in our remembrance as the pasture to which was taken each evening, more than a century ago, our ancestor's old mare—the first horse used in Salford and district in a gin to turn the mill which perched or straightened the nap on the back of the fustian pieces. From Broughton Bridge, right and left of the new cut—Great Clowes Street— were fields. In the centre of one stood a mansion on an artificial raised mound. Being thus the exceptional house above the floods, it was called " Noah's Ark," and was the residence of James Whitlow, solicitor, of St. James' Square, Manchester."

Let us stroll again with Proctor through Greengate as he remembered it, and with the maps of 1819 and 1824 as accompaniments. Starting from a range of picturesque cottages in Green Vale, a large superior house with extensive garden enclosed within a high brick wall was the residence of a family of Hollands, of whom Mr. James Holland was Borough Reeve in 1805. They were silk and cotton manu-facturers. Green Bank was entered at Blacklock's Brow, named from the dwelling of the Blacklocks, the calico printers.

Robert Blacklock, who died in 1813, aged 83, was the earliest calico printer in Lancashire. Bedford Street, which first appears in the Directory for 1800, was lined with small white cots, tiny, but extremely cosy. On Wheat Hill 'was the home of the Sandfords (a connection preserved in Sandford Street). A little beyond Back Davies Street, the road on the same side as far as Broughton Bridge was skirted first by the wooden railings of a small plantation and next by a rail of strong timber guarding the meadows. The field nearest the bridge was the usual recreation ground during the dinner hour for the hands engaged at the adjacent silk mill, where the working hours, as at other factories at that time, ranged from six in the morning to eight at night, and where children as early as their eighth year worked full time with the adults.

The opposite side of the road was more closely inhabited, both along the frontage and up the bank side. Near the bridge a delta of vacant land divided the highway from the footpath leading to the Adelphi, and behind this rose the better-class homesteads, with pleasant gardens, covering Richmond Hill. Mr. Clowes' Bridge was then comparatively new. There were a few shops, and the Broughton Tavern and sundry streets and squares elevated on the side of the brow. Particularly attractive was Green Bank Terrace (on the site of the present Free Library), with long gardens descending to the footpath, extending from Blacklock's Brow to Paradise Hill. Between Richmond Hill and Broken Bank was Shaw Brows, crowned with small groves of trees, its elevated, undulating surface having numerous brooks and ponds wherein the boys of the town fished and bathed. The Brows were beginning to be dotted with detached residences— "The Cottage," Mr. Holland Ackers' "The Bank" (whence Bank Place and Bank Street) and " Brown Hill," the home of Mr. John Bury, timber merchant and brewer, who gave his name to the newly-made Bury Street. Mr. Bury's place of business, for more than thirty years, was the Theatre or Riding School in Water Street. He died in 1811 at a ripe old age. A near neighbour to Mr. Bury was Mr. Joseph Harrop, founder and first editor of the *Mercury.*

In the year 1794, William Cowdroy, a compositor and editor, of Chester, settled in Greengate, and also opened an office in St. Mary's Gate, Manchester, whence he published the *Manchester Gazette.* Cowdroy was a man of rare genius, and, in the words of a contemporary—a poet, a wit, a facetious companion, an unshaken patriot, a kind father, a firm friend, and a truly honest man. One of his sons, William, in 1803, set up Salford's earliest printing press at 27, Bury Street, whence he published *The Gleaner, Harvest Home*, and similar romantic and once-popular literature intended for the amusement of domestic circles. The literary editor of *The Gleaner* was James Watson, then in his brief hey-day as a tavern wit and theatrical poet and writer. One of the pictures in *The Gleaner* illustrating " An Eastern Tale," and signed " C. Calvert, del " is probably the earliest specimen of that artist's work. A friend and neighbour of the Cowdroys (who are all buried along with many other Salford families of the time, in St. Mark's Churchyard, Cheetham Hill) was John Slack, who, in 1790, started the first engraving business in Salford at Princess Street, Gravel Lane. Devoting himself at first entirely to pictures, the business eventually became more of a commercial concern, announced in the Directory of 1820 as " engraver to calico printers."

Bury Street was then a fashionable place of residence ; one of its more noted dwellers being the venerable educationist, Mr. John Hampson, whose Academy was attended, amongst others, by Sir James Watts, of Abney Hall, founder of the famous Manchester firm. A relative of the schoolmaster was Thomas Hampson, who was responsible for building the street which bears his name off Oldfield Lane. and where he died in January, 1825, the same year that omnibuses first started to run from Pendleton to Manchester. Thomas Hampson was the first secretary of the Lancashire Agricultural Society.

In October, 1824, a terrible accident took place at Mr. Nathan Gough's Islington Spinning Mill. About nine o'clock in the morning, whilst the people were all at work, the iron beam on which one compartment of the fire-proof floor of the top storey rested broke suddenly, and crashing through each floor from top to bottom of the mill, which was six storeys high, killed nineteen people and seriously injured an equal number.

In 1825 the Town Hall was nearing completion, together with St. Philip's Church ; Silk Street, Peru Street and Adelphi Street were being spaced out ; at the top of Springfield Lane new dwellings for the industrial population were in course of erection opposite the Salford Poorhouse—opened in 1793. It

OAK HALL, CROSS LANE. SITE IS NOW OCCUPIED BY THE CATTLE MARKET.

was a sign of the times that Green Bank was now beginning to be called Broughton Road, and trowels were being so actively plied that the wealthier burgesses, fond of more rural surroundings, were already trekking across the Irwell into Broughton.

The mad lust of industrialism rushed upon the town, ruthlessly sweeping away in its onrush all that did not conform to the strictest utility. The sweeter aspects of life counted for naught, and all that was pleasant and gracious was overwhelmed by a flood of ugliness to serve the purpose of the hour. Such is the penalty the iconoclast exacts from posterity. Booth Hall, the ancient residence of the family whose name is for ever woven with the best traditions of Salford's past, was pulled down along with other similar buildings in Greengate in 1825, and at the same time the Salford Cross was removed. A few years before, at the coronation of George IV., the Cross was the scene of festivities truly Hogathian. Oxen and sheep were roasted here and distributed with loaves of bread and barrels of strong ale, after a great procession of trades and school children. The popular liveliness culminated in the most boisterous merriment, and small wonder that the waste of food and liquor was far greater than the enjoyment thereof. The late Mr. Ben Mullen made many attempts to trace what became of the Cross after removal, and finally discovered that the base had been carried to Knolls House, in Higher Broughton, to serve as a sundial pedestal, but had afterwards disappeared from there, no one knew where. In the same way an effigy of Charles I. that formerly adorned the Church of the Sacred Trinity was relegated to the obscurity of a local builder's yard and lost. Salford would to-day be rich in records of its age-worn past if only our forbears in those days had but cared enough.

Passing through Bell Gates at the end of Greengate would have brought us in those days to Stanyhurst and the Town Fair. Ballads written and sung by the minstrels of the day of the diversions and characters of Salford Fair are in many collections. " The humours of Salford Fair," wrote Mr. Aston, " and the whole train of itinerant agility, wonders of creation, and Mr. Punch's wooden family divert the lads and lasses at a cheap expense of wit or money." There, in 1811, Sieur Rea, the then celebrated conjuror, in his obituary styled with mock solemnity, "His Imperial Majesty Sieur Rea, Emperor of Conjurors," laid aside his cups, and balls and cards and died at the Red Lion Tavern (now the Raven Hotel) in his sixty-seventh year. In 1812, Mr. Kite, one of the most popular showmen of the time, was seized with fatal illness at his circus in the King's Head yard, and another great figure of the Fair was Mr. Polito, the forerunner of " Sir " George Wombwell and his famous menagerie.

A quaint character, not only at the Fair, but about the town all the year round was James Bagot, popularly known as " Old Chelsea Buns " from his vending of these popular delectabilities of his own baking. He would saunter forth each day from his bakehouse in John Street loaded with his freshly-made wares, and wherever he went, up and down the streets and over the Old Bridge into Manchester, his cheery call of " Hot Chelsea buns ! Hot Chelsea buns !" would bring eager customers—grown-ups and children alike— hastening towards him. Many an artist found in his picturesque figure an engaging subject, and the scissors of the silhouette-makers were kept busy, especially at Fair-time, supplying the demand for mementoes of one whose personal popularity was no whit less than that of his tasty buns.

Apart from the cock-pit and the Fair, the most popular holiday events in Salford in those days were the balloon ascents. The first (on the anniversary of the King's birthday, April 23, 1824) took place at the Cloth Hall, when the younger Sadler went up alone, and after a stormy voyage alighted at Monk's Heath, near Knutsford. Five months later the aeronaut perished near Blackburn. On Monday, October 16, 1837, Mr. Chas. Green ascended in his great Nassau balloon from the Gas Yard in Lamb Lane. He had two passengers, Mr. Chas. Taylor and a man named Carpenter, whose ascent was singular. Green had just got into the car to try the power of the balloon, before starting, and the men at the ropes mistaking his instruction relaxed their hold, with the exception of Carpenter and a soldier, who were carried up with the balloon. When about ten feet up the soldier let go, but Carpenter held on, and when about one hundred feet up succeeded in swarming up the rope with great agility into the car. The Royal Nassau made a further ascent from the same yard a week later, when Mr. Green was accompanied by five passengers who paid twenty guineas each for a journey of forty miles. The quantity of gas taken by the balloon on that occasion was 83,710 cubic feet. At a third ascent in the same year, a lady, Miss Ann Brougham, was one of the seven passengers, and Colonel Sir Michael Creagh was another ; the balloon arriving safely at Overton in Cheshire.

The Old Cloth Hall stood on a portion of the ground that is now occupied by the Exchange Railway Station, but of this building, beyond the site, I have been unable to obtain any particulars. Early in the last century a new hall was erected in Stannyhurst. On a substantial plinth of sandstone, a collonaded front of plain classical columns faced the river. The interior comprised a large market hall with commodious cellars for storage below.

The opening of the Cloth Hall was advertised as follows :—

" On the second day of May, 1814, the new Yorkshire Cloth Hall will open, when there will be exposed for sale by the real manufacturers, a choice assortment of woollen cloths, pelisse cloths, blankets, etc.

" The principal entrance, up the Spread Eagle Gates, nearly opposite the Old Bridge."

This building still exists on the south side of Victoria Bridge, but it has suffered considerably from adaption to suit later purposes.

It is appropriate that at one of the inns in the Blackfriars district, now the Black Lion Hotel, the great national organisation of the Fair people—the Showmen's Guild—was inaugurated.

CHAPTER II.

The Road of Seven M.P.'s.

STANDING back from Broad Street, as though timorously retiring from the rush and clangor of one of the heaviest trafficked streets in the land, is the old Georgian mansion of Belle Vue, known to-day more aptly and officially as " 25, Leaf Square," and first occupied by John Leaf in 1796. John Leaf was in the yarn trade, with a place of business at Salford Cross, and this property was a delightful and convenient abode wherein to entertain his friends. Belle Vue in those days was surrounded by a small park, bounded by the Salford-Bolton highroad on the south and Strawberry Road to the Bury and Bolton Canal as far as Bedlam Bridge (now Frederick Road Bridge) on the western side, and so along the canal to Cock Robin Bridge, from whence south to the main road again.

In 1805 John Leaf became one of the parties to a political lawsuit, and had to find a very large sum for costs. He sold off numerous plots of the estate on chief rents, and projected to develop the property on the lines of a London Square as William Jones was doing at New Windsor. The purchaser had built the long row of houses on the western side up to the level of the first floor windows when funds gave out, and on John Leaf fell the burden of finding the money to complete. Hence the terrace on the opposite side where the Secondary School now stands was never proceeded with. John Leaf continued to live at Belle Vue House until his death in 1840, when it was occupied by his brother-in-law, Robert Ellis Cunliffe, grandfather of the late Sir R. E. Cunliffe, C.B., Solicitor to the Board of Trade, and father of Thomas Potter Cunliffe, a quaint character still remembered by many Pendleton residents. This Thomas was never known to wear an overcoat, the substitute being a sleeveless cape that almost reached his knees, worn always in conjunction with a silk hat.

John Leaf's daughter-in-law, Nancy, was the daughter of Sir Thomas Potter, who built Buile Hill Hall, and to whom the citizens of Manchester were largely indebted for their charter of incorporation. Nancy Leaf lived for many years in Acton Place, on the Crescent, and later at Belle Vue Cottage, a house standing in a large garden at the end of George Street, Pendleton, and which afterwards became Pendleton Academy.

In 1831 the Crown was induced to give Pendleton Green for the site of a new Church of Saint Thomas, the old church in Brindle Heath Road, erected in 1766, having become too small for the increased population. The ancient Maypole was removed from the Green to a piece of waste ground in Ford Lane, nearly opposite a house called " The Priory."

The first incumbent of the old St. Thomas' was the Rev. James Pedley, M.A., of whom the *Gentleman's Magazine* wrote at his death in 1825 : " No man could exceed him in attachment to the Constitution as established in Church and State." Besides being Vicar of Pendleton for forty-nine years, he was at the same time for over forty years a master at the Grammar School.

Facing the Green was a stately residence called Gore Hill, entered by some handsome iron gates in Gardner Street, and occupied by Alderman Joseph Ashworth, an early pioneer of popular education and a partner in the " Pendleton Pow Mills," in Croft Street, built by Taylor & Weston in 1780. Mr. Ashworth was succeeded at Gore Hill by one of our great local benefactors, Sir Elkanah Armitage.* Adjoining Gore Hill, on the plot of land now covered by Pendleton Town Hall, were two white cottages, in one of which, occupied by Mr. Thomas Littlewood, a Salford draper, an atrocious crime took place on April 16, 1817—the housekeeper and servant maid being murdered by burglars, who were run to earth in Free Nook Field, Seedley. The four malefactors were tried at Lancaster and executed.

If the process of industrialisation over a century ago was robbing the centre of the town of its more pleasant amenities,

---

* Born at Failsworth in 1794, Elkanah Armitage had a most remarkable career. Beginning life as a hand-loom weaver he gradually worked his way to great wealth through the mills he established at Pendleton, where, at the time of his death, two thousand workpeople were employed. In 1857 he unsuccessfully contested Salford as a Liberal in opposition to Mr. W. N. Massey. He rests in the great cemetery at Weaste, his funeral procession, in 1876, being a most impressive sight—half a mile long and made up of a hundred carriages. He was knighted for his services during the Chartist disturbances.

it was creating at the same time a new order of merchant princes, who found both pleasant and convenient habitation in the western suburbs. Here they built their stately residences in charming surroundings, close enough at hand to their mills and warehouses to direct the mainsprings of their fortune and at the same time to render their meed of personal service to the town and community, which they recognised as entitled to claim a substantial portion of their active interest. Manorial lord, yeoman merchant, or Victorian manufacturer, in whatever form his age presented him, the local magnate was always a true citizen living in close relationship to those directly and indirectly dependent upon him. The problems of communal life in these latter days would be more readily solved were it possible to re-establish this personal contact of a past time.

During the last century there was no necessity to flee the smoke and find residence in delectable Cheshire, North Wales, or the Lakes, even had transport been so convenient as it now is, for nowhere could be found more desirable a dwelling-place than the western outskirts of Salford then provided. Wide breadths of undulating turf swept by a gentle health-giving wind from the Irish Sea, and dotted with luxuriant growth of beech, chestnut and elm ; a subsoil of gravel and red sandstone ; a view superb in its range over the beautiful expanse of Cheshire to the distant hills. Small wonder that noble mansions grew up on such a favoured site or that Eccles Old Road housed at one time no less than seven distinguished Members of Parliament.

At Fairhope lived Mr. Thomas Agnew, founder of the famous firm of art dealers. Mr. Agnew's wife was the daughter of William Lockett, the first Mayor of Salford, and he himself occupied that same office in 1851, the year of the Great Exhibition in London. On their marriage, the Agnews lived at Richmond Hill, in those days a charming enough spot, which had its name from its resemblance to the famous Surrey view-point, and later they acquired an estate on the Eccles Old Road, where the house " Fairhope " was built as the family residence. It was during Mr. Agnew's mayoralty that Queen Victoria and the Prince Consort visited Salford, and were received in Peel Park by 80,000 children of the Sunday Schools of the district, the first demonstration of its kind that had ever taken place. The Queen's delight

at her welcome is recorded in her diary.* William
Agnew, eldest son of Thomas, lived, on his marriage, at No. 11,
The Crescent, removing later to Hopefield on the Fairhope
Estate, and in 1867 to Summer Hill. Thomas Agnew was
recognised and acknowledged as one of the greatest world
authorities in the Fine Arts. In addition to membership of
the firm of Thomas Agnew & Sons, he was a partner in
Bradbury, Agnew & Co., the proprietors of *Punch*. His great
friend was Sir John Tenniel, tne celebrated cartoonist, and
during his residence Summer Hill was a rendezvous for many
of the greatest figures in painting, music and politics.
Leighton, Millais, Burne-Jones, Leslie and Fred Walker ;
Gladstone, Harcourt, Morley, Fawcett, Rosebery, Granville,
Lord James of Hereford and Lord Edward Cavendish ;
Santley and Halle, Edward Lloyd, Madame Normanda Neruda,
and Piatti, the great player of the violincello—all were frequent
guests at Summer Hill, which became a Grand Salon of all
that was brilliant in the artistic and intellectual life of the
Victorian era. In 1895 Sir William Agnew was created a
Baronet. Summer Hill was presented, in 1921, to the Corporation of Salford by Sir George Agnew, the present Baronet,
whose many benefactions to his native city, which he
represented in Parliament from 1906 to 1918, will be readily
recalled.

Adjacent to Fairhope, on the easterly side, was the mansion
of Claremont, a handsome Georgian residence set in a beautiful
estate, which was formerly the residence of Colonel Ford,

*The Royal Party, including Her Majesty the Queen and His
Royal Highness the Prince Albert, the youthful Prince of Wales,
the Princess Royal and the Duke of Wellington, arrived at Peel
Park from Worsley on October 10 to receive an address from the
Borough of Salford. The scene in the Park was described in the
journals of the day as " the most original and striking spectacle ever
presented to do honour to Royalty in any age." The entry in the
Queen's diary concerning the event is as follows : " We went into
Peel Park before leaving Salford, the Mayor having got out and received
us at the entrance, where was, indeed, a most extraordinary, and, I
suppose, unprecedented sight—82,000 school children—Episcopalians,
Presbyterians, Catholics (these children having a small crucifix
suspended round their necks), Baptists, and Jews (whose faces told
their descent), with their teachers. In the middle of the Park was
erected a pavilion, under which we drove, but did not get out, and
where the Address was read. All the children sang " God Save the
Queen "—the director being placed on a very high stand, from which
he could command the whole assembly in the Park."—(Martin's
" Life of Prince Consort," Vol. 3). A picture of this remarkable scene
is in the Royal Museum and Art Galleries.

H

who raised the Manchester and Salford Light Horse Volunteers. On the death of Mrs. Ford in 1821, Claremont was purchased by Mr. B. A. Heywood, of Clifton Hall, one of the founders of Heywood's Bank. Acresfield, contiguous to Claremont, had in the previous year been presented by Mr. Heywood to his nephew Benjamin, and so began the association with Salford of a family who for more than a century have enriched and ennobled the life of the town. When his uncle died in 1828, Benjamin Heywood removed to Claremont. Three years later, on the passing of the Reform Bill, he was elected to represent South Lancashire in Parliament. Owing to ill-health, Mr. Heywood did not see his way to stand at the succeeding election. During his brief career as a Parliamentary representative he earned from all sides unstinted admiration for his ability and devotion, as the following tribute from a leading article in the *Manchester Guardian* for May 14, 1831, will shew :—

> " To use the language of adulation is as alien from our principles as it is repugnant to our pride, but neither will we abstain from saying what we believe to be the truth, viz., that if personal affability and kindness of disposition, steadiness of purpose, consistence of conduct, unbending integrity, a sound judgment and a cultivated mind, if these qualities and endowments will befit a man for the performance of such duties as devolve upon a representative of the people, then have Mr. Heywood's constituents in general every reason to feel assured that he will justify the regard they have evinced towards him."

Although his own parliamentary career was short, Mr. Heywood retained firm friendships with friends he made during that time ; and Brougham, Palmerston, Morpeth and Lord John Russell were frequently entertained at Claremont. In 1838, on Melbourne's recommendation, Her Majesty created him a baronet. A niece of Sir Benjamin married the Rev. G. H. Sumner, afterwards Archbishop of Canterbury, and was the founder of the Mothers' Union. In 1855, Sir Benjamin built " Light Oaks " as a residence for his son, Arthur, whose married life tragically terminated within a year, when the house was closed for a time, ere another son, Edward, took up residence there. To the munificence of

Mr. Edward Heywood this district owes one of the finest examples of modern church building in the Church of St. Augustine, Pendlebury.* The Church of St. Anne, Brindleheath, is another monument of the religious devotion of this family, being erected by Mrs. Charles Heywood in memory of her husband, whose residence was at Chaseley, a house adjoining Claremont, built by Mr. Robert Gardner, a well-known merchant, whose name is preserved in Gardner Street, Pendleton. Still another son of Sir Benjamin was Oliver Heywood, whose philanthropy and civic devotion was a conspicuous feature of the latter part of the century.

Hope Hall, previously referred to as the home of the Bayley family, became afterwards the residence of Sir Elkanah Armitage, and later of another Member of Parliament in Mr. H. J. Roby.

Facing Hope Hall and Fair Hope, on the opposite side of the Eccles Road, were two other notable houses, " The Weaste " and " Weaste Hall." In 1570, John Gawen of Worsley and Robert Barlow of Little Hulton were under bond to allow Thomas Tyldesley and Margery his wife to occupy the mansion house called " The Weaste," in Little Bolton. " The Weaste," which during the last century was the home of the Tootall family, was demolished in 1900, but Weaste Hall still stands, and was for many years the residence of Mr. Henry Lightbowne, another distinguished figure in local affairs, and who introduced into Salford the manufacture of wallpaper.

Adjoining Buile Hill, the residence of Sir Thomas Potter, later of the Bennett family, and now the Salford Natural History Museum, was Hart Hill, with its handsome Elizabethan style mansion erected by Mr. John Dugdale, who opposed Brotherton for the parliamentary representation of Salford in 1835. In Hart Hill Meadow were buried a number of the plague victims in 1590. A cousin of Mr. Dugdale, also named John, was the builder of another noble mansion house, " Irwell Bank," on the Eccles New Road, at Ladywell. The Dugdale cousins were great characters. The one at Irwell Bank was known as " Ould John Stink o' Brass," and, despite his wealth, which he freely spent in good works, he was so indifferent to his personal appearance that he perpetually wore quite shabby clothes. When anyone chided him on the

* See *Architectural Review* (New York), March, 1899.

matter he would reply : " Ah ! well ; it doesn't matter ; everyone knows me." When on his visits to London or elsewhere, his friends there also remarked on his appearance. His comment invariably was : " Ah ! well, it doesn't matter ; nobody knows me."

He spent £50,000 on the building of Irwell Bank. The great stained-glass window of the hall was presented to old John by the choristers of Manchester Church as a token of their regard. On his death in 1886, the house was sold to the widowed Lady Annette de Trafford, who used it as a Dower House until her death in 1922.

A happy playground of Salford folk for half a century or more has been Swinton Fields, the tree-crowned stretch of open moor to the north-west of Eccles Old Road. Swinton Moor was originally held along with Wardley manor by the Knights Hospitallers, and later by Whalley Abbey. On the suppression of the monasteries these lands passed to the Tyldesleys, who sold them to the Sherringtons, from whom they passed to the Downes family by purchase. In 1581, Sir John Radclyffe of Ordsall claimed Swinton Moor as part of the lands of Whalley Abbey in Monton, granted to the Radclyffes at the Dissolution, and obtained a grant of a portion of the Moor, a connection perpetuated by the name of Radcliffe Park Road. John Downes, who succeeded to the Wardley and Swinton lands about 1642, was a prominent Royalist, and married the daughter of Sir Cecil Trafford. Trafford was a staunch Protestant, and took up the study of theology in the hope of converting his son-in-law. As a result, he himself became a convert to the Roman Church. John Downes left a son and a daughter. Roger, the son, was a friend of Rochester, and after a dissipated career in London, was killed on London Bridge in course of a brawl with the Watch. The daughter, Penelope, married Richard Savage, Fourth Earl Rivers, a dissolute noble, who was one of the first to join William III. on his landing in 1688. Their daughter, Elizabeth, married the Fourth Earl of Barrymore, and had a daughter, Penelope, who contracted a loveless marriage with General Sir James Cholmondley. The poor lady, seeking relief from this " union de convenance," was driven to clandestine meetings with her true lover on Swinton Moor, and these assignations being discovered by her husband, she was divorced as an adultress in 1737. Twenty-three years later she sold her estates locally to Francis, Duke of Bridgewater, and, lonely and childless, she died in 1786. The ghost of poor Lady Pen. is said to haunt the Fields, and could the ancient elms crowning the ridge of the wind-swept moor but speak, they would perhaps tell of the unfortunate lady keeping her love-lorn tryst beneath their friendly shade. Cholmondley and Penelope Roads still preserve her memory in our midst.

All that wealth and beauty once gave has met its inevitable hour before industrialism's unceasing advance, until even Swinton Fields are threatened by the march of events. The green lawns of Claremont and Acresfield are covered by the trim villas of an ever-growing population's demand for room to live. Light Oaks, by the generous gift of Sir Percival Heywood, has become a delightful public park ; and the proud mansion of Irwell Bank, now empty and deserted, gazes sorrowfully over forge and factory, timber stacks and petrol tanks. Wraiths of a pleasant company hover about its great bare rooms, and its weed-grown terraces sadly whispering " Ichabod ! " but the hooting sirens of big steamers, passing to and fro at the garden end, give answer that the glory is not departed—only transformed.

CHAPTER III

Down South.

IN an erstwhile farmhouse kitchen a sweet-faced old lady chatted of South Salford as she knew it in the days of her youth. Looking over that district to-day, with its myriads of small houses and densely-packed streets, the great docks and some of the largest cotton mills in Lancashire, it is difficult to realise that within living memory it was a peaceful, retired spot where beauty lingered in picturesque array. But in that room flooded with golden sunshine from the wide, open casement, a singularly bright and peaceful chamber from which, though but a stone's throw away, the roar of Regent Road seemed completely shut out, one of those odd surviving dwellings tucked away amidst the smoke-grimed wilderness of modern Ordsall, there was an echo and a vision of a less hurried and sweeter day. "There be folk that have ne'er a good word for Salford," the old lady said, with almost a challenge in her tone, "but it were bonny enough when I were a lass. It's just men that's spoiled it all."

An arresting thought, surely, as we watch to-day the unchecked encroachments on our fast-disappearing country-side—factories moving into lower-rated areas wiping out the green fields; overgrown towns spreading their canker ever wider and wider; God-given beauty spots replaced by the pretty-prettiness of modern housing schemes, appalling in their incongruity. How can these ever compensate for our thoughtless rejection of Nature's endowments in what will soon be, in memory alone, a green and pleasant land. The ills of present-day existence are chiefly aggravated by the manner in which the people have been imprisoned in bricks and mortar and divorced entirely from the subtle influence of the countryside and the wind on the heath. And having devastated what once was fair and joyous, blind, blundering thoughtlessness disguised as "Progress"—save the word—leaves behind the trail of slums and hideous havoc, and stretches its destructive length ever further afield. Is it not time to call a halt to this spreading evil and compel authorities to reconstruct sanely and pleasantly for work and living, the quarters of existing towns ruined by the mad march of industrial development ? Ordsall cries its moral loud and long.

Less than a century ago the southern portion of Salford presented a typical picture of pastoral England—a peaceful, pleasant place of agriculture and husbandry. Spreading cornfields interspersed with rich meadows and pasture lands ; cattle browsing by merry streams ; bracken-hung rocky cloughs ; black and white farmhouses peeping out from between their sentinel trees. Its desirability as a dwelling-place had long before attracted the attention of the prosperous merchants of the town, and already the slopes of Ordsall Hill were dotted with their attractive abodes.

The drawback was lack of access. The Plan of Salford in 1740 shews the only way into Ordsall then was by way of Ordsall Lane, the picturesque but narrow thoroughfare that ran from Chapel Street to the Old Hall. The bad condition of English roads in the eighteenth century led to the establishment of Turnpike Trusts to remedy the deficiencies of existing roads and to supply the need for new ; and early in the last century a number of public-spirited men obtained the power under a special Act of Parliament to construct a road from Hulme to Eccles, crossing the Irwell by a new bridge. This road and bridge were opened to traffic in 1808, and named Regent Road in honour of the Prince Regent. A toll was charged for both passengers and vehicles ; turnpikes being erected and the maintenance of the road and bridge placed in the hands of trustees. Regent Bridge formed the fourth link between the two towns. In 1778 the Old Salford Bridge had been widened by taking down the dungeon and extending the piers and arches ; and the New Bayley Bridge, opened to traffic in 1785, had been made toll-free in 1803. The original Blackfriars Bridge still existed as a wooden footbridge until, in 1820, it was replaced by a new erection of stone. It was impossible to enter or leave the town without paying toll except by the Old Salford or the Bayley bridges.

A story is told of one man who tried to escape paying toll but was caught in the act. He determined on revenge. Going to the Regent Bridge one night he roused the bridge-keeper from bed and said he wanted to pay the toll. The keeper, from the window, being naturally loth to dress and come down to collect a half-penny, bade him go free. The passenger was insistent, however. Severely ruffled, the keeper came down, only to find himself the victim of a practical joke. The anxious payer had vanished !

The toll from all the Salford bridges was eventually taken off in response to popular agitation. By an Act which received Royal Assent on August 14, 1848, it was provided that when the principal monies due and owing for the construction of Regent Road and Bridge shall have been reduced to £6,000 the tolls taken at the Bridge Gate shall absolutely cease.

With the making of the Regent Road, the route hammered out two thousand years before by the feet of the Roman legions once more became a main road, that great east and west highway that now bears one of the heaviest traffic burdens of any road in the Kingdom ; and yet, again, it was to resound with the echo of martial tread. In 1819 the Infantry Barracks were built on Regent Road, and after a lapse of a thousand years Salford became once more a garrison town. The military association was further strengthened later, when, on the portion of the road beyond Cross Lane, arose the fort-like building of the 6th Royal Lancashire Militia Barracks. Both these barracks are gone : the homes of the legionnaires of industry are reared over the erstwhile quarters of the sons of arms ; the echo of children's play resounds in the tree-hung acre of what was once the barrack square, but in the memory of old inhabitants lives yet the stirring scenes of a day now past when, every Sunday morning, the redcoats passed in all their splendour and to the thrilling music of drum and brass band to church parade at St. Philip's and St. John's.

Amongst those who took the lead and bore the main financial burden for the making of the road and bridge was Mr. James Hall—" Quaker Hall " as he was generally known—who lived at " Sunnyside," on Ordsall Hill (where Camerons' works now stands) and who operated a fustian mill on the bank of the river. Born in humble circumstances in 1749, Mr. Hall raised himself to great wealth, and became one of the most influential worthies in the town. He took an active part in 1785 in securing the repeal of the fustian tax. There was consternation in Lancashire when Pitt imposed this duty, and the master dyers and bleachers announced that " they were under the sad necessity of declining their present occupation till the next session of Parliament." Mr. Hall was typical of that new order of magnates who found their opportunity through the Industrial Revolution, bringing to the support of strong natural talents an amazing fund of perseverance and industry. Unfortunately, they had little appreciation of anything that did not conform to strict utility, otherwise "Quaker Hall" would not have been guilty of that act of vandalism—the destroying of Ordsall Cave to save his land from antiquarian trespass. A wit of the time, in a vile pun, is said to have exclaimed: "Take him, Hall in Hall, we shall not see his like again."

Besides Hall's Mill, one of the earliest works to invade the suburban retreats of South Salford, began its operations in 1792, when Worrall's Dye Works was founded. This factory has been the corner-stone in the development of Ordsall, and from the first beginnings, with 200 hands, has grown the present great business—the largest of its kind in the world—clothing the women of two hemispheres in velvets of character and exquisite colouring made from cotton yarn. Worrall's and Ordsall are almost synonymous terms, the firm and the district having developed simultaneously, and a depression in one was immediately felt throughout the other. The founder of the firm, Mr. James Worrall, had remarkable genius as a mechanic, which enabled him to perfect inventions that gave him advantages unknown to other firms. Long before the State or the Municipality concerned itself with matters of public education, firms like Worrall's made many earnest efforts to provide for the social and moral improvement of their workers. In Ordsall, Worrall's provided a Reading Room and Library, a Club for Working Men, and both Day and Sunday Schools. Mr. Jas. Worrall, jun., resided at Ordsall Hill, adjoining "Quaker Hall," and throughout his lifetime took a keenly-active interest in the affairs of the town as Councillor, Alderman and Magistrate. In 1861 he was elected Mayor.

The houses on Ordsall Hill were approached through a handsome pair of gates giving on to a well-made gravel carriage drive banked on both sides by a splendid array of rhododendrons, where Sussex Street now is. In addition to the residences of "Quaker Hall" and Mr. Worrall, there was another large house there, occupied at various times by Attorneys Foster and Prescott and by Colonel MacGregor (afterwards General Sir Duncan MacGregor, K.C.B.), father of the well-known Rob Roy,* and with whom, as Major of the 31st Regiment, originated the command which produced such a display of heroism on the part of the men during the burning of the " Kent Indiaman " whilst on its voyage to India. At the road end of this drive was the house of Mr. Jerry Lees, a notable townsman who took a prominent part in the construction of Regent Road, and adjoining this another large residence, occupied for some time by Dr. Crowther, who gave his name to the adjoining street. At the corner of Ordsall Lane was " Barclay Place," where lived Mr. George Bradshaw, the originator of the Railway Guide. Proceeding up the road, where is now Clarence Street was the house of Mr. Alexander Fyfe, the civil engineer, separated by a tree-shaded path leading up the hill from the still existing house shewn on the 1740 plan as in possession of Nathaniel Bolton, but at the time we are now considering, the residence of one Harry Brownbill, a quaint old character as industrious as the day was long, who operated the Tanyard beyond the Barracks. Where now stand the Public Baths was " Ash Cottage," with its " paradise of a garden," as old residents tell, and the residence of Lot Gardner, reputed to be a gentleman of " great accomplishments and able speech," a model merchant, and after Canon Stowell, the best orator in the town. Past the Barracks was an ancient white-washed inn lying in a hollow and with a bowling green attached. From its sign of the ' Lord Nelson," its history as an alehouse presumably dated from the days of Trafalgar. The Free Library now occupies the site, and a still existent group of old cottages known as Brownbill's Fold used to overlook the bowling green and afford entrance to the tanyard. Higher up the road were some large houses in extensive grounds, used as a hospital by the Military, and beyond these, stretching to Goodier's Lane, were the Old Borough Gardens.

---

*John MacGregor (Rob Roy) was born January 24, 1825, and died at Boscombe in 1892. A wrangler at Trinity College, Cambridge, in 1844, he was called to the Bar in 1851, but he did not practise. In the latter year, at the time of the Great Exhibition, he had the inspiration to found the Shoe-black Brigade, to create useful employment in cleaning the muddied boots of visitors to the Exhibition for the slum boys of London who flocked around the entrances begging and making themselves a nuisance. He was the pioneer of canoeing in Britain, making tours throughout European waters in his " Rob Roy " canoe. The account of one of these journeys, published in 1866, as " A Thousand Miles in the Rob Roy Canoe " made him famous.

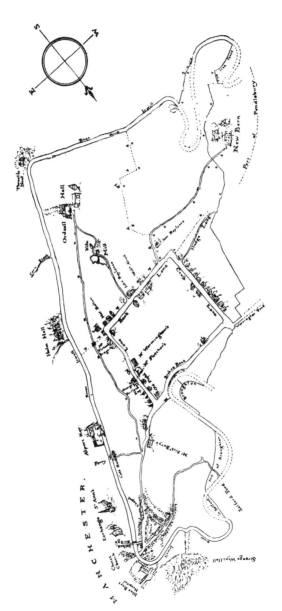

HILL'S PLAN OF SALFORD IN 1741.

On the northern side of Regent Road, between Oldfield Lane and the river, the builder had been busy in the erection of fine blocks of more modest dwellings for the working people of the town. Trafalgar Place and its vicinity may be largely slums to-day, but then they were pleasant enough habitations, and streets are still spoken of by such names as " Well Meadow " that to-day officially bear more prosaic though possibly less inapt designations.

The aforementioned footpath over Ordsall Hill, later made into New Oldfield Road, after passing by " Sunnyside," led to Ordsall Clough, where was the remnant of the Cave, thence by the Skating Pits to Ordsall Lane and Ordsall Gardens—a somewhat notorious pleasure resort. By crossing the fields at the end of the footpath was reached the Fighting Hollow, In this natural green-clothed amphitheatre, for generations would gather farmers and tradesmen, gentry and lads of the town ; aye, and women, too, it is said—patrons of the Fancy all—to watch and cheer, whilst within a roped-in square men strove together with bare fists for a little personal glory and a great love of a manly game.

Do not think, however, that our grandfathers were entirely crude and barbarous in their pleasures. Cock-fighting and prize-fights were by no means their only diversions. They were great horticulturists as well. I have heard old people tell with pride of the splendid kitchen gardens that stretched beyond Ash Cottage Grounds as far as the Barracks wall, tended by working men who spent their leisure thus when their day's work in the factory was done. The popularity of allotments was greater even then than now, and rivalry in the glory of the garden ran high. It was this keen interest, doubtless, that led the Corporation to inaugurate the Peel Park Show, the first municipal enterprise of its kind in the country, and which has now grown into the famous Salford Flower Show, a unique institution for an industrial city.

Almost every working man in those days was an enthusiastic oarsman, and the river bank was lined with numberless boathouses. Of the thrilling contests on the old river and the skill in watermanship shewn by the Salfordians of generations agone, the late Mr. James Corbett has told in his book " The River Irwell." The Salford Regatta was a famous event, and crowds would line the river on both sides of the course between Regent Bridge and Throstle's Nest to watch with keen enthusiasm the best oarsmen of the country in competition, and afterwards join with true Lancashire vim in the revels of the Fair on Sunnyside Fields. Is there any Salfordian even of these later days who does not thrill with pride at the name of Mark Addy, " the Salford Hero," whose heroism has passed into a tradition to inspire for all time the youth of his native town.

The district of Ordsall was in the Parish of Christchurch, and Canon Stowell, realising that he was not persohally able to keep pace with the growing development, began to cast round for ways and means of building a new church to serve the needs of the southern district. A scheme was originated by which a number of moneyed men of the true, practical Christian type undertook to make an annual payment by which a sufficient fund would be raised to build a certain number of churches in the new populous areas. As a result of this, on the 30th day of August, 1841, the foundation stone of the Church of Saint Bartholomew was laid by Squire Egerton, ancestor of the present Lord Egerton of Tatton. Squire Egerton was the ground landlord of the district, and the " beau ideal " of an English country gentleman. Of him it was said that no lordship could have conferred upon him a greater dignity and nobility than he already possessed. Canon Stowell had a curate, whom the late Mr. Hindshaw describes as " a sprightly little fellow ; grave, withal, as a judge ; so solemn that he always looked a sermon before he spoke it ; a plucky, aggressive party who seemed to entertain a correct notion of, and was ready to intimate what your duties were, as well as to act upon what were his." To the Rev. James Moore the worthy Canon committed the charge of the new vineyard, and the task was set about with typical alacrity. It is recounted that he paid a visit to old Dr. Taylor (the famous " Oldfield Lane Doctor "), and made the old bone-setter stare with all his eyes by asking him for £500 towards the erection of the church. On recovering from his surprise and calming down, he gave Mr. Moore a draft for £100. Had he been asked for £100 he would certainly not have given more than £20.

A Sunday School was started in a loft over Brownbill's Tan Yard, whilst money was being gathered for increased and better accommodation. Eventually, and through the munificence of local Churchmen, headed by Squire Egerton,

Day Schools were built in Regent Street and the Egerton Schools in Tatton Street. Later, as the growing demands of the population made it necessary, the Parish of St. Bartholomew became divided, and four daughter churches, with full equipment of schools, now minister to the spiritual needs of the district. Stowell Memorial, as its name indicates, stands to the memory of the great evangelist, whilst the beautiful churches of St. Clement, St. Cyprian and St. Ignatius are the gifts of the Egerton family. There are, in addition, in Ordsall to-day two Roman Catholic Churches and three Free Churches.

About 1850 the great industrial invasion of Ordsall really commenced, pouring a continuous stream of humanity into the district. On every hand the high places literally were being laid low, the crooked places made straight. Every depression in the ground surface was filled in, and on the levelled ground the builder set to work throwing up house after house, and street after street, in interminable sequence. Private mansions were razed, the villas of Regent Road were fronted with shops, the Old Hall itself was hemmed in until streets and cottages took the place of its moat and lawns, and great cotton mills frowned down upon it.

But an even mightier change was still to be effected in South Salford as the great dream to canalise the old river grew gradually nearer to realisation, until the day came when the sea was brought into its very midst, and on the site of the old Milefield where the lads of Ordsall were wont to train their athletic prowess, great ships came sailing into Salford Docks, and the languages of half the world came to mingle with the native tongue.

If the spirit of John Radclyffe ever roams in these later days his manor lands, what must his thoughts be as he ponders on the amazing transformation ? Four-square, his ancient hall still stands as he built it nigh six centuries ago, but sentinelled now by towering mills wherein his own townsfolk weave fabrics more wondrously splendid than ever the looms of Flanders knew, and gazing through the dark lozenged window panes he sees, instead of the high wind-stirred trees of Ordsall Woods, the towering masts of tall sea ships sailing up to his very walls, and bearing thence their cargoes over the horizon to lands he never wot of when first he dreamed in the long ago of founding a race of craftsmen in his own home town. Methinks he'll know he did not dream in vain.

CHAPTER IV

The Religious Revival of the Nineteenth Century.

IF it is in times of crisis that a man often finds his soul, there is no doubt the series of deep-stirring national events that marked the later Georgian era bred in the English nation a new moral earnestness that swung the pendulum in full from frivolity to a new puritanical enthusiasm. John Wesley had kindled a new sense of personal religion, but it remained for the blasphemous antics of the revolutionaries of Paris and the threat of French invasion to startle Englishmen from the religious apathy of the previous century, and to rouse in them a new crusading spirit for duty, decency, and the things of God. From the highest to the lowest, the people were moved with a deep strain of evangelical piety, too full and overflowing to be contained within a National Church, weakened by subservience to the State and the spirit of preceding times. We learn from one authority that in the Sabbath Schools now beginning to be established, " anxious listeners at first, and then zealous proselytes, were drawn thence from cottages in quiet nooks and dingles . . . working men were often found to possess a rude poetic talent which rendered them popular preachers."

These Sabbath Schools were first introduced into Salford in September of 1786, and they rapidly gained public favour. They bred many an earnest man who, filled with missionary fervour, sought to appease the spiritual desire of the expanding populace by the establishment of a multiplicity of mission schools and conventicles.

One of the most curious of these was established by William Cowherd, a man of many accomplishments and professions, who was described in the journals of that day as " classical scholar, chemist, author, preacher, astronomer, student of optics, and doctor." Formerly an Anglican curate, he fell under the influence of Swedenborg, whose writings he assisted to translate into English. In 1800 he left the Church and built for himself a meeting-place in King Street, where he drew around him a devoted band of adherents. It was at first known as " Christ Church," but Cowherd objected to churches being called " by the names of men," and in 1809 he began to describe his sect as Bible Christians, imposing on his members that they should abstain from flesh foods and from intoxicating liquors. Thus there were formed in this Salford chapel the very first vegetarian and teetotal societies of the western world, and from here was published by Joseph Brotherton, then officiating as minister to the congregation, the first tract on temperance.

Cowherd died in March, 1816, and was buried in the churchyard in King Street, his tomb, at his own request, being inscribed : "All feared, none loved, few understood." The following year, 1817, forty members of the Salford organisation landed in Philadelphia and founded a Bible Christian Church in that city. Thus the principles of vegetarianism were first introduced to America, eventually leading Dr. Kellog to conceive the idea of the great sanitarium at Battle Creek.

A local news sheet of September, 1804, contains the following :—

" Common decency has rarely been more wantonly outraged than on Thursday se'nnight, at the burial ground of Queen Street Chapel, Salford. The corpse of a young woman having been brought there for interment, a dispute respecting the grave took place between the friends of the deceased and the attendants of the chapel, when a scene of uproar and brutality took place among the lowly mansions of the dead which would have disgraced the most barbarous times. The degrading spectacle continued for more than an hour, and terminated in the preparation of a new grave and interring the body without the sacred rites being performed. A man is said to have had one of his ears nearly bitten off by an adversary in this violent affray."

All over the town churches and chapels of varied denominations came rapidly into being. A Salford Dorcas Society was formed in 1822 ; two years later, at a meeting in Gravel Lane, a Samaritan Society for the relief of distress was formed. In 1835 the Order of Rechabites came into being at a meeting held at Meadowcroft's Temperance Hotel in Bolton Street. The Humane Society for the Hundred of Salford was founded at the instance of Thos. Butterworth Bayley in 1797.

One winter's morning in the "twenties," as the Yorkshire stage drove into Salford and pulled up for a change of horses at the King's Head Yard, it bore amongst its passengers a young Manx clergyman on his way to take up his first curacy at Huddersfield, and as he gazed from his high-perched seat over the mushroom growth of small houses wrapped in November mist, he was heard to declare his thankfulness that his pastoral charge lay elsewhere. But the hand of Fate takes little account of our likes and dislikes, and Hugh Stowell little knew that within that self-same town of Salford the die of his ministerial career was already cast, and that there he would labour with great gladness as the Rector of Christ Church in Acton Place for a space of more than forty years. In 1826 he began his connection with the town as Rector of St. Stephen's, and two years later took to wife a Salford girl, the daughter of Mr. Richard Ashworth, barrister, of Pendleton. In a vault beneath the church where he so long officiated lie his remains, and the graceful Romanesque spire rising above The Crescent and the Stowell Memorial Church in the Eccles New Road keep alive the name and fame of one of the most dominant forces in the evangelical movement of the century.

The passing of the Catholic Relief Act in 1829 was another indication of the spirit of tolerance which was taking possession of public opinion in all matters of religious life. Roman Catholics were admitted to the full rights of citizenship, and permitted to organise themselves territorially.

Although there must have been in Salford and its immediate environs a large number of adherents of the Roman Church throughout the seventeenth and eighteenth centuries, no Catholic Church is known to have existed in the town, those who held to that faith presumably meeting in secret. With the passing of the 1829 Act, two Sunday Schools were established, one in Bury Street and the other in Charlestown, yet several years were to elapse before the Catholics of Salford were in a position to build a Church. In October, 1843, in a school chapel built on the spot now occupied by the chancel of St. John's Cathedral, Mass was publicly celebrated in Salford for the first time since the Reformation. Inspired by Dr. Sharples, co-adjutor bishop in the Lancashire district, it was determined to erect within Salford a great church worthy in due course to become the cathedral of a Roman Catholic diocese covering the Hundreds of Salford and Blackburn.

Planned by M. E. Hadfield, the foundation stone of the church was laid in the Whit-week of 1844, and although opened in August, 1848, it was not actually completed until 1853. By a striking coincidence, the building of this, the first post-Reformation Roman Catholic Church in Salford was begun in the same year that Salford was incorporated.

With unprecedented solemnity, eight bishops and 130 priests taking part in the ceremonial, in the presence of the Earl of Arundel and Surrey, Sir Thomas and Lady de Trafford, and all the Catholic gentry of the county, the Church of St. John the Evangelist was formally opened. In the course of his sermon, Dr. (afterwards Cardinal) Wiseman said that this fine church, so reminiscent of the noblest Catholic traditions, would be found worthy of the great events soon to take place within its walls. Here stood—built by the pence of the people and the pounds of the gentry—a church worthy of being a cathedral—but three years were to elapse before this proud ambition was realised.

After the ceremony, the bishops met in the Salford Town Hall to consider the advance made towards the creation of a Roman Catholic hierarchy in England and Wales, and to determine their future policy. On December 29, 1850, the Roman Catholic Diocese of Salford came definitely into being, and on June 25, 1851, Dr. William Turner, who had been appointed by the Pope to be the first Bishop of Salford, was consecrated in St. John's Cathedral by Cardinal Wiseman. Dr. Sharples, the builder of the cathedral, was originally chosen for the office of bishop, but he died on the eve of the issue of the Papal Bull.

St. John's Cathedral, with its 240 ft. high spire, one of the most familiar landmarks of the city, is a noble edifice which ranks amongst the scarce architectural glories of modern Salford, and would perhaps attract greater attention were it not hidden on one side by unsightly property. Perhaps in the near future this may be removed, and with the completion of the still unfinished Cathedral House, the final worthy touches given to an imposing pile. The Cathedral is in the Decorated style, with a sanctuary of three bays, the groined roof of which is copied from that of Sawley Abbey ; at the back of the High Altar is a magnificently-canopied screen in Caen stone, 34 ft. high ; between the bays of the sanctuary, on corbels surmounted by richly-crocketed canopies are figures of SS. George, Augustine, Jerome, Edward, Ambrose and Gregory ; the east window, of seven lights, is 40 ft. high. The Chapel of the Blessed Sacrament, built in 1884, forms a south transept, divided from the main building by a wrought-iron screen, and is beautifully enriched with an elaborate treatment in marble and alabaster ; against the south wall is a large picture symbolic of prayer. At the east end of the north choir aisles is the Lee Chantry, founded by Daniel Lee, Esq., J.P., whose canopied tomb occupies a recess in the north wall. On the south side of the Lady Chapel is the Leeming Chantry, founded by John Leeming, Esq., another great benefactor to the Church, who is buried within. Around the clerestory of the Cathedral are ranged the arms and mottoes of the various Roman Catholic bishops associated with Lancashire from early times.

Adjoining the Cathedral is what was formerly the Bishop's House, but is now the administrative headquarters for the Salford Diocese. Bishop Turner's official residence was at Marlborough House, New Windsor, on part of the site now occupied by the Royal Technical College.

The See of Salford has been successively occupied by eminent men. Dr. Turner was succeeded by Dr. Herbert Vaughan (later Cardinal Archbishop of Westminster, and whose memory will always be cherished for his noble efforts in the cause of the denominational schools, the Education Act of 1902 being largely the fruits of his labours. The third bishop was Dr. Bilsborrow, who was succeeded in 1903 by one whose world-wide fame as a classical scholar was only equalled by the reverent regard in which he was held by all classes of the local community, irrespective of creed—Dr. Louis Charles Casartelli. The present bishop, who worthily sustains the high esteem of his predecessors, is Dr. Thomas Henshaw, who may be claimed as a Salfordian entire, inasmuch as he was born at Swinton and received his education at the Salford Grammar School attached to the Cathedral.

In the general process of moral improvement there naturally arose a strong desire for a wider system of popular education. For centuries the people had been content to remain illiterate ; the arts of clerkship were irrelevant to the common life as they pursued and understood it. In places, the Elizabethan Grammar Schools, privately established and endowed, kept steadily aflame the light of learning, and "in every village marked with little spire, there dwelt in lowly shed and mean attire " private schools where the unruly youth of the community were trained with book and birch. Amidst the welter of social and political unrest evoked by the French wars, the Church awoke to her ancient office as the teacher of the people, and as in the old days she had gathered her children within the monastery walls to read, learn, and inwardly digest, so now, in the nineteenth century, she interpreted the spirit of the new renaissance by providing the first elementary schools.

It is probable that schools fulfilling the needs of their times have always existed in Salford, from the first early beginnings when the Chantry Priest, in the time he could spare from his priestly office, devoted himself to instructing the youth of the town. An entry in the Port Mote Records tells of Sir John Radclyffe requiring the repair of the road to Ordsall that " his littel babes " might go with safety " to school at William Debdale's," and in the eighteenth century there was the well-known school of the Rev. John Clayton at the corner of Gravel Lane, called St. Cyprian's. It is interesting to know that we have still in existence in the city one of the first voluntary elementary schools—the National School in Great George Street. This was built in 1812 and organized on the lines laid down by the great pioneer of popular education, Dr. Andrew Bell. It was known at first as the " Model School," and people came from far and near to inspect and study its organisation.

In the same street stands another monument of the earnest desire for enlightenment in those stressful days, the original buildings of the Salford Working Men's College. Along with its companion Pendleton Mechanics' Institute, in Gardner Street, these establishments had their genesis in gatherings of working men paying a small weekly subscription to provide themselves with a meeting place for study and a reading room where books and newspapers they could not afford of themselves would be available for common use.

The Salford Working Men's College was established at a meeting held in the Mayor's Parlour at the Town Hall, in May, 1858. For some years before this there was in existence near Trinity Church a Mechanics' Institute, the success of which prompted its members to the idea of forming a College " to enable working men to improve their education and acquire knowledge." Under the leadership of Mr. E. R. Langworthy the scheme quickly matured, and not for the first time did Salford become a pioneer. The College was confined to students over 18 years of age, and instruction was provided in book-keeping, mathematics, Latin and French, grammar, composition and elocution, mechanical and general drawing, chemistry, geography, geology and natural history. The College was to be self-supporting, each student paying 1s. 6d. subscription for a term of three months, and an additional fee of 6d. per term per class. A novel feature was that the students were given the power of electing representatives on the Council of Management. In its first year the College enrolled over 300 students, most of whom attended during the evenings only. Within its walls were trained many men who rose by its aid from humble beginnings to worthily play their parts in the Borough affairs, and in an even wider sphere. Amongst them were Dr. William Diggle and his brother, whose home was a cottage on the canal side at New Windsor, and both of whom achieved distinguished careers in the Church, the former becoming Lord Bishop of Carlisle.

Although the buildings still stand, the College ceased its useful activities some years ago, but the work of technical education is carried on in the splendid buildings in Peel Park of the Royal Technical College, opened by the present King and Queen, when Duke and Duchess of York, in 1896. What a great service to the still urgent necessity for adult education would be rendered could the old Salford Lyceum be revived and housed in the Great George Street building.

To-day Salford has 129 elementary schools, four central schools and seven secondary schools, all organised and conducted on the most up-to-date systems. As she has led the way educationally in the past, Salford still maintains her reputation. In the finely-equipped Nursery School in Hulme Street she has established another " Model School," visited from all over the country and abroad by those who are anxious to learn from this pioneer of how to care for children, educationally and physically, during their nursery days.

May the new generations, in their wider opportunities through the wonderful educational equipment of the city to-day, shew results at least equal to those of the past.

At present (1930) the Salford educational system is in

process of complete revision in accordance with the Hadow Report. A striking commentary on the development of public education during the last half-century is seen in the comparison of figures for the Education Rate. In 1880 the Salford School Board's expenditure was £5,500. The estimates for the financial year 1930–31 reach a total of over quarter a million pounds.

If there is one institution more than another that claims the unbounded affection of all Salfordians it is that noble house of healing—the Salford Royal Hospital. The organised treatment of the sick as a communal task was first inaugurated at a meeting held 6th of May, 1790, when it was resolved to institute a hospital. Patients were at first attended at their own homes till a house was taken near Salford Bridge. In 1795, the Bath Inn, at the Lady Pirle Well, was purchased for £1,800 and fitted up as a lying-in hospital. A Ladies' Auxiliary provided bed linen to those in need of it, and clothes for new-born infants. This hospital was in 1856 removed to Manchester and re-named St. Mary's Hospital. In May, 1827, on a requisition signed by thirty gentlemen, the Borough Reeve and Constables of Salford and the Constables of Pendleton called a town's meeting, at which it was resolved to establish a general hospital for the relief of the sick poor of the town. A building in Bank Parade was taken and opened in September of the same year. The first president was Mr. William Garnett, of Lark Hill. Mr. Thomas Heywood, of Swinton Park, the eldest brother of Sir Benjamin Heywood, and an accomplished antiquary, was the first treasurer. One of the first physicians was Dr. Thomas Harland, of Bank Street, who had an extensive practice in Salford and the surrounding towns, and was married to a niece of Mr. John Dugdale. Harland was a member of the medical staff for 45 years, but Mr. John Boutflower, one of the original surgeons of the Hospital, who died in 1889, served on the staff for the remarkable period of 62 years, and his son, Mr. Andrew Boutflower, still continues the unbroken record of his family's service to the Hospital of over a century. Mr. John Bout-flower came to Salford early in the century to take over the practice of Dr. Drinkwater in Greengate. The " Good Samaritan " window in the main corridor of the Hospital was erected by Mr. Boutflower from a legacy left him by an appreciative patient. In 1829 a plot of land at the corner of

Adelphi Street was acquired from the Duchy of Lancaster at an annual ground rent of £29 10s., and the first stone of the original portion of the present hospital was laid on April 23, 1830. King George IV. authorised the designation of "Royal" to be used in the title of the Hospital, and became a subscriber of 25 guineas a year. This subscription was continued by William IV., and by each succeeding Sovereign.

Many of the most distinguished names in the Salford of the last century have been associated with the Hospital, and rich was the measure in which it was remembered in the benefactions of a past generation. The most notable of these was that of Mr. John Pendlebury, whose executors, in 1885, handed to the Trustees the sum of £28,275, which made possible the great extension from 62 to 127 beds. From 1836 to 1872, Mr. Humphrey Nicholls, an eccentric but most excellent gentleman, whose habit it was to call upon the secretaries of certain charities and leave rolls of bank-notes, endowed the Hospital with money and properties totalling in all over £16,000. Besides its generous friends amongst local magnates, a succession of whom would be more than welcomed to-day, "Salford Royal" has had, in the past, some quaint receipts. In 1837, the Salford Reform Association gave £46 10s. as proceeds "for shewing the Pavilion"—whatever that may have been—and in the same year, the Stewards of the Conservative Ball contributed £60. A Mr. Ormerod gave £6—wagers won on Mr. Brotherton's election ; and in 1840 a guinea was received from a person for "an assault on the House Surgeon." In 1850, £1,000 was received on the dissolution of the Society for the Prosecution of Felons ; £765 was handed over as the proceeds of a Ball, and £1,200 came in 1869 from the balance of the Lord Mayor of London's Cotton Famine Relief Fund. A new ward was endowed, at a cost of over £20,000, subscribed by the citizens, as a memorial to the Salford men who gave their lives in the Great War of 1914–1918. This was opened by the Duke of York in November, 1922.

The total number of patients treated at the Hospital since its opening in 1827 has been 1,639,719 ; the average annual number at present being 49,885. Despite the fact that the city possesses in the Hope Infirmary one of the largest hospital units in the country, as well as Municipal Hospitals at Ladywell, Drinkwater Park, Nab Top and Seedley Terrace, the service of Salford Royal to the city and the districts for miles around grows with the years, and a vast new extension is now projected. Let the citizens of this great city see to it that they are no less mindful of the cause of suffering humanity than their fathers were, and by their benefactions help to make their Hospital as noble a monument to twentieth century Salford as during the nineteenth it has given the retort direct to those who would credit that period with nothing but selfish materialism.

That infantile welfare is now a subject commanding the earnest attention of the whole nation is a further credit that belongs to Salford. The Salford Ladies' Public Health Society was founded by a number of public-spirited women of the city who, by the establishment of Maternity Centres and Day Nurseries, served by the highest medical and nursing skill, pioneered a work amongst their poorer-circumstanced sisters which, by their efforts, has now become regarded as one of the nation's chief obligations.

To enumerate all the social effort that is being carried on in what one distinguished lady worker calls "this very live and human Salford of ours," would fill a volume in itself, and probably in no city in the land can a finer record be shewn. To care for the sick and needy and those who fall by the wayside has ever been the truest religious expression. God grant that Salford men and women will never be one whit less responsive to like service in His Name in the future than in the past.

The following list indicates the settlement of the various Nonconformist Churches in Salford :—

1790.—Wesleyan Methodists. Gravel Lane Chapel.

1797.—Congregationalists. One John Joule built a chapel at New Windsor. Services held in 1817 in the Cloth Hall led to the formation of a church in Chapel Street, a secession from which resulted in the foundation of the Richmond Church.

1807.—Independent Methodists formed a church in Cook Street.

1809.—Bible Christians, founded by William Cowherd, in King Street.

1812.—Unitarians built a chapel in Jackson's Square (now covered by Exchange Station).

1815.—Swedenborgians had a New Jerusalem Church in Bolton Street.

1824.—Welsh Calvinistic Independents took over the
    Unitarian Chapel in Jackson's Square, the latter
    body having built a new church in Dawson's
    Croft.

1833.—Baptists established a church in Great George Street.

1847.—Presbyterian Church of England built a church in
    Chapel Street.

1866.—Welsh Calvinistic Methodists built Salem Chapel
    in Rigby Street.

1869.—Primitive Methodists took over the King Street
    Chapel on removal of Bible Christians to Cross
    Lane.

CHAPTER V

The Social and Political Developments of the Nineteenth Century.

WHEN, in January, 1805, incendiaries set fire to Ollivant's factory in Bury Street, and to Rowleys' Mill in Oldfield Lane, it was symptomatic of the unsettled condition of the poorer classes at that time. The " Industrial Revolution " had, indeed, increased national prosperity, but it brought no small amount of individual misery in its train. For centuries the back-bone of the community had been the sturdy master-craftsmen, weaving their own designs into cloth on their own hand-looms, as their fourteenth century forbears had been taught by the first settlers from Flanders. With the coming of the steam engine and the power loom there was no longer a market for the more costly, although more durable, hand-woven cloths, and the hand-loom weavers were forced into becoming slaves of the factory, their independence killed, their spirit broken, their prosperity vanished. The minds which had found active expression in creative artistry on their own looms were driven to more sinister designs as the factory bell rang them in at five in the morning to serve the undiscriminating god of cheap production enthroned on the power loom.

There was famine, too, to add to the prevalent distress. A series of bad harvests and poor seasons increased the price of food and dimmed the agricultural outlook. Into the towns came a constant stream of men of the plough, with their families, seeking—vainly enough—a better job in the factories. Natural resources decreasing, manufacturing production overserved, food at a premium, and wages lowered by the surplus of cheap labour, starvation stalked menacingly through the towns of Lancashire.

Under ordinary circumstances Government action would have relieved the situation, but the shadow of Napoleon lay heavy on the land and engrossed all the attention of the State. But starvation is a hard master, and, deprived of natural relief, in Salford, as in all the manufacturing towns, men turned to riot to vent their distress, and avidly seized upon the suggestions of the politicians that these evils would all be removed by a reform in parliamentary representation. From the labouring classes in Lancashire came a loud and importunate demand for the supreme legislative power—the power of universal suffrage. This agitation had its culmination in the unfortunate events of August 16, 1819, at St. Peter's Fields in Manchester. Deep gloom seized upon the public mind and party animosity reigned triumphant. With the accession of George IV., whose coronation was celebrated by a gorgeous procession through the town and great festivities at Salford Cross, symptoms of returning prosperity caused a moderation of political ardour, and plans began to be developed for improving the town.

Within a year or two, however, dispiritedness fell again on the whole country, and a mysterious sickness claimed an increasing toll of victims in the insanitary purlieus of the badly-built and huddled-up industrial districts. Out of the depression felt by agricultural and manufacturing interests alike rose again the cry of Reform " and when, in 1831, a new Parliament was elected, after an excess of rioting that shook the whole land, it was pledged to the hilt to the passage of a Reform Bill. In this Parliament we, in Salford, have a particular interest, inasmuch as the representatives of Lancashire therein were Lord Stanley (afterwards the thirteenth Earl of Derby), and one of our own townsmen, Mr. Benjamin Heywood, of Claremont. It is recorded that, following the election at Lancaster, Mr. Heywood returned with a great cavalcade of friends, and was met at Irlams-o'-th'- Height by a procession of one hundred horsemen and many carriages. At Pendleton, two bands and a multitude of persons on foot, carrying flags, joined the procession. " When the procession had passed beyond The Crescent the crowds became more dense at every step, and the scene presented by that part of the road, from the movement of the procession and the animation of the people, was exceedingly striking, whilst the effect was considerably heightened by the church bells at that moment commencing merry peals."

Mr. Heywood's parliamentary career was a short one as, owing to ill-health, he did not offer himself at the 1832 election, but he successfully pleaded the claim of Salford to one member of its own, and rendered invaluable assistance in the drafting of the other Lancashire divisions.

OLD BLACKFRIARS BRIDGE.

In December, 1832, therefore, the newly-enfranchised Borough of Salford proceeded to elect its first representative. There were two candidates. The Conservatives nominated Mr. William Garnett, of Lark Hill, "a gentleman of unblemished integrity and moral worth, well known for his strong Conservative views in politics and his munificent hospitality, delighting to gather his friends around the table of his spacious dining-room." The Radicals put forward Mr. Joseph Brotherton, the minister of the Bible Christian Church. It was an exciting time this election. Heads were broken in violent scuffles, especially in the neighbourhood of Oldfield Lane, where the Conservatives had their headquarters at the Spinners' Arms. The election lasted two days, and cost in expenses £250 15s. 6d. Mr. Brotherton was elected by a majority of 194, the figures at the close of the poll being : Brotherton, 712 ; Garnett, 518.

In 1835, after Melbourne's abrupt dismissal, Mr. John Dugdale was the Conservative nominee, but again Mr. Brotherton was elected. Two years later Mr. Garnett came forward again and was only beaten by the narrow margin of two votes. It is a tradition that at this election Mr. Garnett voted for his opponent, but at the persuasion of his friends Mr. Brotherton voted for himself, and thus secured the verdict.

For twenty-five years Mr. Brotherton continued to represent the Borough, until his death, which occurred with painful suddenness in an omnibus as he was journeying along The Crescent on January 7, 1857. Only five days previously he was inspecting the new cemetery at Mode Wheel, and chose his own burial space ; and there he was laid to rest, the first interment in that vast " God's Acre," where now over 280,000 of his fellow-townsfolk sleep their last around him. A fine monument was erected over his grave, and a statue to his memory in Peel Park bears his now world-famous utterance in the House of Commons :—

" My riches consist not in the abundance of my possessions but in the fewness of my wants."

In 1843 Mr. Garnett was appointed High Sheriff, an office previously occupied in 1801 by Colonel Ackers, also of Lark Hill. Processions were the delight of those days, and we are told, as illustrating the high esteem in which Mr. Garnett was held, that on setting out from Lark Hill to attend the assizes he was accompanied by " a most splendid procession, consisting of upwards of sixty carriages containing several hundred gentlemen of all shades of politics, also the various town's officers."

The Reform Bill of 1867 gave Salford two members, and at the election in that year two Conservatives, Mr. C. E. Cawley and Mr. W. T. Charley were returned. By the Reform Bill of 1885 the representation of the Borough was again increased, and the three constituencies of North Salford, South Salford and West Salford formed ; the fluctuations of political fortune falling in the ensuing election on two Liberals and one Conservative.

In his novel " Sybil," Disraeli has sketched most realistically, from his own observations, the life of the people in the Lancashire manufacturing towns during the early years of the reign of Queen Victoria. Gradually—slowly perhaps, but none the less surely—improvements in life and living were taking place, due to the growing prosperity of industry and the effect of ameliorative social effort. The history of Salford during this period is a perfect reflex of what was generally taking place, and it reveals that despite occasional setbacks, and political disputes such as the Chartist riots and the Fenian outrages and disturbances, a higher standard and greater happiness of life and living was becoming effective amongst the industrial population. In Peel Park stands a monument to the great agitation that occupied the years from 1839 to 1846—the statue of Sir Robert Peel, bearing as inscription the words he uttered before quitting office after he had carried through the Repeal of the Corn Laws :—

> " It may be that I shall leave a name sometimes remembered with expressions of goodwill in the abodes of those whose lot it is to labour, and to earn their daily bread by the sweat of their brow, when they shall recruit their exhausted strength with abundant and untaxed food—the sweeter because it is no longer leavened by the sense of injustice."

In the Coalition Government of 1919–1923 Salford had the honour of providing a Cabinet Minister, when Sir Montague Barlow, K.B.E., the representative of South Salford, became Minister of Labour.

CHAPTER VI

Peel Park and the Irwell Floods.

WHAT caused more excitement and concern to the good folk of Salford than the exigencies of politics were the floods which regularly, at varying intervals, would inundate the lower-lying portions of the town. The old river, winding its sluggish way, nowadays hardly seems capable of anything approaching a flood, but even within fairly recent times it has very thoroughly lived up to its name of " the winding torrent."

There is on record an extraordinary flood in 1616, called from the day " Lambard's Flood," in which the water suddenly rose many yards " plumme above the ordinary course," that men stood on Salford Bridge and laded up water with a little piggin, which called forth the pious reflection : " It is an easy matter with God to drowne a towne ; yea, a world." And there was, too, the great flood of 1649.

In 1837 the old river rose to such a height that New Bayley Street was under water, and cattle, furniture, and even a baby in its cradle were washed down the river. Mrs. Linnaeus Banks has made use of this incident in one of her well-known novels. Three years later there was another flood that did enormous damage, and in 1843 a temporary footbridge near the New Bayley was washed away by the force of the waters. For a short space the river behaved itself ; a temporary respite that was broken by another severe inundation in February of 1852. All floods within the last century sink into insignificance beside that of 1866, a year that old inhabitants still refer to as " the year of the Great Flood." On Tuesday, November 13, rain began to fall, and continued without ceasing for three whole days. At seven o'clock on the Friday morning the gardeners were walking along the footpaths in Peel Park, and three hours later the same footpaths were three feet under water. By six o'clock that night the river had risen fourteen feet above its normal level. Mills on the river bank were brought to a standstill, and the workers had to escape as best they could. At noon,

I

the house of the head gardener in Peel Park was inaccessible, the greenhouses were completely wrecked, and the gardener and his family had to be rescued from the roof of the house by boat. Between The Crescent and Broughton Suspension Bridge stretched one great sheet of water ; down Lower Broughton Road poured a swiftly-flowing river, and even in Strangeways, from Grove Street to the Assize Courts, water was knee high by noon. Residents in the Polygon had to take boats to the Griffin Hotel to join the omnibuses, but ere long the omnibuses ceased to run. As the early winter darkness fell, grave terror came upon the Lower Broughton district. The street lamps could not be lighted, and by the eerie flickering glow of torches, rescue parties in carts and boats, headed by the Mayor (Mr. Pochin), working with frenzied zeal, succeeded in delivering seven hundred people from their wrecked homes to comfort and shelter hastily and readily improvised at the Town Hall, the Workhouse, the Gas Offices and St. John's Catholic Schools. Only one life was lost. A man tried to make his way across Duke Street, opposite Grosvenor Terrace ; loosing his footing, he was swept away and drowned. His body was seen floating about the water that covered a field in the neighbourhood, but it was impossible to reach it.

By Saturday morning the danger began to subside, and on Sunday the angry river was back in its ordinary course. Over eleven hundred acres of land in Salford was flooded, and property valued at over a million pounds was destroyed or largely ruined, whilst a grave danger to public health arose from the deposits of sludge left all over the flooded area. An obelisk erected in Peel Park marks the height the flood reached at that point.

The construction of the Ship Canal has largely solved the question of such a disaster recurring, there being now an ample channel below Regent Bridge to provide an outlet for any excessive downstream flood. The upper reaches of the river could be effectively controlled and made to provide revenue and delightful recreation for the people if the late Mr. James Corbett's scheme for a Salford water park was carried into effect. This scheme embodies the creation of a series of six-mile-long pools from Ringley Fold to the Adelphi Weir, each pool emptying into the one beneath it by sluices, and thus by daily flooding with new water gradually effecting the purification of the river. The Salford Council, ever since their first incorporation in 1844, have creditably devoted themselves to preventing the pollution of the river by manufacturers, and by constructing the first municipal works for the treatment of sewage, they set an example to all other authorities in the watershed who were pouring their untreated sewage into a stream that less than a century ago flowed through Salford almost as pure and unfouled as the moorland spring in which it has its birth in the hills above Bacup. In 1862 the Corporation of Salford promoted an Act of Parliament enabling them to establish a River Conservancy Committee and to take proceedings against anyone polluting the river. They appointed the first river inspector, and adopted measures which considerably stopped the abuse. It was largely through these pioneer efforts that in 1891 a wider authority came into being in the Mersey and Irwell Joint Conservancy Board.

Peel Park entered into the possession of the Corporation in 1846. In the year 1835, through the exertions of the Member for Salford—Mr. Joseph Brotherton—Mr. J. Silk Buckingham and Sir Thomas Potter, of Buile Hill, a Bill was passed through Parliament enabling local authorities to provide public parks and levy a rate for their maintenance, and in 1841 Parliament went so far in encouragement of local effort as to grant the sum of £10,000 to be distributed amongst those towns which sought to provide themselves with public parks. Carlyle lent the advocacy of his pen to the movement urging the setting apart of some "green ground with trees upon it, for the summer holidays and evenings of industrious men." The burgesses of Salford and Manchester, in August, 1844, held a joint public meeting, as a result of which two estates were bought in Manchester, and in Salford the Lark Hill estate was purchased from Mr. William Garnett, who was retiring to his Westmoreland seat of Quernmore.

Lark Hill—delightfully suggestive name—occupied the site of Acres Hall, the ancient home of the Acres family, and hereon, in 1792, Colonel James Ackers, a distinguished local merchant prince, built the comfortable-looking Georgian mansion destined later to become the first Free Library. It was purchased by Mr. Garnett in 1826, and he agreed to sell to the Parks Committee for £5,000, less £500, which he deducted as his subscription to the fund. A grant was made by the Government, and Sir Robert Peel himself subscribed £1,000. On Saturday, August 22, 1846, the Park was opened with great festivities and handed over to the Corporation. Out of compliment to the Prime Minister it was named Peel Park. Shortly afterwards, the original seven acres of Lark Hill were enlarged by the purchase of 25 acres of meadowland adjoining, from Mr. J. P. Fitzgerald, at £235 an acre, and in 1869 a further five acres were purchased at £500 an acre for the purposes of cricket and similar games. In 1896, by the gift of the David Lewis Trustees, a further 25 acres adjoining Peel Park were presented to the Corporation for a recreation ground. In 1900 the 18 acres of the Meadows were acquired, and in 1910–12, fourteen and a half acres at Wallness and Broken Bank were added. There cannot be many industrial cities with almost 100 acres of open park-land in their very heart, and the impression this creates is well borne out by the remark of a Swiss lady visiting the city recently when she said that Salford was the only town in England that conveyed the idea of *une grande terre.*

On many occasions Peel Park has been visited by Royal and distinguished people. The notable visit of Queen Victoria and Prince Albert in 1851 has already been referred to elsewhere in these pages, and a second visit was paid in May, 1857, when His Royal Highness unveiled the statue of the Queen, which had been erected to commemorate Her Majesty's earlier visit. "It is with pleasure," Prince Albert said, "that I inaugurate this statue which loyalty has erected on the spot where the Queen met for the first time your Town Council, in the presence of 80,000 children enjoying the blessings of school education . . . May succeeding generations, seeing the Queen's statue in the midst of this park, find in contemplation an assurance that where loyalty and attachment to the Sovereign as the representative of the institutions of the country are linked to an ardent love of progress, founded upon self-reliance and self-improvement, a country cannot fail to prosper under favour of the Almighty."

In July, 1869, the park was visited by the Prince and Princess of Wales, on which occasion it is recorded that the Princess wore "a short costume dress of blue satin, flounced half-way up the skirt with a white grenadine tunic, over which was a blue sash en panier. Her bonnet was likewise of blue, trimmed with lace." In those days the dress of the mere male called for attention equally with that of the ladies, and we are told that the Prince " was dressed in a frock coat of the fashionable blue and light trousers, and wore a black hat." A striking feature of the proceedings, which caused the Princess to exclaim, "What a pretty sight," was the guard of beauty comprised of 33 young ladies of the best families in the town " uniformly attired in dresses of white net trimmed with mauve ruches and fringes, and blonde lace bonnets trimmed with mauve and wild roses," and each holding a choice bouquet. As King Edward VII. and Queen Alexandra the park was honoured by a further visit in 1905.

On November 30, 1860, the Empress of the French visited the park, and that the ancient spirit of chivalry still flourished in the town is shewn by an incident that happened on that occasion. The day was wet, the road was muddy, but with a gallantry that would not have been surpassed by the worthy courtier of Queen Bess, a well-known gentleman of the town doffed his overcoat for the Empress to step upon as she alighted from her carriage.

Benjamin Disraeli was a visitor in April, 1872, and the suitability of Salford as the venue of a Great Exhibition Hall was first mooted by the Earl of Derby on his visit to the park in 1874.

Their Majesties King George the Fifth and Queen Mary have twice visited Peel Park, the first occasion in 1896, as Duke and Duchess of York, to open the Royal Technical College, and again after their ascent to the throne in 1913, when they were received in a wonderful pavilion of blue and gold on the very spot where Queen Victoria and Prince Albert had been received sixty-two years before. Here, too, H.R.H. the Prince of Wales was received on his visit in 1921.

The visits of Queen Victoria were commemorated by the erection of the Victoria Arch at the eastern entrance to the park, from a design by T. G. Barker, a Salford architect. The western entrance is through some handsome wrought-iron gates, made in Rome, and presented to the city by the Earl of Ducie on the demolition of Strangeways Hall.

The fine statue of Queen Victoria in white Sicilian marble is faced by a similar one of the Prince Consort, erected in

1874.   On the eastern terrace are statues of Sir Robert Peel,
in bronze (erected in 1852) ; of Joseph Brotherton, in bronze
(erected 1858), and of Richard Cobden, in Campanella marble
(erected 1867).   Curiously enough, all the statues are by the
same sculptor—Matthew Noble.   On the same terrace, and
forming with the statues a sculptured collective grouping of
the three estates of the realm—Royalty, the middle classes,
and the industrials—are two figures, one of the boy shoeblack,
and the other, the work of an operative carver of the town, a
life-like presentment of the old-time boy chimney sweep.

CHAPTER VII

A City of Achievements.

THE development of Salford during the last century has been rather akin to that of the celebrated literary character who " just growed." In consequence, there is ample ground for quite reasonable criticism of it as haphazard and one-sided. Nevertheless, although there is very much to deplore, there is, at the same time, quite a great deal of cause for wholesome pride in the pioneer spirit that has been very markedly manifested in numerous phases of its administration. Not once, but over and over again during the last hundred years Salford has stood in the vanguard of progress, beckoning onward to wider visions and expanding traditions. Yet so strangely content have we been to let our light stay hidden under the proverbial bushel that it is small wonder little is known of what has been attempted and done, and Salford is casually dismissed in the popular mind as a soulless and sordid product of the industrial age. The community that hesitates to show a legitimate pride in its own accomplishments has only itself to blame when it is ignored or despised. Let us review, therefore, some of our city's more notable achievements in an otherwise depressing period.

Every schoolboy has learned that Pall Mall, in London, was the first street in the world to be lit by coal gas. This credit actually belongs to our own Chapel Street. When Winser was commencing his breathless campaign to persuade London to the advantages of utilising the discoveries of Lebon, and Sir Walter Scott in literary circles and Sir Humphrey Davy amongst the scientists were pouring ridicule upon the project which even Napoleon described as *une grande folie*, a Salford manufacturer, Mr. George Lee, of the firm of Phillips & Lee, had arranged with William Murdoch the inventor of the art of coal-gas manufacture, to light his house in Chapel Street and portions of his cotton mills (now known as Trinity House) with the new illuminant. By 1807, the year in which Winser succeeded in lighting Pall Mall, the whole of these mills and the neighbouring Chapel Street were already lighted by gas. In 1809, on the occasion of the Royal Jubilee, a vast crown, with innumerable jets, was erected on the roof of the mill, and presented, when lighted up, an object so exceedingly beautiful that it has been said so fine a display of ornamental illumination has never since been seen.

Ten years later, the Town Commissioners took over the works which Messrs. Appleby, Brain, Fisher & Clay, all of Salford, had erected on the site of Warmingham's Orchard in Clowes Street, and from which practically the whole of the town of Salford was lighted. So Salford courage and enterprise led the way in one of the most important of industrial developments when other towns, not even excepting London, were still nourishing their fears and prejudices.

To-day the ocean laps the feet of our city, and great ships bring the merchandise of the seven seas to and from the quays of Salford town. Few people know, however, that so long ago as 1844 Salford was acknowledged and treated as a port, and that the mighty dream that had its realisation in Daniel Adamson was first born in the mind of a Salford wine merchant. William Gibb was persuaded that since Salford, by the Irwell, had communication with the sea, it ought to be made a port of entry for customs purposes, and he agitated his demand so energetically that it was conceded. (Thank you, Mr. Gibb, for a lesson we do need to take to heart in pressing our legitimate demands to-day.) Bonding warehouses were established at Trinity House, and in July, 1844, the same year as the town was incorporated, the first cargo, consisting of wine and spirits, imported by Mr. Gibb, was brought up the river in a flat called " The Express." A public dinner was given Mr. Gibb and a service of plate value £500 presented to him as an expression of gratitude for the service he had rendered the community. By a curious coincidence, this successful effort on a small scale to utilise and improve the navigable route between Salford and the sea had its fuller culmination, exactly fifty years later, when Queen Victoria came to Salford to formally open the Ship Canal.

More, perhaps, than any other agency, the Municipal Free Library has been the great means of educating and elevating the masses in the unprecedented growth of population in the nineteenth century. It is not generally known that the greatest part in the inauguration of the Free Libraries movement was played by the Borough of Salford. Indeed, although John Ruskin—never very lavish in his compliments to Lancashire people and places—indicates by his passing allusion to the point in " Fors Clavigera " that he, at any rate, recognised the significance, from a national point of view, of the part Salford had played, there has been an extraordinary reluctance to accord Salford the credit that is undeniably hers—the honour of being the first town in the country to establish a municipal Free Library.

In the year 1844, a number of public-spirited men, including the Member of Parliament for Salford, Mr. Joseph Brotherton, met together to discuss means of providing greater amenities for the continually-growing population, and particularly to improve popular taste in matters of art and science. As a result of this meeting, Mr. Brotherton drew up the draft of a Bill which he laid before Mr. William Ewart, M.P., " for encouraging the establishment of museums in large towns." This eventually became the Museums Act of 1845, under which any town with 10,000 inhabitants was allowed to erect a museum of science and art out of the rates.

Salford had, in the mansion at Lark Hill, the most suitable possible building for the purpose, and immediately established a museum therein, supplying books—as an adjunct to the Museum—although this was not so provided in the Act ; in other words, a library was formed. Canterbury and Warrington did likewise, but whereas in each of those places a charge was made for loan of the books, Salford made her library free. So successful was the experiment that Mr. Brotherton, in conjunction with the Mayor, Mr. Edward Ryley Langworthy, determined to institute a Library on a more ambitious scale, and after enlisting cordial and financial support from various townspeople they brought the matter before the Council. By a resolution of June 13, 1849, the Salford Borough Council founded the first unconditional free municipal public library in the United Kingdom, and was the first town to levy a rate for library purposes.

On July 21, 1849, Her Majesty the Queen, " having taken into her Royal consideration that she was Lady of the Manor of Salford," indicated her gracious consent to become Patroness of the Salford Museum and Library, and commanded that it should bear the designation of Royal Museum and Library. His Royal Highness Prince Albert likewise signified his intention of becoming Patron of the institution.

The Public Libraries Act of 1850 was framed almost entirely on the principles adopted for the establishment of the public free library in Salford, and it is worth noticing that for seven months prior to the passing of that Act the Library of Salford had been open, free to all-comers for twelve hours out of the twenty-four of each secular day in the week. The benefits conferred by the Act were gradually seized upon. The earlier towns to adopt the measure were Norwich, in September, 1850 ; Winchester, in December, 1850 ; Bolton, in March ; Liverpool, in May ; and Manchester, in August 1852 ; Cambridge (May), Blackburn (September), and Sheffield (October) in 1853. Whereas all these and subsequent municipal free libraries have been born of the 1850 Act, the Act itself was begotten of Salford, and this town must for ever take high rank amongst the pioneers of popular movements for the amelioration of the lot, and the elevation of the status of the working classes of this country.

It is a peculiar fact that in the early days " book-learning " was not considered the thing for women, and although a special reading-room, nicely furnished even to a mirror, was specially provided for their use, the attempt to attract the women and girls was a failure.

Salford has not been content to rest upon her laurels, and still to-day she holds a premier place in the museum world. Out of the original exhibits have developed the wonderfully-arranged collection at Peel Park and Buile Hill. (Will not another Langworthy arise amongst our public-spirited manufacturers to provide the desperately-needed extensions to the former building ?) The Schools' Museum Service was the first successful attempt in the world to bring the museums into active co-operation with the educational system, and whilst Salford's ideas are being extensively adopted on the Continent of Europe, the majority of English towns lag woefully behind.

That the Salford Museums are performing a most useful service in developing the intellectual life of the people is seen from the fact that they are visited by more than a quarter of a million people every year. Nearly thirty millions of people have passed through the turnstiles of the Museums since their inception, and yet this remarkable service involves for maintenance and administration a charge of only a half-penny on the rates. Brotherton and Langworthy have indeed been justified in the oft-commented appreciation and understanding of the Fine Arts that characterise the working-people of Salford in the present day.

Salford was the first town to establish a public swimming bath when the Adelphi Baths were opened in 1855. She was first in the field in the provision of a public sanatorium. In technical education—an important matter in a community that earns its bread by the sweat of its brow—Salford has taken, too, a prominent part. Proud of our town in very truth we have just cause to be! Let those who scoff so readily and so cheaply whenever the name of Salford is mentioned point to any other town in the country through that can show an equally proud record of remarkable achievement during the truly remarkable period when Victoria was Queen.

CHAPTER VIII

Literary and Scientific Associations.

A S the last hundred years of Salford's history have been great with achievement, we may look to find them rich in personality. And we shall not be disappointed. The century is graced with lives well lived and laid down without fear ; men and women who, in many cases, have attained more than a local fame, plain citizens who, in following the gleam that shines afar have illumined their day and generation. Elsewhere we have told of several of these and their activities in various spheres, and turning to the field of literature and science it may be a surprise to many to know how full and varied has been the contribution this town of grey industry has made, through her sons and daughters, to the higher arts.

To-day the neighbourhood of Islington Square is, alas ! the very reverse of a fashionable district, but it is not so long ago since it housed the opulent merchant and the man of letters. Here, in 1849, Frances Hodgson Burnett, creator of " Little Lord Fauntelroy," that classic so dear to Victorian hearts, and whose " Lass of Gowrie's " is one of the best stories of Lancashire life ever published, first saw the light of day,* and John Edward Taylor, who established the foundations of the *Manchester Guardian*, was likewise a native of this same parish, spending his childhood in Islington Street, and removing on his marriage to the adjoining Sidney Street.

Lower down, in New Bayley Street, was born on Christmas Eve, 1818, a boy who was destined to become one of the greatest scientists of the century, John Prescott Joule. Delicate from birth, Joule early shewed a profound interest in scientific studies, particularly in regard to electricity. He was placed by his father under the instructorship of Dr. John Dalton, and a laboratory was built attached to the house where the youth could carry out his researches. At the age of nineteen he invented an electro-magnetic engine, and in the course of examining its performance he adopted a definite scientific unit based on the amount of electricity required to decompose nine grains of water in one hour. From this he

* She later went to live at Seedley, and in her autobiography described her garden there as the " back garden of Paradise."

was able, in 1840, to state the law according to which heat is produced in a conductor by the passage of an electric current. In 1843, in a paper read before the British Association at Cork entitled " The Calorific Effects of Magneto-electricity and the Mechanical Value of Heat," he expressed the conviction that whenever mechanical force is expended an exact equivalent of heat is always obtained. His findings were further elaborated in a memoir presented to the Royal Society in 1849, and later, Joule was entrusted by the British Association with the task of deducing the mechanical equivalent of heat from the thermal effects of electric currents. He was associated with Lord Kelvin in other important research work, and was responsible for the practical method of surface-condensation, which is regarded as the most important improvement of the steam engine since the days of James Watt (Encyclo. Brit., xv., 523). All his life a victim of ill-health, Joule was nevertheless permitted a long and useful career, and his eminent services to science only ended with his death in October, 1889, at the age of 71.

A brother of the scientist, who acquired fame in another branch of the arts was Benjamin St. John B. Joule, sometimes spoken of as the " Father of Modern English Church Music."

It is something of a coincidence that the year that saw the birth of Joule saw also, in the previous April, the death of another Salfordian whose extraordinary talent has enriched mathematical and scientific knowledge. Dr. Henry Clarke has been referred to in a previous connection, but it would be remiss not to mention here the notable contribution this man of remarkable attainments made to science and philosophy. Son of an honoured burgess of the town, Mr. Thomas Clarke, Dr. Clarke was born in Salford in 1743, and at the early age of thirteen began to evince a striking propensity for matters scientific. In 1777 he published his famous " Tabulæ Linguarum," a series of grammatical tables covering all languages, classical and antique ; " A Treatise on Perspective," and " The Rationale of Circulating Numbers." His intimate understanding of the higher branches of mathematics was combined with an amazing classical knowledge, which his facile pen turned to account in " Virgil Re-vindicated," " An English Translation from the original Greek of the Works of Aratus the Cilician," and a number of like publications which he issued between 1799 and 1809. " An Introduction to Geography " and " The Seaman's Desiderata, or Concise Rules for computing the apparent time at Sea," were other works from his pen, which shew the extraordinary range of his interests and learning. He was, besides, an expert mechanic. Yet despite his great accomplishments he was the most unassuming and sociable of men. He died from apoplexy at Islington, in London, at the age of 75, a few months after retiring from the position of Professor of History, Geography and Experimental Philosophy at the Royal Military College, Sandhurst.

Eaton Hodgkinson is another great mathematician whom we can claim as a Salfordian by adoption if not by birth. Born at Anderton, in Cheshire, in 1789, he persuaded his widowed mother to invest her capital in a pawnbroking business in Salford. Here the family removed when Eaton was 22, and in the leisure time he could snatch from the business, he devoted himself to scientific studies, for which he had shewn a marked propensity as a boy at school, at which time his great hobby had been the making of sundials. A man of profound rather than brilliant intellect, his whole life was devoted to experimental research, and engineering text-books bear witness to the many important mechanical formulæ he discovered. In fact, it is safe to say that no man has ever made greater contributions to engineering science, and but for his experiments and discoveries, modern bridge building would never have attained its remarkable perfection. Spending his life for the advancement of science in the service of mankind without desiring or gaining pecuniary reward, he died at Eaglesfield House, Higher Broughton, in June, 1861, in the seventy-second year of his age, rich in the recognition by the most eminent scientific societies and authorities of his great merits and abilities, and having the happiness of seeing within his own lifetime the fruits of his labours applied to the construction of some of the world's greatest engineering achievements.

In the spring of 1839 a remarkable new poem took the English-speaking world by storm. Extravagantly praised and mercilessly condemned, its author was ranked by some as greater than Browning. The poem was bought and read with avid interest on both sides of the Atlantic, and Tennyson and Lytton were amongst those who swelled the chorus of its praise. It was in St. Stephen Street, at the house of Wilmot

THE NEW BAYLEY. ON THE LEFT IS THE LYING-IN HOSPITAL WHICH OCCUPIED THE SITE OF THE
SPAW HOUSE AND THE LADY PIRLE WELL.

Henry Jones, that twenty-year-old Philip James Bailey wrote " Festus," and whence he sent forth to an astonished world this poem that Bamford declared would " one day be esteemed an honour to the town."

George Macdonald, the poet and novelist, lived for some years at 2, Camp Place, Broughton, and from the neighbouring Fenny Place, Ralph Waldo Emerson wrote in a letter dated November 5, 1847 :—

> " At last, and only this day for the first time, I am established in my own lodgings on English ground, and have a fair parlour and chamber into which both the sun and moon shine, and into which friendly people have already entered. I mean to make this my centre."

Here the great philosopher loved to gather around his table the ardent young men of independent thought, and with his fine graciousness of manner and an ineffably sweet smile, listen to the enthusiastic discourse of his guests. At one of these gatherings he read his then unpublished lecture on " Plato."

Abraham Stansfield, the Lancashire author, and a botanist of note, often described as one of Nature's noblemen, was also a native of Salford, and Harrison Ainsworth spent a large portion of his early life at the house of his aunt in Adelphi Terrace.

It is to a Salford man—George Bradshaw—that the Railway Time-table owes its introduction. An engraver by profession, Bradshaw issued several maps of the inland waterways on which steam packets plied, and in 1839 he first published Bradshaw's Railway Time-tables. Born at Windsor Bridge, Bradshaw lived later at Barclay Place, a house formerly standing at the corner of Ordsall Lane and Regent Road.

Frederic Shields, the painter and decorative artist, lived for a time at Ordsall Hall. Sir Henry Haworth both lived in the town and was the representative of South Salford in Parliament, a constituency that in later times had also Hilaire Belloc for its member. Hulme House, on The Crescent, was the home of George Woodburne, the legal writer.

Joseph Kay, the economist, and for sixteen years Judge of the Salford Court of Record, was born at Ordsall Cottage in 1821. William Thompson Watkin, the authority on Roman remains, was a native of Salford, as were also William Harrison the distinguished Manx antiquary, and Henry James Holden the artist. Salford also has its prototype of Samuel Rogers in Paul Moor Jones, the banker-poet, who lived at Somerville House, Irlams-o'-th'-Height.

Salford claims its contribution to the epic of the Dark Continent, inasmuch as the wife of David Livingstone was the daughter of a Salford home. To her devotion and helpfulness he paid his famous tribute : " A straightforward woman was she : the best spoke in the wheel of home." About 1790 there settled in Salford a Scotsman from Perth named Robert Smith, who married Mary Gray, of York, and took up residence at a house in New Windsor. Here was born a daughter, Mary, who married Robert Moffatt, and it was their daughter, Mary, who changed for the great missionary-explorer his conception of the marital state.

Turn whither we will, in any branch of life's service and the influence of Salford men and women is encountered. Modern banking owes much to the genius of Sir Edward Holden, long an honoured burgess of Salford town. Away in the United States, at Rochester, is the world's most remarkable monument of modern medical science founded by Robert Worrall Mayo, a native of this town.* When the motor lifeboat flings through the sea on its errand of succour, we remember it was the genius of a Salford man, James Corbett, a former Borough engineer, that evolved the principle of the unsinkable boat.

In the story of woman's emancipation, the name of Emilia Pankhurst will ever be honoured, and it is to this Salford woman the credit belongs that her sisters in Britain now enjoy the full rights and responsibilities of citizenship.

Here, too, more than one novelist has found fertile material for his pen. Guy Thorne, in " When it was Dark," depicts people and places whose acquaintance he made during his father's vicariate at St. Thomas', Pendleton, and Leaf Square holds remembrances of the lovable figure of the Rev. Francis Ffolyatt and his troublesome but amusing family in the pages of Gilbert Cannan's " Round the Corner," a novel in which the author has found incident for his story in the High Church riots at St. Paul's, Ellor Street in the " 'seventies." Harold

---

*He was born at Lower Bentcliffe, and baptised at Eccles Parish Church where his sons erected a beautiful window to his memory in 1929. The Mayo family played a considerable part in the industrial development of South Salford in association with their relatives, the Worralls.

Brighouse, himself a Salfordian, has woven a whole series of plays out of Salford life and character, sparkling with the wit and humour of everyday types.

'Tis a strange contradictory old place, this Salford of ours, whose soul even industrialism has not completely killed, and where the breath of romance still lingers in " gentle thoughts and mild desires " awaiting some author's depicting pen. There are havens of quiet in the heart of the bustle and rush, fragrant with the genteel atmosphere of a bygone day, like the graceful bow-fronted houses in Hulme Place, from whose doorways one almost expects to see emerge My Lady in her crinoline, attended by elegant periwigged swain.

Amidst the sedate Georgian houses of Encombe Place lingers memories of the spare thoughtful figure of Edward Lee Hicks, scholar and cleric, friend and disciple of John Ruskin, who, in " Fors Clavigera," was not unconscious of Salford's efforts in the Free Library and Museum movement. Something of the spell which Salford weaves over those who serve her is reflected in Dr. Hick's own words before leaving St. Philips' for the Bishopric of Lincoln, when he said : " Perhaps I shall never have a greater opportunity of preaching and living the Gospel of Jesus Christ than I have had here in Salford, and now that the opportunity is passing from me, I wish that I had used it better and accomplished more."

CHAPTER IX.

Incorporation.

ONE of the most momentous steps forward in the progress
of modern Salford took place on the 16th of April,
1844, when by Royal Charter the Borough was
incorporated and the people elected their first Town Council.

It has been said that Englishmen learned the responsibilities of citizenship at their own gates. The political
liberty and the constitutional sense that has made England
a pattern for the nations of the earth was nurtured and
developed originally in the Port Moots—those early nurseries
of municipal government—for long enough before any central
Parliamentary system came into being. " A nation may
establish a system of free government," says De Tocqueville,
" but without the spirit of municipal institutions it cannot
have the spirit of liberty."

Through the seventeenth and eighteenth centuries the
boroughs of England largely lost the privileges of popular
government until there was little enough to be envied in the
position of a corporate borough, and where a town was fairly
well governed, as Salford was, under its Borough Reeve and
Constables, there was certainly no inducement to change its
status. By the passing of the Municipal Reform Act of 1835,
the government of the boroughs was given back to the people,
securing to them absolute control of their own affairs and the
means of supplying their own wants through Town Councils
annually elected by popular vote.

The Reform Act of 1832, having admitted the people to a
share in managing the business of the nation, it was a natural
corollary that they should also be given the management of
their own local affairs. The great object of the Act of 1835,
in the words of Lord John Russell, was " to open a free course
to the beneficial operation of those subordinate bodies in the
government of the country which were provided in our
ancient institutions as an essential counterpoise to the central
authority." Truly the heritage of local administration
deserves better respect than it for the most part receives.

The old Commissioners of Police, in whom was vested the
government of the town, were men of energy and public

spirit, and, to a certain degree, far-sightedness. Their duties were carried out in an exemplary fashion, and the burgesses had little to complain of regarding administration. During the first forty years of the nineteenth century, however, the borough had made remarkable progress both in population and assessable value, and the Commissioners decided that since this advance was likely to continue, it was desirable in the best interests of the borough and its status, that it should take advantage of the wider opportunities of local government provided by the Municipal Corporations Act. A petition was duly presented to the Privy Council and the Charter of Incorporation granted. It provides " that the inhabitants of the Borough of Salford . . . and their successors shall be for ever hereafter one body politic and corporate—in deed, fact and name—and that the said body corporate shall be called the Mayor, Aldermen, and Burgesses of the Borough of Salford."

The powers and duties of the Mayor, Aldermen and Burgesses were defined in the circumlocutory fashion of legal terminology, and a description given of the boundaries of the four wards into which the town was to be divided. These wards were to be called Blackfriars, Crescent, St. Stephen's and Trinity, and each ward was to return six councillors.

Although the Parliamentary Borough of Salford included the townships of Pendleton and Broughton, the Municipal Borough extended no farther west than New Windsor, and included only that small portion of Broughton lying south of the river. On October 21, 1847, thirty-eight ratepayers and property owners in Broughton, " gentlemen of the highest respectability and station in society "—a somewhat redundant expression, as it was a town joke that all the respectability of those days dwelt in Broughton—petitioned the Corporation regarding the possibility of that township being included within the Borough. As a result, the Town Clerk was instructed to prepare a Bill for promotion in Parliament " to extend the boundaries of the Municipal Borough of Salford so as to include the whole of the Parliamentary Borough, or so much thereof as may be found most desirable and beneficial for all parties." This aroused great commotion. The inhabitants of Pendleton were annoyed that they had not been previously consulted, and the ratepayers of Broughton in public meeting assembled cast ridicule on the " 38 gentle-

men of the highest respectability and station in society "
who had presumed to speak in their name, and passed a
resolution that the Corporation of Salford had been guilty
of " an unwarrantable interference in the affairs of their
neighbours." The Corporation's tactical error had been their
undoing, and the Bill was withdrawn.

The question was revived in 1851 by a report which was
published by Mr. Robert Rawlinson, superintending inspector
to the General Board of Health. Mr. Rawlinson had been
sent down from London in response to a petition signed by
359 residents to hold an enquiry into the sanitary state of
the township of Pendleton. His report was a formidable
indictment of the township authorities regarding sanitation
and water supply. Pendleton folk then began to realise what
a mistake they had made in rejecting Salford's overtures.
As a result of efforts made by Mr. Joseph Brotherton, M.P.,
negotiations were renewed and a Bill again promoted, which
passed the committee of the House of Lords. Broughton
then became annoyed at the financial provisions, and a petition
was forwarded to the House of Lords declaring that
amalgamation was " unnecessary, uncalled for, and calculated
to injure the property and increase the rates of the township."
Counsel for the Corporation added fuel to the fire of indignation
by describing the inhabitants of Broughton and Pendleton as
" semi-savages." Pendleton, however, despite wounded
feelings, agreed to still support the measure, but Broughton
presented a divided front, with the result that the Select
Committee of the House of Lords decided to pass the Bill,
but leaving Broughton out. The mutilated Bill was withdrawn, but reinstated following negotiations, and on June 14,
1853, the Royal Assent was given to the " Salford Extension
and Improvement Act, 1853."

By the Act, general committees—that is, committees
composed of representatives of all the districts—should have
control of all matters relating to the Borough generally, but
the management of the highways and streets was vested in
district committees for each township. Each district
committee was to have power to levy an Improvement and
Highway Rate for its district separately and independently,
to borrow money on the security of such rate, and to appoint
and pay its own officers. The Town Council were to have no
control at all over the internal arrangements of the districts

except in so far as it was obliged to formally confirm the proceedings of the district committees. This " trinity without unity," as it was styled, lasted until 1891, in which year an Act was passed bringing all three districts under one general system. The Act of 1853 fixed the number of members of the Council at 64, which figure is still retained.

In accordance with the provisions of the Local Government Act of 1888, Salford was created a County Borough in April, 1889. The Charter of Incorporation established a Court of Record in which debts up to £20 were recoverable. A separate Commission of the Peace was granted the Borough in 1870 and renewed in 1886. Quarter Sessions were established in 1899.

The year after the Charter was granted, the Corporation thought it a proper thing to ascertain the boundaries of their domain, and led by Mr. William Lockett, last of the Borough Reeves and first Mayor, the boundaries were formally perambulated and staked out according to the Ordnance Survey. Although it is not recorded that the civic fathers were treated to any of the indignities common to such occasions in other places, they apparently did not again repeat the event.

On August 30, 1825, Lord Bexley, Chancellor of the Duchy of Lancaster, laid the foundation stone of the Town Hall— that plain, familiar Doric-fronted building which was originally erected by public subscription. In 1834 it was acquired by the Police Commissioners for the sum of £5,000, and on the borough being incorporated, it was taken over and enlarged to provide the additional accommodation called for by the increased municipal administration. At the time of its erection, and for many years subsequently, a vegetable market was held on the flags in front of the buildings, and in the rear the butchers had their stalls. Both these markets were swept away as additional accommodation became imperative. If one may hazard a serious criticism of the municipal rulers since incorporation it is their extraordinary failure to provide a Town Hall fitting to the dignity and status of the Borough. More than £100,000 have been spent in repeated additions to the Bexley Square buildings, with no other result than to create what has been rather aptly, if forcibly, described as " a d——d rabbit warren." Halls for the Broughton and Pendleton districts were provided in 1854 and 1867 respectively.

A few figures of a general kind will illustrate the enormous progress Salford has made since the Charter of Incorporation was obtained. According to the census of 1841, the three townships together had a total population of 70,224 ; ten years later it had increased to 87,523, and the continuous growth since is shewn below :—

```
1861............................102,449
1871............................124,801
1881............................176,235
1891...............         ...........198,139
1901............................220,957
1911............................231,380
1921............................244,675
```

Equally striking is the advance in rateable value from £140,010 in 1841 to the present figure of £1,345,759.* It is interesting to note that prior to the extension of the Manchester boundaries in 1885, the area of Salford exceeded that of her neighbour by almost a thousand acres. The rapid development of the last thirty years is seen from statistics prepared in 1894, which shew that of the area of the borough then, 1,200 acres were occupied by dwellings, business premises and streets ; 2,600 acres were private park lands ; and 1,400 acres were in use as agricultural land. What a comparison with to-day, when every available yard of land is built over, and the area is the most congested in the country outside the London area.

As the old town grew beyond measure in both population and importance, it became increasingly obvious that she was entitled to the recognition of a higher status, and so, in 1926, His Majesty King George the Fifth, Duke of Lancaster and Lord of the Manor of Salford, was graciously pleased to issue a Royal Edict elevating the Royal and Ancient Borough to all the rights and dignities of a city.

During the period since her Incorporation, Salford has been fortunate in the devoted service of many eminent sons. It would be invidious to quote names, but a glance through the roll of ex-Mayors will eloquently reveal how nobly the industrial leaders of a generation now gone, " men furnished with ability, giving counsel by their understanding, by their

---

*Under the Provisions of the Local Government Act of 1929, the net Rateable Value has been reduced to £1,118,688.

knowledge wise in their instructions," served their inheritance and left a name behind them in civic service whose glory shall never be blotted out.

In later years this high tradition of civic devotion has languished somewhat, due, in part, to the fact that the men of business have sought their habitations further afield, and take not the same personal interest in local affairs that their predecessors did. Immersed in their personal affairs, occupied by the multifarious ramifications of modern business, repelled by the rancour and partisan bitterness which nowadays sour municipal elections, many men stand aloof from civic administration who, by their business training and creative ability, have an invaluable contribution to make towards the efficiency of local government. Yet local government, intimately touching, as it does, the immediate interests of the population at so many points, offers a far wider and more satisfying sense of public service than the House of Commons does ; and the growth of municipal activities, involving the welfare of a great populace and the control of millions of pounds of public money demands that the best brains of the community should be applied to the direction of municipal affairs.

It ought to be more clearly realised that citizenship does not end with the paying of rates, but that upon every man of character who owes attachment to the place, whether by residence or by business location, devolves a great duty of personal service to the city. By ignoring that duty they shame their citizenship, and draw upon themselves an unpleasant reflection in the measure by which the city falls below the standard of propriety.

Mayhap the day is not too distant when it will be generally recognised that party politics have no place in municipal affairs, and that the stupid strife of contesting factions is a heavy brake on the wheel of civic progress. There is undoubtedly, an overwhelming need for some reform in the process of public elections whereby it would be possible to secure the most able citizens, irrespective of creed or politics, as the directors of municipal affairs. Whether such reform comes soon or late, the city demands immediately, and without further tarrying, the service of those citizens most qualified to serve her. Even the Apostle Paul was proud to confess himself a citizen of no mean city. Salford, by her history and achievements, is certainly not unworthy to stand within the line of the great tradition, and in these days, when an even greater Salford is waiting to be called forth by the living faith of her citizens, can those who are heirs to her responsibilities as well as her glories remain deaf to her call, or will they not rather, with noble examples to spur them on, learn and labour truly that when called by the common voice to the service of the city they shall be found not wanting in the quality of their devotion ?

CHAPTER X

The Town in 1844.

IN an interesting little volume published at the time of the Incorporation Jubilee in 1894 are preserved several recollections of old inhabitants of the town as it was fifty years before.

"I have seen a marvellous change in Salford," said one old inhabitant. "Talking to my young friends of angling in the Irwell below Peel Park, and of bathing in the same locality, they imagine I am romancing. But I remember these things well; although I admit at once that I was not myself tempted to bathe where it was so exposed. I can hardly say that the water was clear then, but it was fit to bathe in, and a lad would have no fear of being poisoned on the one hand or buried in mud on the other."

"In districts other than Broughton," he proceeded "the town had not grown to anything like its present dimensions, and it was a more cheerful place to live in. I remember fruit trees bearing blossom in The Crescent, which was then the abode of the well-to-do; Leaf Square being another favourite place with this particular class. Oldfield Road was a narrow, crooked, unpaved street; Cross Lane was as rural in appearance as if it were far removed from a town, and Pendleton, though it had toll-bars on both its main roads, was little more than a name, in a residential sense. Regent Road had been laid out early in the century, but, of course, it was not the busy place it is now. The centre of Salford, however, was already beginning to give indications of congestion. I remember, during the Cotton Famine between 1861 and 1863, visiting the people in a block of property near Chapel Street and the present Blackfriars Street. The houses had originally been pleasant cottages, but now there was a family in each room, and the people were evidently extremely poor. Another place I visited at the same time was Birtles Square, in Greengate. The Square consisted of a number of lofty buildings, forming a court, with two or three culs-de-sac running from it. Nearly every room, I found, was occupied by a separate family. Some of the rooms were approached by a common staircase going to the top ; others by an exterior gallery, and those overlooking the river by a wooden gangway. All the people were wretchedly poor, and the place struck me as being a veritable human rabbit-warren. One side of Birtles Square has since been taken down to allow for the extension of some rubber works, and other property which I have mentioned was taken down for the Blackfriars Street improvement.

" Reverting to the changes at Cross Lane, I may mention, that opposite Park Place there was a large square field now covered with cottage houses, in which the children of the tenants in Park Place could have their recreation. A great change has also taken place on the other side of Cross Lane, in the district of which West Liverpool Street is the centre. About where the Buck Hotel now is there was a house in which the owners of the adjacent estate resided, but all around was pasture land, with the exception of two or three cottages, called Woodbine Cottages, where the Bible Christians have their church now. A stream of pure water ran through the district, and, strange as it may seem now, when the land is covered with bricks and mortar, there was then a plentiful growth of watercresses.

" In what is now called Liverpool Street there stood, on the northerly side, a long row of large houses which never seemed to have been occupied ; and a little lower, on the opposite side, there were some houses which tradition said had been built with the idea that they would be required for the L. & N.W. Railway. Those were the days when railway enterprises were new, and when there was perhaps more speculation than now in trying to cover the route of a new line in advance. In the case under notice, however, the property was not required ; the railway company were able to avoid it, and the property owner's little enterprise proved a disastrous one."

As memory is sometimes treacherous, it was thought well to call a second witness to tell what he remembered of Salford as it was half a century before. His story confirmed that of the previous narrator and supplemented it as follows : " Fifty years ago the older residential parts of Salford, eastward of Oldfield Road and the Adelphi, were already almost entirely built over, and the only open spaces remaining were already laid out for building. The Infantry Barracks in Regent Road were surrounded by open fields, but brickfields at various points overshadowed the beginning of building operations. The Woollen Cloth Hall at Victoria Bridge was a busy cloth market. Greengate Market, near the site of the ancient Market Cross, was still in use, and also the Meat Market in Chapel Street. For several days, twice a year, the Cattle Fair or Dirt Fair, as it was called, occupied Blackfriars Street and Chapel Street, and the Cattle Market was beginning to flourish in Cross Lane. Fruit and vegetables were sold in the Borough Market opposite the Dispensary, at the end of Oldfield Lane. As to travelling facilities, we had, of course, no tramways then. Mr. Greenwood's two-horse omnibuses ran on the Pendleton route, and Mr. Turner's on the Broughton routes, at fourpenny and sixpenny fares. All the present lines of railways were in use, but they have been widened considerably since then, and one or two new stations have been erected. To and from the Packet Landing Place in New Bayley Street there came and went many passenger boats and light traffic boats, towed by trotting horses to and from Runcorn and Warrington. The river was then much used for boating. There were large numbers of row-boats on hire, and some half-dozen small steamers carried holiday-makers from the town down the river. The Manchester and Salford Regattas were amongst the best-patronised meetings of their kind, both for amateur and professional oarsmen, and sailing races were sometimes included in the programmes. There were only four works and no houses at all along the racing course between Regent Bridge and Throstle's Nest Lock. Broughton and Pendleton did not form part of the borough at the time the Charter of Incorporation was granted. Broughton was a comparatively isolated and retired residential suburb, approached only through toll-bars at Strangeways, Broughton Bridge, and the Suspension Bridge. Residents were allowed free passage at Broughton Bridge toll-house, and as the population increased the toll-collector's memory for faces was severely taxed. In Northumberland Street, Higher Broughton, a Zoological Gardens struggled for existence. There an infant who afterwards became Stipendiary Magistrate of Salford sustained a serious wound inflicted by one of the wild animals whilst his nurse's back was turned, the marks of which he retained until his death. Pendleton fifty years ago included a number of cottages surrounding the cotton mills and bleachworks, but its main area was occupied by mansions in park-like grounds. The water supply was almost entirely obtained from wells or springs, and in dry summers serious inconvenience and injury to health ensued."

In the *Salford Reporter*, in a series of articles during 1880, the late Mr. John Plant, then Curator at Peel Park, gave the following glowing account of one portion of Salford as it appeared in his time : " The prevailing taste and hobby of the working classes in Salford during the first half of the century, particularly the mill hand-weavers and operatives of a similar employment, was for the cultivation of old-fashioned English flowers in their plots of gardens or in their cottage windows, and of show vegetable produce, all of which were possible when the town atmosphere was clean and sweet. Up to the year 1840, or thereabouts, the fruit trees in the gardens belonging to the fair mansions forming The Crescent were famous for the abundance and excellence of their fruits ; the orchards were crowded with peaches, nectarines, magnum-bonum plums, cherries, pears, etc. Even now (1881) several of the jargonelle pear trees are struggling to make believe they are not dead. They show a sprinkling of green leaves every spring, but neither blossom nor, of course, bear fruit. The few pear trees lingering in Peel Park have not blossomed for several years. In the long garden at the back of No. 24, formerly in the occupancy of Mr. ——, there was a grand jargonelle pear tree, the sight of which in the spring-time was a treat to behold, and drew crowds of people to Back Hulme Street to look at it. An old resident says there were very good vines, which bore very fair grapes, covering the sunny sides of the garden walls, whilst the gooseberries, raspberries and such-like fruit were as excellent for quality and quantity as were ever grown ; in fact, each mansion was like a luxuriant farm in the country, with its independent home supplies of fruit and vegetables."

Mr. Plant, in illustration of the state of the river in those days, gave the following quotation from a letter he had received from a gentleman who lived in The Crescent from 1837 to 1850 : " I remember seeing fly-fishing in the Irwell from the spit of sand at the sharp bend of the river just below the Dispensary end of the Adelphi Road, and, when the river was in flood, crowds of persons assembled along the iron rails guarding the broken willow bank to watch parties of men dragging large bag-nets of fish. Many kinds of fish were thus netted, but trout were only caught with the fly-rod."

" In those days," says another account, " there was no more cosy, beautiful-looking residence within the Borough of Salford than Lark Hill. Situated on the elevated natural terrace of the river, the old-fashioned square mansion, standing in its own grounds, presented a very striking appearance from The Crescent as well as from the low meadow-lands of Lower Broughton. Here and there in the grounds there were clumps of trees which provided a shade from the sun, and everywhere there was, in addition to garden flowers, a rich growth of foxgloves, ferns and wild flowers. The house was built in 1792 by Colonel Jas. Ackers, a prominent man in public affairs, whose title was derived from his command of the Manchester and Salford Volunteers. Retiring in 1826 to the South of England, Colonel Ackers sold Lark Hill to Mr. William Garnett."

Beyond Lark Hill, on the westerly side, was another handsome mansion, Marlborough House. Between this and the canal at New Windsor was a square of stately terraced houses occupied by the well-to-do classes, and known as Marlborough Square. Marlborough House was occupied by Dr. Turner, the first Bishop of Salford, as his official residence. It was eventually demolished to make way for the Royal Technical College which now occupies the site.

" I recollect well," an old gentleman told the present writer recently, " my father's description of the Adelphi district in his young days, when the fields and hedges were white with cloths spread over them by the bleachers of the mills on the river bank ; " crofting," as it was called." The old name for bleachers was " whitsters," whence is derived our present Whit Lane, originally " Whitsters Lane."

Flowering fruit trees ; fishing in the river ; cloth bleached in the sun in an atmosphere free from smuts—what devastating changes have been wrought in Salford within two and three generations ! In the words of the quaint old workman philosopher, Tubby Wadlow in " Hobson's Choice," " The force of life we have to-day in Salford is indeed a challenge at the hands of our renovation."

CHAPTER XI

These Later Years.

I N surveying the history of Salford during the years that have passed since the Charter of Incorporation, one is impressed by three things, and the first of these is the amazing industrial development.

At the time of incorporation, the manufactories of the town included a flax mill, silk mills, calico printing and dyeworks, engraving and machine works, and cotton factories on an extensive scale. To-day, though cotton and engineering and the dyeing and patterning of fabrics are still amongst her dominant industries, thousands of her people find their living in the transport trade, three-quarters of the rubber textile industry of the country is centred in her midst, and, due to the special quality of her natural waters, added to the fact that long ago she remitted the tax on all malted grain entering her boundaries, she is still famous, as in ancient times, for Salford ale, and is, indeed, one of the chief brewing centres of the kingdom. The Salford of to-day has over a thousand factories and workshops, and through her great docks and her strategic importance as the hub of the arterial road system of Lancashire, she has become an invaluable distributing centre for overseas produce and a significant link in Empire trade. Well is her title of the " Gateway of the Industrial North " deserved, and in vivid contrast to the little insular town of a century ago, the sights and sounds of Salford streets in this our time reveal in their curious cosmopolitan character a moving, speaking picture of the world in miniature.

The commercial development of this district owes an incalculable debt of gratitude to the magnificent enterprise of the Duke of Bridgewater who, in 1758, obtained an Act of Parliament to make a canal from Worsley to Salford. Later, the plan was altered and the course of the canal taken across the River Irwell by an aqueduct at Barton, and thence through the township of Stretford.* In 1791, a canal was

---

* It is interesting to recall that the very first steamboat in the world, seven years before the American experiment which claims the credit, was built at Worsley, and used on the Bridgewater Canal, with engines by Messrs. Sharratt, the Salford engineers.

made from Bolton to Salford, largely following the course of the upper reaches of the Irwell. The transport of goods and passengers by these inland waterways was a vast improvement on the pack-horse system along the rough roads, and trade was consequently better facilitated. An even greater improvement came in 1830, when Stephenson's invention of the railway engine enabled the construction of a railway from Manchester to Liverpool. Actually, the commencing point of this line was from a station a few yards over the Salford boundary, and the first stopping place was at Ordsall Lane, where the rails crossed the road by a level crossing, within a stone's throw of the terminating point of the Salford and Bolton Canal, and ran for a length of four miles right through the town to Eccles, at which place the Lady Well on the Gilda Brook at the Salford boundary, traditionally ascribed as the place where St. Patrick and St. Germanus baptised their first converts, was utilised for watering the engines.

In 1838, a new railway was opened from Bolton to Salford, with its terminus at New Bayley Street, and in 1884, the Lancashire & Yorkshire Railway constructed their Liverpool express line. Herein Salford lost a great opportunity. Street levels were lowered, and huge unsightly viaducts constructed across the streets, for which the railway companies paid a grossly inadequate sum of £34,000 as compensation, promising, at the same time, to make their main terminal station within the Salford bounds. The promise was carried out, literally, by building the Exchange Station on the very extremity of the borough, and with the main approach direct into Manchester. As in many other things, it was Salford's fate to bear the inconveniences whilst another reaped the benefits. What a different story might have been written of the Chapel Street district to-day if only the Corporation of those days had had the acumen to insist—as they might reasonably have been expected to—that the terminus should be at New Bayley Street instead of the present Exchange Station.

The second point of expression is the striking efficiency of the municipal services ; indeed, it is generally recognised that in respect of these the Corporation has been not merely content with taking a prominent part, but has consistently acted as a leader amongst the municipalities of the country.

Particularly noteworthy is the improvement in public health. A deplorable account of the heritage of early

K

industrialism is given in Sir Robert Rawlinson's report of 1851, wherein he says, " The foresight, intelligence, and activity of local authorities have not kept pace with the general prosperity of the country." Sir Robert points out how acres of land had been covered with houses and whole streets formed without any adequate attention being paid to sewerage and drainage. Houses had been thrown up to provide for the rapid increase in population, " slight in structure, imperfect in plan, crowded at the back ; provision for stowing refuse being made in the most objectionable places, often close upon living rooms or immediately beneath sleeping-room windows. New streets remained undrained, and were not paved, cleansed, lighted or regulated, so that they speedily generate nuisances of the most dangerous and worst kind." The report, however, goes on to state that " this wretched state of things is not peculiar to this district, but is common to the whole Kingdom where any extent of cottage building has been made."

The average of annual mortality in the period 1841–51 in the Salford registration district was 28 per 1,000 of population, although this compared favourably with Manchester's 33 per 1,000 and Liverpool's 34 per 1,000. The sanitary sins of the early days—the narrow courts, the back-to-back houses (often rejoicing in grandiose names, such as Shafton Place, that emphasised in their incongruity the squalor they designated), the faulty drainage, the open cess-pools, the neglect of all precautions against infectious disease—have been largely swept away. Salford was almost the first authority in the Irwell watershed to construct intercepting sewers and works for the treatment of its sewage ; and the Mode Wheel Sewage Works have served as the model for the sewage systems of several American cities. Noisome cellar dwellings and filthy privies have been abolished ; vast street improvements involving the demolition of the worst slums in the older parts of the city have been carried out. Efficient sanitary inspection, the scientific treatment of epidemic disease, and the education of the public in elementary hygiene have been inaugurated, and a system of public hospitals established which place at the service of the poorest man and woman in Salford medical and surgical skill that was not available to a nobleman even when George IV. was King. So successfully, in fact, has the Corporation of Salford laboured, that despite the drawbacks consequent on the congested condition of its area, the standard of public health in the city will compare not unfavourably with many a seaside resort. Incredible, perhaps, but true ! and its present low mortality-rate will prove that Salford is far from being the black spot its detractors would have folk believe.

At one time the work of protecting the town from the ravages of fire was a spare-time job for policemen and other volunteers. To raise the alarm, the bell of Trinity Church was rung, and often it was quite half an hour before the Brigade could get to work. Compare these comic-opera-like conditions with the extraordinary efficiency of the present Central Fire Station, admittedly one of the finest and most effective service units of its kind in the Kingdom, and we realise how vast has been the improvement in a comparatively short space of time. This mark of high efficiency, indeed, is characteristic of all branches of the City Police Force, in whom are vested the ancient duties of watch and ward. Few cities of the size of Salford, with far less peculiar problems, can shew so low a record of crime, a tribute not only to the integrity of the population, but equally to the firm, yet not unkindly, regulating sway of the local men in blue. Despite the increased complexities induced by the docks and the cosmopolitan influence thereby created, it has not been necessary to increase the City Police Force in unison with the growth of population, scientific administration and control having been so efficiently applied. The Salford Police Force justifiably enjoys, in an unusual degree, the confidence and friendship of the citizens. Particularly in regard to the handling of the immense problems of traffic control, the Salford Police, under the direction of the present Chief Constable, have upheld the reputation of Salford as a pioneer, and most of the improved ideas making for safer road conditions have been first inaugurated in this city.

As the home of gas lighting, the city has made equal progression in taking advantage of later scientific developments, and her Electricity Generating Station at Agecroft ranks as one of the four most efficient modern stations in Great Britain. And so the same proud record of striving for the best distinguishes practically every department of the extensive network of public services by which Salford seeks the improved physical and social condition of her vast population.

The Town Council formed under the Charter of Incorporation has done its work so well, despite the omissions and commissions common to all fallible human organisations, that one can the less understand the third point of expression, and that is the failure to grasp more surely, and develop more widely the self-centred possibilities of the town.

Like an over-patient Cinderella, absorbed in her work-a-day tasks, Salford in these later days has concerned herself too little with external appearances, and accepted too easily a modest stillness and humility. With a charity that may be enviable—but is certainly not businesslike—she has allowed her sister towns to occupy the limelight, and hidden her own light under the proverbial bushel. Is it to be wondered that such modesty has been taken at its own valuation, and that she has suffered accordingly from scant recognition and from the easy criticism of the ill-informed ? Cinderella may linger too long in humble garb and remain unnoticed when Prince Prosperity passes by.

But a new spirit stirs within the ancient town " squatting on Irwell's banks," as the late Mr. Balfour Browne once described her. The forest of factory chimneys lifting themselves where once the greenwoods waved, is a symbol of another age—campaniles of industry summoning to wider ambitions. With a unique strategic position as a commercial and industrial centre, and with vast undeveloped resources, naught can stay the city's destiny if her citizens be but conscious of the present, faithful to the past, and alive to the future yet to be.

*   *   *   *

And now, gentle reader, our journey is ended, our story is told. We have walked back on Time to where, out of the mists, this Salford of ours was born. We have seen its changing forms through youth and unperishing age, through weal and woe, rising to greater strength out of every adversity. Hoary by the measure of the receding years but virile with the impulse of an eternal youth, striding ever forward to nobler achievements, this ancient city is an essay in civic evolution from whose enduring permanence we are brought to understand that a city is not of bricks and stone, but of the spirit of unconquerable man. Out of the conflicts of every age the flame of the spirit issues forth, fortified by experience and chastened by mistakes. Hopefully we look forward to the great days still ahead when, fed by increasing opportunities and fanned by the understanding devotion of all her children, our city shall shine forth like a beacon on a hill—a model and inspiration for all that is best and highest in civic life, honoured Mother once more of the great district to which she once gave her name.

There is a certain famous novel in which Salford life and character is well delineated, and wherein the idealistic soul of the city is made to speak, as indeed it does, from one of its humblest workers. " I see the day when life on Irwell's banks will be more radiant and lovely . . . God in the people. And the people, not one class but every class, a unity, making and remaking things nearer perfection."

With this thought to guide us into the new dawn of another age, who can foretell the glory of the Salford yet to be ?

Epilogue.

ON the terrace of Peel Park a Man is standing, gazing over the sleeping city. A wandering wind, laden with the clean breath of the distant moorlands, stirs the trees and ripples the surface of the river. The scudding cloud-drift plays hide and seek with the scattered stars, and the pale moon enchants the night with her cold radiance. Except that the trees are now pinched and shrivelled, and the western torrent a turgid, murky flow, and the stretching wilderness a congested human hive, it seems to the Man that he has stepped back through the mist of ages and stands here, as in the beginning, a lonely nameless adventurer listening to the voice of the Great Spirit urging him to build. Yet out of the one many have been begotten to labour for a space and pass forward, bequeathing the endless task to those who follow after and to countless generations still unborn. To what end and to what purpose.

Suddenly, like the sighing of the wind, still voices float upon the silence of the night, and the man realises he is not alone. Out of the shadows, phantom forms press around him, and he feels himself drawn into the magic of the night. In this stifled midnight hour the spirits of those who have laboured in the past awaken to live and walk again where once they loved and served. Brython Chief and Saxon Thane, quest-borne Knight and centurion of Rome, kingly Alfred and the pious Confessor, bluff Earl Ranulph and proud Del Bothe, gallant John Radclyffe, leading his illustrious line ; Stanleys and Molyneaux, Ralph Byrom and Dr. John, Hugo de Burun and his cowled monks, beloved Humphrey and his no less noble grandson—a wondrous company of splendid souls—gathering again in the darkened hours to see how the trust they bequeathed is being fulfilled.

Like a flash of light in the darkness, the man realises the truth—the past is never dead. In an old city like this there is an historical continuity ; a transcendental soul that passes from one generation to another ; an imperishable spirit that draws the present into living communion with the strivings of distant days.

And as they pass, with unechoing tread, through the silent streets, the Man grows uneasy with shame at the judgment of their voiceless comment. He sees the city for the first time, as it appears to them ; sees the squalor where once was beauty ; the misery where once was joy. With advantages of science and knowledge that they knew nothing of, he and his generation have created nothing but this dismal dreariness, a drab oppression almost too hideous to be borne. Was this a worthy dwelling-place for a proud people, for the sons and daughters of a city that boasts a lineage of over a thousand years of freedom ; whose citizens were freemen when others were bondmen and serfs ? The city that never knew the oppression of a feudal lord suffers more grievous penalties now—the overwhelming oppression of poverty, ugliness and want. The place that should be the home of a happy populace has become a prison from which the more fortunate seek a glad escape, and thousands who should be contributing to the building, languish in a soul-destroying environment. Happy, promiseful lives caught up in the deadening drift. Tired lives choked with heartbreak, passing out whence they came. The Man feels the fierce, passionate accusation of it all. Clamant and defiant comes the challenge from the living past, finding an echo in the depths of his soul, a feeling for his own city.

In a radiance of thought drawn, it seemed, from those who bore him company on this night's pilgrimage, he saw the city as it might be, the mirror of all the hopes and aspirations of its children from the dawn of time. A city of happy homes, pleasantly set ; of spacious streets and fine buildings ; of busy factories humming with the zest of a work-proud people ; of schools teaching the everyday arts of natural necessity. A city of families bound in an abiding brotherhood, sharing a common name and serving a common heritage. A city of order and fitness where all things are consecrate to the common weal and the glory of God ; a city welling with the spring-tide of life.

" Our tools were crude, but we wrought in love," said the Voice of the Past. And beyond the vision the man saw the boundless opportunities waiting to be utilised, the practical means by which the mirage-like ideal would become the glad reality, if only he and his fellow citizens would care and will and work. To care with all the passionate devotion of bygone days ; to interpret, in modern form, and with the aid of modern advantages, the mighty spirit of love.; to work out by the common effort of the whole community the great traditions of a wondrous heritage, until this grey old city glowed beacon-like with the radiant, creative spirit of a people seeking perfection.

A gentle stillness fell as the Man stood again on the terrace of the park. The world seemed for a moment hushed, and though it was yet dark there came a faint lightening in the eastern sky. The grey waste imperceptibly widened, and, in its spreading, the Spirits of the Past faded from sight. A rushing murmur woke the world to life and fresh activity. Just a fanning wind it seemed, but the Man knew it was the " Amen " of this hidden company of days long past, as in the light of dawn, with heart upraised he prayed : " GRANT US THY GRACE, O LORD, THAT IN THE STRENGTH OF THY PURPOSE WE MAY BUILD TRUE."

SALFORD CITY REPORTER LTD., PRINTERS, SALFORD.